D1233474

JOSEPH PRIESTLEY, SCIENTIST, PHILOSOPHER, AND THEOLOGIAN

Joseph Priestley, Scientist, Philosopher, and Theologian

Edited by

ISABEL RIVERS AND DAVID L. WYKES

OXFORD
UNIVERSITY PRESS

OXFORD

UNIVERSITY PRESS

Great Clarendon Street, Oxford OX2 6DP

Oxford University Press is a department of the University of Oxford.
It furthers the University's objective of excellence in research, scholarship,
and education by publishing worldwide in

Oxford New York

Auckland Cape Town Dar es Salaam Hong Kong Karachi
Kuala Lumpur Madrid Melbourne Mexico City Nairobi
New Delhi Shanghai Taipei Toronto

With offices in

Argentina Austria Brazil Chile Czech Republic France Greece
Guatemala Hungary Italy Japan Poland Portugal Singapore
South Korea Switzerland Thailand Turkey Ukraine Vietnam

Oxford is a registered trade mark of Oxford University Press
in the UK and in certain other countries

Published in the United States
by Oxford University Press Inc., New York

© Oxford University Press 2008

The moral rights of the authors have been asserted
Database right Oxford University Press (maker)

First published 2008

British Library Cataloguing in Publication Data

Data available

Library of Congress Cataloging in Publication Data

Joseph Priestley, scientist, philosopher, and theologian / edited by Isabel Rivers
and David L. Wykes.

p. cm.

Includes bibliographical references (p.) and index.

ISBN 978-0-19-921530-0

1. Priestley, Joseph, 1733–1804. I. Rivers, Isabel. II. Wykes, David L.

BX9869.P8J73 2008

540.92–dc22   2007036921

Typeset by SPI Publisher Services, Pondicherry, India
Printed in Great Britain
on acid-free paper by
Biddles Ltd., King's Lynn, Norfolk

ISBN 978–0–19–921530–0

1 3 5 7 9 10 8 6 4 2

Contents

Notes on the Contributors and Editors

W. H. Brock is Emeritus Professor of History of Science at the University of Leicester. He has published extensively on the history of chemistry, scientific periodicals, and the development of scientific education. His books include *From Protyle to Proton* (1985); *The Fontana History of Chemistry* (1992); *Science for All: Studies in the History of Victorian Science and Education* (1996); and *Justus von Liebig* (1997). He is currently writing a biography of Sir William Crookes. He was President of the British Society for History of Science, 1978–80, and edited *Ambix*, 1968–83.

G. M. Ditchfield is Professor of Eighteenth-Century History, University of Kent, Canterbury. His publications include *George III: An Essay in Monarchy* (2002); *Theophilus Lindsey: from Anglican to Unitarian* (1998); *The Evangelical Revival* (2002); and a large number of articles and chapters in books on the movement to repeal the Test and Corporation Acts, the anti-slavery movement, the role of the House of Lords, and other eighteenth-century subjects. He has contributed many lives to the *Oxford Dictionary of National Biography*, of late eighteenth-century churchmen, dissenters, politicians, and controversialists. Volume I of his two-volume edition of the *Letters of Theophilus Lindsey* has been published by the Church of England Record Society (2007).

James Dybikowski was Professor of Philosophy at the University of British Columbia. He has published *On Burning Ground: An Examination of the Ideas, Projects and Life of David Williams* (1993), and co-edited (with Miguel Benitez and Gianni Paganini) *Scepticisme, clandestinité et libres pensées: Scepticism, Clandestinity and Free-thinking* (2002). He has published numerous articles on Greek philosophy as well as on eighteenth-century thought, especially the free-thinking tradition. He has edited special issues of *Enlightenment and Dissent*, including one devoted to the philosophy of Samuel Clarke (1997), and is currently the journal's co-editor with Martin Fitzpatrick.

Martin Fitzpatrick was Senior Lecturer at the Department of History and Welsh History of the University of Wales, Aberystwyth. He was co-founder and co-editor with D. O. Thomas of *The Price–Priestley Newsletter* (1977–81) and *Enlightenment and Dissent* (1982–). He has published many articles and chapters in the field of Priestley studies and on the Enlightenment more generally. He was senior editor of and a contributor to *The Enlightenment World* (2004), and co-editor with Nicholas Thomas and Jenny Newell of *The Death of Captain Cook and Other Writings by David Samwell* (2007).

Jenny Graham is an independent scholar living in Cambridge. She spent many years in America and did much of her research in the American Philosophical Society in Philadelphia. She has published *Revolutionary in Exile: The Emigration of Joseph Priestley to America, 1794–1804* (1995); *The Nation, the Law and the King: Reform Politics in England, 1789–1799*, 2 vols (2000); and several articles in *Enlightenment and Dissent*.

Alison Kennedy gained her doctorate in history from the University of Stirling in November 2006. Her thesis is a study in intellectual history related to the classical historian and philologist John Kenrick, entitled 'John Kenrick and the Transformation of Unitarian Thought'. Her research interests remain focused upon radical Unitarian theology and its relationship to secular ideas.

Isabel Rivers is Professor of Eighteenth-Century English Literature and Culture, Queen Mary, University of London, and Co-Director of the Dr Williams's Centre for Dissenting Studies. Her books include *Reason, Grace, and Sentiment: A Study of the Language of Religion and Ethics in England, 1660–1780*, 2 vols (1991–2000); and *Books and their Readers in Eighteenth-Century England*, 2 vols, editor and contributor (1982, 2001). She has published many chapters and articles on seventeenth- and eighteenth-century literature, religion, and philosophy, and is currently writing *Vanity Fair and the Celestial City: Dissenting, Methodist, and Evangelical Literary Culture in England, 1720–1800*.

David Wykes is Director of Dr Williams's Trust and Library and Co-Director of the Dr Williams's Centre for Dissenting Studies. He is an associate editor of *The Oxford Dictionary of National Biography* and contributor of 52 articles. He edited *Parliament and Dissent* with Stephen Taylor (2005), and has published many essays and articles on dissenting and Unitarian history. He is currently writing a book on *Religious Dissent after Toleration, 1689–1715*. Together with Knud Haakonssen, Isabel Rivers, and Richard Whatmore he is planning *A History of the Dissenting Academies in the British Isles.*

Preface

This new study of Joseph Priestley is the first publication to result from the work of the Dr Williams's Centre for Dissenting Studies, established in September 2004 as a collaboration between the School of English and Drama, Queen Mary, University of London, and Dr Williams's Library, Gordon Square, London. The objectives of the Centre are to promote the use of the Library's unique holdings of puritan, Protestant nonconformist and dissenting books and manuscripts; to encourage research into and dissemination of these resources; and to increase knowledge and understanding of the importance of puritanism and Protestant dissent to English society and literature from the sixteenth century to the present. The book has its origin in a one-day conference on Priestley held at the Library on 5 March 2005 to launch the Centre. It is not, however, a collection of conference proceedings, but a carefully structured volume of essays which seeks to re-interpret Priestley's extraordinary range of interests and re-establish him as a major intellectual figure in Britain and America in the second half of the eighteenth century.

Isabel Rivers
David L. Wykes

The Dr Williams's Centre for Dissenting Studies
London

List of Abbreviations

APS	American Philosophical Society
Anderson & Lawrence	R. G. W. Anderson and Christopher Lawrence (eds), *Science, Medicine and Dissent: Joseph Priestley (1733–1804)* (London: Wellcome Trust/Science Museum, 1987).
BCL	Birmingham Central Library
BCA, JWP	Birmingham City Archives, James Watt Papers.
Bowden & Rosner	Mary Ellen Bowden and Lisa Rosner (eds), *Joseph Priestley, Radical Thinker* (Philadelphia, PA: Chemical Heritage Foundation, 2005).
Bradley	James E. Bradley, *Religion, Revolution and English Radicalism: Nonconformity in Eighteenth-Century Politics and Society* (Cambridge: CUP, 1990).
CUP	Cambridge University Press
DWL	Dr Williams's Library
ECCO	Eighteenth Century Collections Online
EHR	*English Historical Review*
E&D	*Enlightenment and Dissent*
ESTC	English Short Title Catalogue
Golinski	Jan Golinski, *Science as Public Culture: Chemistry and Enlightenment in Britain, 1760–1820* (Cambridge: CUP, 1992).
Graham, *Reform Politics*	Jenny Graham, *The Nation, the Law, and the King: Reform Politics in England, 1789–1799*, 2 vols. (Lanham, MD: University Press of America, 2000).
Graham, 'Revolutionary in Exile'	Jenny Graham, 'Revolutionary in Exile: The Emigration of Joseph Priestley to America, 1794–1804,' *Transactions of the American Philosophical Society*, 85.2 (1995), 1–213.

Graham, 'Revolutionary Philosopher', part one	Jenny Graham, 'Revolutionary Philosopher: the Political Ideas of Joseph Priestley (1733–1804), Part One', *E&D*, 8 (1989), 43–68.
Graham, 'Revolutionary Philosopher', part two	Jenny Graham, 'Revolutionary Philosopher: the Political Ideas of Joseph Priestley (1733–1804), Part Two', *E&D*, 9 (1990), 14–46.
Haakonssen	Knud Haakonssen (ed.), *Enlightenment and Religion: Rational Dissent in Eighteenth-Century Britain* (Cambridge: CUP, 1996).
Hist. Jnl.	*Historical Journal*
HSP	The Historical Society of Pennsylvania
JBS	*Journal of British Studies*
JEH	*Journal of Ecclesiastical History*
JP	*The Journal of Political Philosophy*
JRUL	John Rylands University Library, Manchester
Lib. Cong. Mss	Library of Congress Manuscripts
LPN	Literary and Philosophical Society of Newcastle upon Tyne
Mass. Hist. Soc.	Massachusetts Historical Society
Oxford DNB	*The Oxford Dictionary of National Biography*, ed. Colin Matthew and Brian Harrison, 60 vols. (Oxford University Press, 2004) and online at www.oxforddnb.com/
OUP	Oxford University Press
Papers of Jefferson	*The Papers of Thomas Jefferson*, vol. XXVIII, ed. John Cantanzariti et al., vols. XXIX–XXXI, ed. Barbara B. Oberg et al. (Princeton and Oxford: Princeton University Press, 2000, 2002–4).
PMHB	*Pennsylvania Magazine of History and Biography*
P-PN	*Price-Priestley Newsletter*
Proc. Mass. Hist. Soc	*Proceedings of the Massachusetts Historical Society*
PRO, TSP	Public Record Office, Treasury Solicitors Papers
Rivers	Isabel Rivers, *Reason, Grace, and Sentiment: A Study of the Language of Religion and Ethics in*

	England, 1660–1780, 2 vols. (Cambridge: CUP, 1991–2000).
Rutt	*The Theological and Miscellaneous Works of Joseph Priestley,* ed. J. T. Rutt, 25 vols. in 26 (London: George Smallfield, 1817–32; New York: Kraus Reprint Co. 1972; Bristol: Thoemmes, 1999) (the first volume is divided into two: I i and I ii).
Schofield, I	Robert E. Schofield, *The Enlightenment of Joseph Priestley: A Study of his Life and Works from 1733 to 1773* (University Park, PA: Penn State University Press, 1997).
Schofield, II	Robert E. Schofield, *The Enlightened Joseph Priestley: A Study of his Life and Work from 1773 to 1804* (University Park, PA: Penn State University Press, 2004).
Scientific Autobiography	*A Scientific Autobiography of Joseph Priestley, 1733–1804: Selected Scientific Correspondence,* ed. Robert E. Schofield (Cambridge, MA: MIT Press, 1966).
Scientific Correspondence	*Scientific Correspondence of Joseph Priestley,* ed. Henry Carrington Bolton (New York, 1892; New York: Kraus Reprint, 1969).
Schwartz & McEvoy	A. Truman Schwartz and John G. McEvoy (eds.), *Motion Towards Perfection: The Achievement of Joseph Priestley* (Boston, MA: Skinner House Books, 1990).
TUHS	*Transactions of the Unitarian Historical Society*
WMQ	*William and Mary Quarterly*
WPL	Warrington Public Libraries

Introduction*

David L. Wykes and Isabel Rivers

The Revd Dr Joseph Priestley died on the morning of 6 February 1804 in the isolated township of Northumberland, Pennsylvania, at the age of 70. Despite the remoteness of the place in which he died, Priestley was no obscure minister of religion, but one of the most remarkable thinkers of the eighteenth century, whose life encompassed an extraordinary range of interests. He is celebrated as the first to discover the properties of oxygen, together with a number of other core gases; the first to identify carbon dioxide and invent soda water and thus carbonated drinks; and the first to demonstrate some of the basic processes of photosynthesis. He is therefore seen as having revolutionized experimental chemistry. He had earlier made important discoveries in the study of electricity, as a result of which he gained public recognition as a scientist and election as a Fellow of the Royal Society. Priestley is chiefly remembered today as a scientist, but he was far more than that. He was a prolific author, publishing works on grammar, rhetoric, history, and political theory, besides electricity, optics, and experimental chemistry. He was a theologian, a philosopher, an educationalist, a historian, as well as a scientist. Yet none of these interests touch the heart of what he saw as his life's work: his religion and his ministry. His theological writings were crucial to the development of Unitarianism and helped to transform the religious landscape of the late eighteenth and early nineteenth

---

* David Wykes is grateful to G. M. Ditchfield for his comments on an earlier version of the introduction.

centuries. By the time of his death in 1804 he had published more than 200 books, pamphlets, sermons, and essays.

The challenge of studying Priestley is not only that of encompassing the breadth of his extraordinary range of interests, on which he wrote so extensively, but of comprehending the underlying philosophy unifying his ideas. Most recent studies of Priestley's career have been dominated by the problems of identifying and connecting his diverse interests. Indeed until recently it has been difficult to comprehend Priestley and his achievements because his science has been divorced from his other concerns, in particular his religious ideas. The original entry for Priestley in the *Dictionary of National Biography* provided a striking example, with two lives seemingly of two different people: of Priestley the theologian by the Unitarian historian Alexander Gordon, and of Priestley the scientist by the chemist Philip Hartog. Undoubtedly Priestley's wide-ranging interests create particular difficulties for scholars attempting to understand his work, and unsurprisingly many studies of Priestley have maintained a dichotomy between his science and his religion: for example F. W. Gibbs's 1965 biography of Priestley, which focused on his work as a scientist, and John Ruskin Clark's 1990 biography, which concentrated on his theology.[1] Fortunately, there has been a growing recognition in recent decades, particularly amongst historians of science and philosophy, that Priestley's religious beliefs cannot be separated from his other ideas. John McEvoy and J. E. McGuire, in one of the most ambitious attempts to portray the unity and integrity of Priestley's thought (discussed by W. H. Brock in Chapter 2), argue that Priestley's religious beliefs were fundamental to his theological, scientific, and political ideas, and formed the intellectual foundation on which his entire philosophical framework rested.[2]

[1] Golinski, 63, 65; D. M. Knight, ' "Fresh Warmth to our Friendship": Priestley and his Circle', in *Oxygen and the Conversion of Future Feedstocks: The Proceedings of the Third BOC Priestley Conference* (London: Royal Society of Chemistry Publication, 1984), 384–5; F. W. Gibbs, *Joseph Priestley: Adventurer in Science and Champion of Truth* (London: Thomas Nelson & Sons, 1965); John Ruskin Clark, *Joseph Priestley, a Comet in the System* (San Diego: Torch Publications, 1990).

[2] John G. McEvoy and J. E. McGuire, 'God and Nature: Priestley's Way of Rational Dissent', *Historical Studies in Physical Sciences*, 6 (1975), 325–404. See also John G. McEvoy, 'Joseph Priestley, Scientist, Philosopher and Divine', *Proceedings of the American Philosophical Society*, 128 (1984), 193–9.

Though brought up a Calvinist, as a result of his own detailed investigation of Scriptural evidence Priestley became convinced that religious understanding came from a rational interpretation of both nature and Scripture. McEvoy argues that this commitment to 'reason and revelation shaped the basic categories of Priestley's thought'.[3] Other scholars, notably Simon Schaffer, John Money, and Jan Golinski, have sought to understand Priestley's work in relation to his dissenting background and the audiences he addressed.[4] Priestley was above all a religious dissenter, and this fact determined his political and religious outlook and concerns. Recent decades have seen a welcome recognition of the significance of religious issues in eighteenth-century England, and a growing acceptance of the importance of religious dissent and the contribution of rational dissent in particular to political and other reform movements.

RELIGIOUS DISSENT AND THE LAW

Eighteenth-century religious dissent in England dates from the Restoration of Charles II in 1660 and the 1662 Act of Uniformity, which re-established the episcopal Church of England with its bishops, courts, and administration, and required conformity to prescribed doctrine and the Book of Common Prayer. As a result of the political reaction which followed the disorders and excesses of the Civil War and Interregnum the Restoration religious settlement was founded on an uncompromising Anglicanism. Over the next ten years Parliament passed a series of coercive laws for the purpose of suppressing religious nonconformity and enforcing obedience to the Church of England. The legislation included the 1661 Corporation Act, intended to restrict membership of a municipal or chartered

[3] J. G. McEvoy, 'Causes and Laws, Powers and Principles: The Metaphysical Foundations of Priestley's Conception of Phlogiston' in Anderson & Lawrence, 55.

[4] Simon Schaffer, 'Natural Philosophy and Public Spectacle in the Eighteenth Century', *History of Science*, 21 (1983), 1–43; John Money, 'Joseph Priestley in Cultural Context: Philosophic Spectacle, Popular Belief and Popular Politics in Eighteenth-Century Birmingham: Part One and Two', 7 & 8, *E&D* (1988–9), 57–82, 69–89; Jan Golinski, 'The Theory of Practice and the Practice of Theory: Sociological Approaches in the History of Science', *Isis*, 81 (1990), 492–505; Golinski, *Science as Public Culture*.

corporation to communicant members of the Church of England, and the 1673 Test Act, intended to exclude Catholics (but in effect all non-Anglicans) from any civil or military office under the crown.[5] The two acts introduced a new element, the sacramental test: a requirement for officeholders to have received 'the sacrament of the Lord's Supper according to the usage of the Church of England'.[6] This requirement gave rise to the practice of occasional conformity, by which dissenters visited their parish church once a year in order to receive the sacrament and obtain the necessary certificate for the purpose of qualifying themselves for office under the Acts.

'Nonconformity' and 'dissent' are terms defining the legal status of all those Protestant groups and individuals who refused to conform to the Church of England (from the later seventeenth century 'dissent' is the term more commonly applied). These groups had little in common except opposition to the terms of conformity: the term dissent conceals a wide range of doctrinal and other differences, not least between separatists, such as the Baptists, Quakers, and Independents (or Congregationalists), who rejected the concept of a national church and sought 'indulgence' or toleration to allow them to worship freely in their own meetings, and most Presbyterians, who could not accept the terms of conformity, but who considered themselves the heirs of a reformed Elizabethan Church and who hoped in vain for 'comprehension' or inclusion in a more accommodating Church of England with an altered liturgy.[7]

The forms and structure of eighteenth-century dissent were a consequence of the Revolution of 1688, in which the Catholic James II was replaced by his Protestant son-in-law and daughter William III and Mary II. As part of the religious settlement two bills were introduced into Parliament, but the bill for comprehension, because

---

[5] There was a second Test Act (1678) to prevent Catholics from sitting in either house of Parliament.

[6] 25 Car. II, c. 2, 'An Act for Preventing Dangers which may Happen from Popish Recusants' (1673), ¶2, *The Statutes at Large of England and of Great Britain from Magna Carta to the Union of the Kingdom of Great Britain and Ireland* (London, 1811), V, 416.

[7] English Presbyterianism should not be confused with Scottish Presbyterianism or the later Presbyterian Church in England; see C. Gordon Bolam, Jeremy Goring, H. L. Short, and Roger Thomas, *The English Presbyterians: From Elizabethan Puritanism to Modern Unitarianism* (London: George Allen & Unwin, 1968), 19–21.

of the opposition from many churchmen and their Tory allies in Parliament, was lost and only the toleration bill became law. As a consequence all dissenters were forced to obtain their freedom to worship in public from an act intended only to offer a qualified toleration to a despised minority. Modestly entitled 'An Act for Exempting their Majesties Protestant Subjects, Dissenting from the Church of England, from the Penalties of certain laws', the 1689 Toleration Act, by suspending the penal laws against those who refused to attend the Church of England, allowed Protestant dissenters to gather their own congregations, though Catholics and those who denied the Trinity were excluded from the benefits of the Act.[8] Dissenters who took the oaths of supremacy and allegiance, and made the declaration against transubstantiation, were allowed to register their own meeting-places for public worship. Ministers, in addition, had to subscribe to the Thirty-Nine Articles of Religion, which officially defined the doctrine of the Church of England, though they were excused those directly concerned with Anglican church–government and authority. In addition, Baptists were exempt from the part of the Twenty-Seventh Article concerning infant baptism, and Quakers from taking the oaths. The Toleration Act did not remove but merely suspended the earlier penal laws against nonconformist meetings. It therefore fell far short of a full religious toleration: dissenters continued to be discriminated against in many important areas of everyday life and were subject to major political, and indeed civil, disabilities because they were not members of the Church of England. The Revolution also saw a significant number of high churchmen leave the Church after refusing the oaths of allegiance to William and Mary. These nonjurors included the Archbishop of Canterbury, several bishops and about 400 clergy, some of whom formed a separate nonjuring church.

DOCTRINAL DEVELOPMENTS WITHIN DISSENT

In the early years after toleration there was considerable cooperation between Presbyterians and Congregationalists. A scheme for uniting

---

[8] 1 Wm & Mary c18, *Statutes at Large*, V, 516.

the two ministries, the Happy Union, was adopted in April 1691, though it collapsed in London within months amid bitter dissension. Nevertheless, outside London and the major towns, Presbyterians and Congregationalists, having been brought together by the earlier persecution, often continued to meet as a joint congregation because of their loyalty to a particular minister. During the first two decades of the eighteenth century the majority of these joint congregations were to divide, as in most cases the smaller body of Congregational supporters withdrew to establish their own meetings. A common cause of these divisions was the choice of a new minister. Although such disputes involved fundamental disagreements concerning church government and congregational authority that the appointment of a minister or a new assistant highlighted, doctrinal differences were of increasing importance, and in many cases the appointment of a minister whose commitment to Calvinist doctrine came to be questioned led the more orthodox members to withdraw to establish their own meetings. Differences between Presbyterians and Congregationalists, which had originally involved mainly matters of church order, became increasingly focused on doctrine.[9]

The standard statement of doctrinal orthodoxy for seventeenth-century Presbyterians was the *Westminster Confession of Faith* of 1646, adopted by the Congregational churches with modifications in the *Savoy Declaration of Faith and Order* of 1658. The key tenets that were to prove irreconcilable grounds of contention in the eighteenth century were the unity in one Godhead of the three persons of the Trinity; God's eternal decree predestinating the elect to glory and the rest to perdition; original sin and the total dependence of human beings on free grace; and the atonement, or the role of Christ as mediator and sacrifice.[10] These tenets, which overlapped considerably with those of the Anglican Thirty-Nine Articles concerned with doctrine, were loosely and somewhat inaccurately covered by the label

---

[9] David L. Wykes, 'After the Happy Union: Presbyterians and Independents in the Provinces', *Unity and Diversity in the Church: Studies in Church History*, 32 (1996), 283–95.

[10] *The Confession of Faith, the Larger and Shorter Catechisms, with the Scripture-Proofs at Large* (Edinburgh: the University Press, 1855); *The Savoy Declaration of Faith and Order*, ed. A. G. Matthews (London: Independent Press, 1959).

Calvinist, after the French theologian Jean Calvin (1509–64). The break with orthodoxy came over two principal doctrines, predestination and the Trinity; the heterodox labels, again somewhat inaccurate, were Arminian, after the Dutch theologian Jacobus Arminius (1560–1609), for those who believed that grace was offered to all, not just the elect, and that faith was conditional on repentance; and Socinian, after the Italian theologian Faustus Socinus (1539–1604), for those who elevated reason above faith and emphasized the humanity of Christ.[11]

The great seventeenth-century puritan Richard Baxter (1615–91), who feared that the doctrine of the imputation of Christ's righteousness to the elect led to antinomianism, in which the moral life of the elect had no bearing on their salvation, advocated a 'Middle-Way' between Calvinism and Arminianism.[12] This compromise, set out at great length in *Richard Baxter's Catholick Theologie* (1675), a dialogue between a Calvinist, an Arminian, and a Reconciler, was given the label Baxterian. Baxter sought to lessen the number of disputed points dividing Protestants by appealing to reason and the sufficiency of Scripture rather than relying on doctrinal formulas. His theology was to prove attractive to many eighteenth-century dissenters, Congregational as well as Presbyterian, who came to see Scripture as the only authority for faith and reason as the only guide to truth. By also appealing to personal conscience in matters of uncertainty they were led inevitably to tolerate a wide divergence in belief. But efforts to moderate Calvinist orthodoxy were perceived by many as an attack upon fundamental Christian truths, in particular the doctrine of the Trinity. Here there was a growing divergence between Congregationalists and Presbyterians, with some of the latter increasingly drawn in the second half of the century to varieties of anti-Trinitarianism: Arianism, Socinianism, and Unitarianism. Again, these labels were often used loosely or as terms of abuse. Arianism, after the fourth-century theologian Arius, opponent of the Trinitarian Athanasius, designated the heretical belief that the Son was created by the Father and was subordinate to him, though still divine. It is clear that many

---

[11] Rivers, I, 9–11.
[12] See N. H. Keeble, *Richard Baxter, Puritan Man of Letters* (Oxford: Clarendon Press, 1982).

eighteenth-century Presbyterians who questioned the doctrine of the Trinity were Arians. The emergence of a militant Unitarianism, with its insistence that Christ was simply human, occurred only in the last three decades of the eighteenth century, and this was due largely to the efforts of Priestley himself.

The controversy over the Trinity within the Church of England was also to prove influential among Presbyterians. The work that had the greatest impact was *The Scripture-Doctrine of the Trinity* (1712) by the theologian and philosopher Samuel Clarke (1675–1729). As a result of reading Clarke a number of Presbyterians came to have doubts about the doctrine of the Trinity, and Clarke also set new standards of Biblical criticism by his thorough investigation of the Scriptural evidence. Disputes over the Trinity amongst dissenters resulted in the Salters' Hall debate in 1719 concerning the principle of demanding subscription to orthodox doctrine. This was to prove a watershed between liberal and orthodox dissent. Although the division between those who subscribed to the declaration on the Trinity and those who refused was far from being decided on denominational lines, Salters' Hall does appear to have encouraged those who were Calvinist and favoured orthodoxy to identify with the Congregational interest, and those who prized freedom of enquiry and the exercise of reason with the Presbyterians.[13]

In the second half of the century there were increasing tensions between evangelical and rational dissenters, as they were now becoming known. Developments in dissent were significantly affected by the diverse movement usually called the evangelical revival, which had its origins in the 1730s within the Church of England. The Arminian branch of Methodism, under the leadership of the staunch churchman John Wesley (1703–91), had few links with dissent, but the Calvinist evangelicalism of George Whitefield (1714–70) and others revitalized orthodox dissent among the Baptists and Congregationalists. Through the use of itinerant preachers these groups were to establish an astonishing number of new congregations, particularly

---

[13] Roger Thomas, 'The Non-Subscription Controversy amongst Dissenters in 1719: the Salters' Hall Debate', *JEH*, 4 (1953), 174–5, 183ff; Thomas, 'The Salters' Hall Watershed, 1719', in Bolam, *et al*, *English Presbyterians*, ch. 4.

in the growing industrial areas.[14] In contrast the leading Presbyterian congregations in the main towns, by adopting what they perceived to be rational religious beliefs, rejected the religious enthusiasm of the evangelical revival. This rational dissent lacked popular appeal and there was significant loss of members, particularly in the countryside, to the Congregationalists and the Methodists. As a consequence by the beginning of the nineteenth century only about a third of the congregations which had originally been Presbyterian at the start of the eighteenth century had adopted Unitarian opinions. Yet despite the sharp fall in numbers, in most of the major towns by the end of the eighteenth century these congregations had become centres of great wealth and influence, often including members on the fringes of county society.[15] Presbyterians, from being the most orthodox and conservative body of dissenters in 1662, had become by the early nineteenth century a 'body which refused to impose any test or creed and whose only formula was a heterodox insistence upon the single personality of God and the proper humanity of Christ'.[16]

LATE EIGHTEENTH-CENTURY REFORM MOVEMENTS

Attempts to remove some of the main political disabilities experienced by dissenters resulted in a concerted effort during the 1730s to repeal the Test and Corporation Acts, but the motions introduced into the Commons in 1736 and 1739 were comprehensively rejected and no further attempt at repeal was made for 50 years.

[14] David Bebbington, *Evangelicalism in Modern Britain: A History from the 1730s to the 1980s* (London: Unwin Hyman, 1989); D. W. Lovegrove, *Established Church, Sectarian People: Itinerancy and the Transformation of English Dissent, 1780–1830* (Cambridge: CUP, 1988); Mark Noll, *The Rise of Evangelicalism: The Age of Edwards, Whitefield and the Wesleys* (Nottingham: Inter Varsity Press, 2004). G. M. Ditchfield, *The Evangelical Revival* (London: UCL Press, 1998), 106, discusses the increase in numbers.

[15] John Seed, 'Gentlemen Dissenters: The Social and Political Meanings of Rational Dissent in the 1770s and 1780s', *Hist. Jnl.*, 28 (1985), 299–325.

[16] Olive M. Griffiths, *Religion and Learning: A Study in English Presbyterian Thought from 1662 to the Foundation of the Unitarian Movement* (Cambridge: CUP, 1935), 3.

Reformers in the late eighteenth century concentrated at first on efforts to amend the laws concerning subscription, not the sacramental tests. In 1772 a group of Anglican clergy led by Priestley's friend Theophilus Lindsey (1723–1808), who met at the Feathers Tavern in London, petitioned Parliament to abolish subscription to the Thirty-Nine Articles, required of those in Anglican orders upon nomination or promotion. Their objection was to the imposition of religious tests, but it was also linked to a dislike of the Trinitarian theology of the Thirty-Nine Articles. Receiving only limited support within the Church of England, the Feathers Tavern Petition was quickly dismissed by MPs. Lindsey had already resigned his living as vicar of Catterick by the time the petition was introduced again in 1774. On this occasion it was rejected without a division.[17]

The Commons debate on the petition encouraged dissenters who shared a similar grievance to seek relief from the requirement imposed by the Toleration Act for their ministers and teachers to subscribe to those of the Thirty-Nine Articles that were concerned with doctrine. Bills introduced into the Commons in 1772 and 1773 were quickly passed in a thin House, only to be defeated in the Lords. With a general election due before 1775, MPs chose not to alienate dissenters, conscious of their electoral influence in many urban constituencies, but knowing that the strength of the bishops and their supporters in the Lords would ensure the bill's defeat. But the campaign was to reveal a damaging rift between the majority of petitioners who were clearly orthodox, and the principal promoters who were increasingly heterodox in their attitude towards the Trinity. A group of Calvinist dissenters actually petitioned the Commons against the 1773 bill, welcoming the existing restrictions as helping to preserve the doctrine of the Trinity, and indeed insisting that they did not stand in need of relief. Success finally came with the Dissenters' Relief Act in 1779, passed as a result of the government's wish to conciliate dissenters because of the war with America. The Act was more limited than earlier bills and disappointed many dissenters, but

[17] G. M. Ditchfield, 'Feathers Tavern Petitioners (*act.* 1771–1774)', *Oxford DNB*; G. M. Ditchfield, 'The Subscription Issue in British Parliamentary Politics, 1772–1779', *Parliamentary History*, 7 (1988), 45–80.

it offered an important exemption to ministers and schoolteachers from the requirement to subscribe to the Thirty-Nine Articles. In the late 1780s, encouraged by a belief that support for reform was increasing, particularly in Parliament, dissenters renewed their efforts for the repeal of the Test and Corporation Acts and the removal of the sacramental tests for officeholders. Three attempts were made between 1787 and 1790 and all were defeated. In the case of the last a number of former supporters voted against repeal because of their growing fears for the security of both Church and State as a result of the French Revolution.[18]

Late eighteenth-century dissenters experienced discrimination in many important areas of everyday life still controlled by the Church, such as the probate courts, marriage, schools, and universities, as well as the licensing of teachers, surgeons and midwives. Dissenters continued to suffer major political disabilities, particularly as a result of the Test and Corporation Acts, which were not finally repealed until 1828. Nevertheless, despite the provisions of these Acts, it is clear that many dissenters did hold office. It is often assumed that they were occasional conformists, taking the Anglican sacrament in order to qualify for office. Although this was the case for some dissenters, it is clear that such behaviour was increasingly unacceptable to rational dissenters, both because of their opposition on principle to all religious subscriptions, and because of their difficulty in accepting the Trinitarian formulas of the Anglican sacrament. In addition most Baptists, Quakers, and Congregationalists rejected any communion with the Church of England. As a consequence many dissenters must have held office without qualifying themselves. Those who denied the Trinity were even more vulnerable in law since they were specifically excluded from the terms of the Toleration Act, and the Blasphemy Act of 1698 made them liable to up to three years' imprisonment

---

[18] 19 Geo. III, c. 44 'An Act for the further Relief of Protestant Dissenting Ministers and Schoolmasters' (1779), *Statutes at Large*, XIV, 474–5; Ditchfield, 'The Subscription Issue'; Ditchfield, ' "How Narrow will the Limits of this Toleration Appear?": Dissenting Petitions to Parliament, 1772–1773', in Stephen Taylor and David L. Wykes (eds), *Parliament and Dissent* (Edinburgh: Edinburgh University Press, 2005), 91–106; Ditchfield, 'The Parliamentary Struggle over the Repeal of the Test and Corporation Acts, 1787–1790', *EHR*, 89 (1974), 551–77.

and the loss of their civil rights. Although the risk of prosecution for officeholders was small, the sense of insecurity and injustice, 'of symbolic exclusion and victimisation by the state', should not be underestimated.[19]

James Bradley has pointed out that from the mid-1760s dissenters, and in particular rational dissenters, not only felt a growing sense of grievance over the continuing civil and political disabilities they experienced, but were also becoming increasingly alienated from the government as a result of a series of political events. The government's mishandling of the controversy surrounding the MP and popular agitator, John Wilkes (1725–97), led many to question the moderation and sense of fairness of those in power and the legality of their methods. This, together with the failure to offer concessions concerning religious subscription in respect of sacramental tests, and the breakdown of relations with the colonists in America, led to an important change in dissenting attitudes. Their own sense of injustice at the hands of the state and its high church supporters predisposed them to support the American rebellion. What they perceived as the apparent growth in arbitrary power and government in both Britain and America led Priestley and others to link religious opposition with broader ideas about natural rights and the need to resist oppression.[20]

For Priestley the pursuit of truth was never restricted to religion. What was true for rational religion was also true for science, politics, and every other area of life. As a consequence he drew certain practical conclusions from his religious and philosophical beliefs. In general terms they involved a deep-seated commitment to the concept of religious (and therefore political and civil) liberty, and as a result he was opposed to what he saw as religious bigotry and political corruption. He was therefore actively involved in all the major reform movements of his day, the agitation for civil and religious liberty, Parliamentary reform, abolition of the slave trade, and support for the American and French revolutions.

---

[19] John Seed, ' "A Set of Men Powerful Enough in Many Things": Rational Dissent and Political Opposition in England, 1770–1790', in Haakonssen, 158.

[20] Bradley, 38, 89.

COMMEMORATING PRIESTLEY

Joseph Priestley has never lacked for biographers. There are ten or so modern biographies as well as many essays, edited collections, and symposia devoted to Priestley. Many of the studies have been prompted by the major anniversaries of his life, notably the centenary and bicentenary of his birth (1833 and 1933) and death (1904 and 2004), and of the discovery of oxygen (1874 and 1974), as well as the two hundred and fiftieth anniversary of his birth (1983). The bicentenary of Priestley's arrival in the United States (1994) was celebrated in that country. Indeed probably no scientist, let alone minister of religion, has been studied, depicted, or commemorated more often, and perhaps none has been the subject of so many exhibitions. This is itself an indication of the amount of material created and collected relating to Priestley, ranging from portraits and images to manuscripts and printed works, and including even some of his scientific equipment. This material, now mainly held by institutions in Britain and the United States, includes an astonishing number of likenesses, prints, caricatures, and other images. A recent survey identified 16 portraits in oils (including some copies) painted before his death in 1804, the earliest dating from about 1763; four public statues erected in Oxford (1860), Birmingham (1874), Leeds (1903), and Birstall (1912), his birthplace, as well as busts and other sculptures on buildings in London. Many images of Priestley were mass-produced, both in his lifetime and subsequently. There are engraved prints of most of the portraits, contemporary caricatures, portrait medallions in jasperware by his friend and patron the celebrated potter Josiah Wedgwood, and at least eight medals struck between 1783 and the early twentieth century, as well as a commemorative postage stamp issued in the United States in 1983.[21] The surprising feature is not

[21] Robert Anderson, 'Memorialising Scientists: the Case of Joseph Priestley', in Bowden & Rosner, 30–41, who discusses the paintings, statues, and medals; John H. McLachlan, *Joseph Priestley, Man of Science, 1783–1804. An Iconography of a Great Yorkshireman* (Braunton, Devon: Merlin Books, 1983), who attempts a complete survey of the non-print images, but see Derek A. Davenport's review, *E&D*, 3 (1984), 115–16; R. G. W. Anderson, 'Priestley Displayed', in Anderson & Lawrence, 91–6. For caricatures see M. Fitzpatrick, 'Priestley Caricatured' in Schwartz & McEvoy, 161–218; Arthur Sheps, 'Public Perception of Joseph Priestley, the Birmingham Dissenters,

simply the amount and range of Priestley material, but that so much dates from his lifetime.

Although vilified by many during his life—indeed *The Times* shortly before his death declared that 'Dr Priestley's health is said to be in a declining state; his reputation has long been so'[22]—his public standing rose throughout the nineteenth century, leading not simply to his rehabilitation, but to his near canonization. The commemoration of the centenary of his birth in 1833 helped establish this celebrity. A dinner attended by many of the leading scientists in the country was held in London, at which Priestley was acknowledged as 'the Principal Founder of Pneumatic Chemistry' and, in the words of the representative of Cambridge University, 'an honour to his age and country'. Lauded by the scientific establishment, he was even reclaimed by the Royal Society, whose members had largely ostracized him during his later years. It was said that the President, the Duke of Sussex (1773–1843), a royal duke, was only prevented from attending the dinner by indisposition. Not surprisingly, Priestley's fellow Unitarians also celebrated the centenary at a second dinner in Birmingham, the town he was so ignominiously forced to leave by the riots of July 1791. In contrast to the London meeting, which had deliberately ignored all but his scientific achievements, the toasts and speeches at Birmingham sought to praise Priestley's legacy in the cause of political and religious liberty and truth. The *Birmingham Journal* drew a contrast between the obloquy and prejudice Priestley had suffered during his life and the widespread consensus, 30 years later, that he was now numbered among 'the great men' of his age, and 'placed on his proper pedestal in the temple of Fame'.[23]

More surprising was the decision by the University of Oxford in 1860 to include a statue of Priestley in the new University Museum,

and the Church-and-King Riots of 1791', *Eighteenth Century Life*, 13 (1989), 46–64; Samuel A. Tower, 'Stamps: a Tribute to the Man who discovered Oxygen', *New York Times*, 10 Apr. 1983, H36.

[22] *The Times*, 28 Jan. 1804, p. 2, col. C.

[23] 'Centenary Commemoration of Dr Priestley', *The Times*, 27 Mar. 1833, p. 2, col. G; 'Commemoration of the Centenary of Dr Priestley's Birth' and 'Celebration of Dr Priestley's Birth-Day at Birmingham', *Christian Reformer*, 19 (1833), 142–3, 170–85; *Birmingham Journal*, 30 Mar. 1833; DWL, MS 12.56 (46) Printed notice of dinner on 28 March 1833 at Birmingham organized by Old and New Meetings to celebrate the centenary of the birth of Joseph Priestley.

where he was commemorated with the other 'great founders and improvers of natural knowledge'. The statue itself was commissioned and largely paid for by Unitarians. He was also one of the five men of science—the others being Aristotle, Galileo, Newton, and Linnaeus—included on the highly decorative ceramic staircase constructed in the new Victoria & Albert Museum between 1865 and 1871. Priestley's scientific reputation received further recognition with the centenary of the discovery of oxygen in 1874. A statue of Priestley was erected by public subscription in Birmingham, though not without protests from the Evangelicals. T. H. Huxley, one of the leading Victorian scientists and who coined the term 'agnostic', was invited to give the principal speech. In America the occasion was marked by a meeting of scientists at the house where Priestley died in Northumberland, Pennsylvania. This meeting led directly to the founding of the American Chemical Society two years later.[24] Though continuing to be honoured by his fellow Unitarians for his political and religious legacy, by the mid-nineteenth century Priestley's theological outlook had been largely replaced amongst Unitarians by that of the theologian and philosopher James Martineau (1810–1900). As a consequence Priestley's reputation even amongst Unitarians is as a scientist.

W. H. Brock points out in Chapter 2 that it is perhaps surprising that Priestley has been so highly regarded by the Anglo-American scientific community when his scientific theories are perceived to have been so flawed and even the achievement of his greatest 'discovery' has been questioned. Nevertheless Priestley continues to be honoured by the main professional bodies in both the United Kingdom and the United States, and as a consequence his name is associated with a number of prestigious scientific awards. The American Chemical Society has awarded the Priestley Medal since 1922 for distinguished service in the field of chemistry. Priestley figures on the President's badge of office for the British Royal Society of Chemistry. In August 2000 the two Societies unveiled an 'International Historic Chemical

[24] 'Proposed statue of Dr Priestley at Oxford', *Christian Reformer*, NS 16, (1860), 187–9, 446–7; Bernard Lightman, 'Interpreting Agnosticism as a Nonconformist Sect: T. H. Huxley's "New Reformation" ' in Paul Wood (ed), *Science and Dissent in England, 1688–1945* (Aldershot: Ashgate, 2004), 197–8. David Wykes is grateful to Wendy Shepherd and Stella Brecknell for their help with the history of the statues in the Oxford University Museum of Natural History.

Landmark' at Bowood House, Calne (where Priestley undertook his main experiments on gases) to commemorate what scientists see as his work in laying the foundations of modern chemistry. Recognition of Priestley has extended even to business. The British Oxygen Company established the BOC-Priestley conference in 1978, named after Priestley as a result of his work on oxygen. There had been nine conferences by 2003, including the third in 1983 marking the two hundred and fiftieth anniversary of Priestley's birth. In 2002 the American Chemical Heritage Foundation established the Joseph Priestley Society, which holds regular meetings to encourage understanding of scientific and technological advances in industry. The academic interest is evident from the number of conferences, books, and essays on Priestley, and the establishment in 1977 of a specialist journal the *Price-Priestley Newsletter*, renamed in 1982 as *Enlightenment and Dissent*.

SOURCES FOR THE STUDY OF PRIESTLEY

The materials, both primary and secondary, with which to study Priestley are very considerable. In addition to his own enormous output of printed works, in which he often included biographical details, a large body of manuscript material by or about Priestley survives.[25] Despite serious losses in Priestley's lifetime, originals or copies of some 630 of his letters have been located. About two-fifths of the originals are at Dr Williams's Library, London, thus forming the largest collection, and are addressed mainly to his Unitarian friends, Theophilus Lindsey and Thomas Belsham.[26] Other important collections of Priestley's manuscripts are at the American Philosophical Society, Philadelphia (41 letters to Priestley's friend and former student John Vaughan); Harris Manchester College, Oxford

---

[25] R. E. Crook, *A Bibliography of Joseph Priestley, 1733–1804* (London: The Library Association, 1966) is a valuable checklist of Priestley's publications and the different editions, but inevitably excludes works about Priestley published since. John Stephens of Oxford was preparing a definitive bibliography shortly before his death in 2006.

[26] These figures are based on Professor Schofield's preliminary checklist of Priestley's letters with additions. David Wykes is grateful to Professor Schofield for sending him a copy of his list.

(sermons and prayers); Warrington Public Library (68 letters to his eldest son, Joseph jr., and brother-in-law, John Wilkinson); the Royal Society, London (55 letters mainly to the experimental philosopher John Canton and the potter Josiah Wedgwood); Birmingham Central Library (New Meeting congregational records and papers relating to the 1791 riots); Pennsylvania State University (Priestley's memoirs); and Dickinson College, Carlisle, Pennsylvania (family papers). Many of Priestley's letters have been published.[27] In addition a volume of pamphlets, letters, prints, and caricatures was put together in 1860 by the London Unitarian James Yates (1789–1871) in connection with the statue at Oxford. Another important collection was made by the Birmingham industrialist and historian Samuel Timmins (d. 1903) in the late nineteenth century.[28]

The only surviving part of Priestley's diaries, covering some of his final year as a student at Daventry Academy, has been transcribed from shorthand and published.[29] As a consequence his memoirs provide most of the particulars known about his family and education as well as many of the facts concerning his career and later life. They should, however, be used with caution: in many cases the events themselves were written up long afterwards, and some of the details, especially the dates, are contradicted from other sources. Priestley told Theophilus Lindsey in September 1787 that he had begun to write his memoirs to be published after his death. 'I do not mean

[27] The main collections are Rutt, I i and ii (principally theological); *Scientific Correspondence*; *Scientific Autobiography*. DWL, MS 12.12–13, Priestley's letters to Lindsey have been published on microfilm by Microform Academic Publishers, Wakefield. The recent edition of these letters by Simon Mills, of Queen Mary, University of London, is available online at www.english.qmul.ac.uk/drwilliams/. For the letters at WPL, MS 2 Priestley manuscripts, see 'Dr Priestley', *Christian Reformer*, ns 7 (1860), 100–8, 129–45, 202–11; and for a photostat copy of the originals see BCL, MS 621037, 'A Collection of 68 Letters written chiefly by Dr Joseph Priestley to John Wilkinson, 1789–1802'.

[28] Royal Society Library, London, General Manuscript Series, MS 654 'Portraits, Drawings, Original Letters, Anecdotes and other Memorials of Joseph Priestley, LLD., FRS . . . collected and arranged by James Yates, MA, FRS &c.' (c. 1860); BCL, MS 73499, 'Broadsides, caricatures, letters, newspaper cuttings, portraits etc, of, or relating to Joseph Priestley' made by Samuel Timmins. David Wykes is grateful to Judy Dennison, Birmingham City Archives, for information on the make up of this volume.

[29] Tony Rail and Beryl Thomas (eds), 'Joseph Priestley's Journal while at Daventry Academy, 1754', *E&D*, 13 (1994), 49–113.

to make it large'. He explained his purpose in the opening paragraph of his memoirs: 'Having thought it right to leave behind me
some account of my friends and benefactors, it is...necessary I also
give some account of myself.'[30] He must have completed it within
a short period as the end of the first part is dated 'Birmingham
1787'. Within a year of arriving in America in 1794 he added 'A
Continuation of the Memoirs'. The completed work is dated 24
March 1795. The memoirs and continuation were published after
his death by his eldest son Joseph jr., who also added 'A Short
account of the last Illness' of his father taken from a letter sent to
Lindsey, together with an account of his final years. *The Memoirs
of Dr Joseph Priestley, to the Year 1795, Written by Himself: With a
Continuation, to the Time of his Decease, by his Son* was published
in Northumberland, Pennsylvania in 1806, with notes on Priestley's
writings by his fellow radical Thomas Cooper and the Unitarian minister William Christie. Joseph Johnson, Priestley's publisher, brought
out the *Memoirs* in London the same year, with a second volume in 1807 containing Cooper's and Christie's notes. The original *Memoirs* have gone through at least seven editions.[31] They are
awkward for the historian to use because the pagination differs
with each publisher. The *Memoirs* were also republished by Rutt
with extensive notes and transcriptions of many letters. Rutt's annotated edition is therefore to be preferred, both for the additional
notes and the consistency of the pagination in the different reprints.
Whereas Rutt's edition of Priestley's *Memoirs* is to be relied upon,
the surviving correspondence reveals the liberties that Rutt took

---

[30] Rutt, I i, 418–19; *Memoirs of Dr Joseph Priestley, to the Year 1795, Written by
Himself: With a Continuation, to the Time of his Decease, by his Son, Joseph Priestley*
(Northumberland [PA] & London 1806), 1, 114, 128.

[31] *Memoirs of Dr Joseph Priestley, to the Year 1795, Written by Himself: With a
Continuation, to the Time of his Decease, by his Son, Joseph Priestley* (Northumberland
[PA]: Printed by John Binns, 1806; London: Joseph Johnson, 1806). Later editions
were published by Joseph Johnson, London, 1809; James Belcher and son, Birm-
ingham, 1810; Radclyffes & Co., Birmingham, 1833; [British & Foreign Unitarian
Association], London, 1893; H. R. Allenson, London, 1904; abridged edition, Bancroft
Press, Washington, DC, 1964. The most recent edition is *Autobiography of Joseph
Priestley: Memoirs written by Himself*, ed. Jack Lindsay (Bath: Adams & Dart, 1970;
Teaneck, NJ: Fairleigh Dickinson University Press, 1971), but Lindsay omits Joseph
jr.'s 'Continuation'.

when editing the letters, in common with most early nineteenth-century editors, in silently omitting passages, often those of a personal nature, and even conflating different letters.[32]

Because of the range of Priestley's interests and the wealth of source material available, he remains difficult for a single scholar to assess and for nonspecialist readers to approach. Robert E. Schofield, editor of his scientific correspondence and author of the standard two-volume life and of the article in the *Oxford Dictionary of National Biography*, has devoted 40 years to the study of Priestley.[33] His biography, amounting to nearly 700 pages of text, is invaluable for the specialist, but a biographical approach has its limitations, particularly in providing an overall assessment of Priestley and his work. In addition, several major new studies have been published since Schofield finished writing his two volumes. The need is for a new single-volume assessment of Priestley's life and work which is accessible to scholars and students from a wide variety of backgrounds. With this end in view, the editors have brought together the present collection of essays to provide an up to date account of all of Priestley's activities, as a minister, educationalist, scientist, philosopher, theologian, political thinker, and historian, with a summary of his life and an account of his last years in America. They hope that this book will help to return him to his rightful place in eighteenth-century intellectual life.

---

[32] *The Theological and Miscellaneous Works of Joseph Priestley*, ed. John Towill Rutt (London: George Smallfield, 1817–32), 25 vols. in 26. Facsimile editions were published by New York: Kraus Reprint Co. 1972; Bristol: Thoemmes, 1999. The 'Memoirs and Correspondence, 1733–1804' form vol. I part i and ii of Rutt's original edition and were published separately as *Life and Correspondence of Joseph Priestley, LL.D., F.R.S.*, 2 vols (London, 1831–2). We are grateful to Simon Mills for his confirmation of Rutt's editorial practices concerning the correspondence.

[33] *Scientific Autobiography*; Schofield, I and II; Robert E. Schofield, 'Priestley, Joseph (1733–1804)', *Oxford DNB*.

1

Joseph Priestley, Minister and Teacher*

David L. Wykes

INTRODUCTION

Although it is as a scientist and as a radical that Priestley is best remembered, without doubt he himself considered his work as a minister the most important, and it was to dominate the greater part of his active life. Only when he was librarian and literary companion to the Earl of Shelburne during the middle years of his life (1772–80), and after 1794, when he was in exile in America during the ten years before his death, was he neither minister nor teacher. Moreover, contemporaries would have seen Priestley as the leading advocate of Unitarianism and have been well aware of the controversial and polemical works he published attacking the main orthodox Christian doctrines. As Robert E. Schofield has pointed out, Priestley wrote four times as much on religion and theology as on science, with politics and education ranking second. He also established his reputation first as an author in grammar, language, and history.[1] Not only did Priestley's work as a minister dominate the greater part of his life, it gave him the education and training he needed to pursue his scientific and other intellectual interests. His ministry at New Meeting, Birmingham (1780–91) was, in many ways, the defining part of his career, and certainly the happiest period of his life according to his

* I am grateful to Martin Fitzpatrick and G. M. Ditchfield for their advice on this chapter.

[1] Robert E. Schofield, 'Joseph Priestley: Theology, Physics and Metaphysics', *E&D*, 2 (1983), 70, 69.

own account, not least because of the catastrophe of the Birmingham riots of July 1791 which brought it to an end. This chapter examines the changes in Priestley's religious opinions against the background of his life, his work as a minister and teacher, and the impact of his theological and other ideas upon the development of modern Unitarianism.

PRIESTLEY'S EARLY LIFE AND EDUCATION

Priestley was born on 13 March 1733, old style, at Fieldhead, in the parish of Birstall, near Leeds, where his family was engaged in the manufacture and finishing of cloth.[2] His mother died in childbirth when he was 5 years old. His father, Jonas Priestley, having a young family, soon remarried, and Priestley was sent to Heckmondwike to live with his father's childless older sister, Sarah, and her wealthy husband, John Keighley. His aunt was undoubtedly the formative influence on his childhood. His uncle died when he was 12, and his widowed aunt was 'fond of him in the extreme'; 'she was truly a parent to me' 'considering me as her child'.[3] When she discovered his interest in books and natural ability she had him educated with the intention that he should become a minister. He was sent to the local grammar school at Batley, where he was taught Latin and the rudiments of Greek. He learnt Hebrew from his minister, John Kirkby, whose school he subsequently attended and where he had acquired 'a pretty good knowledge' of the classical languages by the age of 16, when Kirkby retired. This was the end of Priestley's

---

[2] The most recent attempt to recover details concerning Priestley's early life is Schofield, I.

[3] Rutt, I i, 4, 6–7; Timothy Priestley, *A Funeral Sermon Occasioned by the Death of the Late Joseph Priestley,... to which is Added, A True Statement of many Important Circumstances Relative to those Differences of Opinion which Existed between the Two Brothers, Joseph and Timothy* (London, 1804), with an appendix of 'authentic anecdotes', 36. For details of Priestley's family, the dates of the death of his mother and his aunt's marriage, see Joseph Hunter, *Familiae Minorum Gentium*, ed. J. W. Clay, Harleian Society, 27 (1894), I, 95; *The Nonconformist Register, of Baptisms, Marriages, and Deaths, Compiled by the Revs Oliver Heywood & T. Dickenson, 1644–1702, 1702–1752, Generally Known as the Northowram or Coley Register*, ed. J. Horsfall Turner (Brighouse, 1881), 327, 220.

formal schooling. Being a weak and consumptive child, he was nearly forced by ill health to give up his studies and follow a trade instead, and he taught himself French, German, and Italian to that end. An uncle found him a place at a merchant's house at Lisbon, but he recovered in time and resumed his studies. In the year or so before he went to the dissenting academy at Daventry, he studied mathematics with George Haggerston (d. 1792), the Presbyterian minister at Hopton near Dewsbury, who in turn had studied at Edinburgh University under Colin MacLaurin, author of one of the best popular introductions to Newtonian science. Priestley himself taught Hebrew to John Tommas, Baptist minister at Gildersome, and he acquired, as a consequence, a pretty good acquaintance with Syriac and was able to read Arabic. Before he was 20 he had read 'the Hebrew Bible twice through, once with points and once without'. He also read in preparation for his training for the ministry W. J. 's Gravesande's *Mathematical Elements of Natural Philosophy*, John Locke's *Essay concerning Human Understanding*, Isaac Watts's treatise on *Logic* and a number of other texts. As a consequence, he wrote, 'when I was admitted to the academy, ... I was excused all the studies of the first year, and a great part of those of the second.'[4]

There is little doubt that from an early age Priestley exhibited an interest in religious matters, or that he was brought up in an orthodox family. His mother taught him the Westminster Assembly's catechism, a series of set questions and answers which formed the principal method of imprinting the orthodox doctrines of faith upon the minds of the young. According to his brother Timothy, at the age of 4 Priestley could repeat all of the 107 questions and answers of the shorter Westminster catechism 'without missing a word': early evidence of both his ability and his orthodox upbringing. While at Batley Grammar School Priestley had defended the doctrine of free will in correspondence with the freethinker Peter Annet (1693–1769), whose shorthand he had learnt.[5] His family attended the Independent

---

[4] Rutt, I i, 7, 8, 13, 14; D. N. R. Lester, *The History of Batley Grammar School, 1612–1962* (Batley: J. S. Newsome & Son Ltd, 1968), 48–53; Joseph Priestley, *Defences of Unitarianism for the Year 1786, containing Letters to Dr Horne, Dean of Canterbury* (Birmingham, 1788), 187.

[5] Priestley, *Funeral Sermon ... of the Late Joseph Priestley*, 35–6; Rutt, I i, 5; Joseph Priestley, *Letters to Dr Horsley, in Answer to his Animadversions on the History of the Corruptions of Christianity* (Birmingham, 1783), p. v.

Chapel at Heckmondwike, keeping the Sabbath strictly, and he was catechized there regularly and publicly. His aunt's household was religious, with family prayers daily, morning and evening. In Priestley's own words,

Thus I was brought up with sentiments of piety, but without bigotry; and having, from my earliest years, given much attention to the subject of religion, I was much confirmed as I well could be in the principles of Calvinism, all the books that came in my way having that tendency.[6]

During these years, however, there are hints that Priestley was moving away from Calvinism, though in a fairly unformulated way, yet still holding to the main orthodox tenets. In about 1749, when he was 16, he had a serious illness, which at the time appeared to be consumption. Already troubled about religious matters, he became convinced as a result of his Calvinist upbringing that a religious experience demonstrating personal conviction was necessary for salvation. He therefore became deeply disturbed when he was unable to find evidence of such an experience. As a consequence he seems to have been in a state of terror for a time, fearing that repentance and salvation were denied him. All this was entirely conventional. Many people were brought to religion by illness or a major personal crisis. Priestley was greatly reassured when he found that there were others, including ministers he knew, who did not hold these orthodox doctrines either.[7]

Before the second half of the eighteenth century there were few if any who openly expressed Unitarian views, but it is clear some ministers in the neighbourhood of Leeds had departed from orthodox Calvinism. They included a number of the ministers with whom Priestley came into contact whilst growing up. He recalled that William Graham (d. 1796) of Warley near Halifax and Thomas Walker (d. 1763) of Leeds were considered 'the most heretical ministers of the neighbourhood'. In addition, George Haggerston, who taught him mathematics, was a Baxterian.[8] When the Independent Church at Heckmondwike was seeking a new minister in 1752 on the retirement of John Kirkby through ill health, those who applied

---

[6] Rutt, I i, 11, 16–17, 19.   [7] Rutt, I i, 12.

[8] Rutt, I i, 11, 12, 15. For the significance of Baxterianism and for the main theological developments in the period see the Introduction.

included John Walker of Ashton-under-Lyne, 'an avowed Baxterian'.[9] 'Being rejected on that account, his opinions were much canvassed', that is widely discussed. Priestley was among those influenced, not least as a result of his private conversations with Walker, who during his stay was a guest of Priestley's aunt. 'We soon became very intimate, and I thought I saw much of reason in his sentiments.' As a result of these debates with ministers and of his own reading Priestley's opinions changed, so that when he applied to the Church at Heckmondwike for membership and admission to the Lord's Supper in 1752, at the age of 19, he was rejected for his unsound opinions on the question of original sin. Subsequently, he was to realize, as a consequence of '[t]hinking farther on these subjects, I was, before I went to the academy, an Arminian; but had by no means rejected the doctrine of the Trinity, or that of Atonement.'[10]

DAVENTRY ACADEMY

Despite being rejected by his church, Priestley remained intent on entering the ministry. Candidates for the nonconformist ministry had to undergo training in preparation for their future careers. Although dissenters could not matriculate at Oxford nor take a degree at Cambridge without subscription to the Anglican Thirty-Nine Articles of Religion, the legal barriers were perhaps less significant than practical considerations, in particular that both universities in defending Anglican orthodoxy upheld values hostile to dissent. Dissenters had therefore established their own academies, intended to provide candidates for the ministry with a higher education similar to that found at

[9] Alexander Gordon identifies Walker as John Walker, a native of Ashton-under-Lyne, who entered Doddridge's academy in 1749; see Alexander Gordon, *Heads of English Unitarian History with appended lectures on Baxter and Priestley* (London: Philip Green, 1895), 105–6.

[10] Rutt, I i, 11, 14–15, 17. For the supposed influence of Walker and Haggerston on Priestley's religious opinions, see 'A Short Sketch of the Life and Writings of the late Joseph Priestley, L.L.D. F.R.S. &c &c', *Universal Theology Magazine and Impartial Review*, 1 (1804), 172; Priestley, *Funeral Sermon... of the Late Joseph Priestley*, 40–1. Priestley himself acknowledged the influence of Graham: Joseph Priestley, *Disquisitions Relating to Matter and Spirit. To which is added, the History of the Philosophical Doctrine concerning the Origin of the Soul* (London, 1777), dedication to Graham, p. vi.

the universities, and so to follow on from grammar-learning. The best were very good indeed, and the ministers they trained were able to hold their own with Anglican controversialists trained at Oxford and Cambridge, but a number founded in the mid-eighteenth century were more noted for their piety than their scholarship. [11]

Because of his lack of orthodoxy, Priestley faced difficulties over the choice of academy. His relatives originally suggested the academy at Plaisterers' Hall, Stepney, run by the highly orthodox Zephaniah Marryat (1684?–1754). Following concern over the spread of Arminianism and the threat to orthodox Calvinism, the academy had been established by the King's Head Society with the intention of training orthodox students for the ministry and maintaining them in their Calvinism. Every candidate supported by the Society was required to subscribe to *A Declaration as to some Controverted Points of Christian Doctrine*, and to undergo regular examination as to their beliefs to ensure their continued orthodoxy. In Priestley's own words,

My aunt, and all my relations, being strict Calvinists, it was their intention to send me to the academy at Mile-end, ... But, being at that time an Arminian, I resolutely opposed it, especially upon finding that if I went thither, besides giving an [account of my] *experience*, I must subscribe my assent to ten printed articles of the strictest Calvinistic faith, and repeat it every six months.

Priestley's stubbornness led to an impasse which might have forced him to give up any idea of training for the ministry: for as he noted, 'My opposition ... would probably have been to no purpose, and I must have adopted some other mode of life'. [12] Fortunately, Priestley's former minister and teacher, John Kirkby, intervened. Determined that Priestley should have a better education than that provided by the orthodox Plaisterers' Hall, he recommended the academy conducted by Philip Doddridge at Northampton instead. Priestley's stepmother, who had served as housekeeper to Doddridge's family, added her voice in favour as well. [13]

---

[11] D. L. Wykes, 'The Contribution of the Dissenting Academy to the Emergence of Rational Dissent' in Haakonssen, 103, 125–6.

[12] Rutt, I i, 21. After Marryat's death the Academy moved to Mile End under the direction of John Conder. The examination of students as to their spiritual state was every three months, not six.

[13] Rutt, I i, 22.

Doddridge's academy was undoubtedly one of the best dissenting academies during the second quarter of the eighteenth century. Indeed, because of the reputation of its tutor, it even attracted
students from Anglican families and from abroad. Before Priestley
could enter the academy, Doddridge died of consumption in 1751
at the early age of 49; the academy then moved to Daventry under
his successor Caleb Ashworth (d. 1775), assisted by Samuel Clark
(d. 1769), but much of Doddridge's teaching and methods was preserved. Priestley was admitted to Daventry Academy as a student for
the ministry in November 1752.[14] There is no doubt that the academy
opened Priestley's mind to new ideas as well as providing him with
the scholarship and knowledge necessary to undertake independent
study in the classics, natural philosophy (science), and philosophy as
well as theology.

The academy at Daventry, unlike many academies of the period,
particularly those conducted on strictly orthodox lines, encouraged
students to weigh up the evidence and think for themselves. Rather
than giving only the orthodox interpretations of controversial questions, the tutors, following Doddridge's example, sought to provide the students with the arguments necessary to defend the truth
against error and heresy. In later academies the method of disputation
became formalized, with the tutor and his assistant often taking up
opposing sides. At Daventry, according to Priestley, Ashworth took
'the orthodox side of every question, and Mr Clark, the sub-tutor,
that of heresy'. Moreover, 'we were referred to authors on both sides
of every question, and were then required to give an account of them'.
Inevitably some students after having heard the arguments both for
and against found it impossible to be reconciled with the orthodox
position. Encouraged to read widely round the subject and to form
his own judgement, Priestley, like many other students, was to apply
these methods when studying Scripture for himself.[15] Moreover the

---

[14] DWL, MS CT1, Minutes of the Coward Trust, 16 May 1738 to 30 Nov. 1752, 139.
[15] Rutt, I i, 23–4; Wykes, 'Contribution of the Dissenting Academy', 128. For an
account of Priestley's studies during his last year at Daventry see Tony Rail and Beryl
Thomas (eds), 'Joseph Priestley's Journal while at Daventry Academy, 1754', *E & D*,
13 (1994), 49–113. For Doddridge's methods and their influence see Isabel Rivers, *The
Defence of Truth through the Knowledge of Error: Philip Doddridge's Academy Lectures*
(London: Dr Williams's Trust, 2003).

students themselves engaged freely in discussing together many of these controversial ideas.

In my time, the academy was in a state peculiarly favourable to the serious pursuit of truth, as the students were about equally divided upon every question of much importance, such as liberty and necessity, the sleep of the soul, and all the articles of theological orthodoxy and heresy; in consequence of which, all these topics were the subject of continual discussion.

From these discussions Priestley found himself adopting what is 'generally called the heterodox side of almost every question'.[16]

It was at Daventry that Priestley first encountered the doctrine of necessity, initially from reading Anthony Collins's *Philosophical Inquiry concerning Human Liberty* (1717). Priestley reprinted the work in 1790. But it was Hartley's *Observations on Man*, referred to 'in the course of our Lectures', which had the most profound influence on his thinking. Priestley saw his introduction to Hartley's work as the event that

produced the greatest, and in my opinion the most favourable effect on my general turn of thinking through life. It established me in the belief of the doctrine of Necessity, ... it greatly improved that disposition to piety which I brought to the academy, and freed it from the rigour with which it had been tinctured. Indeed, I do not know whether the consideration of Dr Hartley's theory contributes more to enlighten the mind, or improve the heart.

Hartley's necessitarian philosophy enabled Priestley to replace the doctrine of man's natural depravity with a scheme that saw man as capable of attaining perfection through the will of a benevolent God.[17] Before he left Daventry it is clear that Priestley had become an Arian, that is he insisted on the worship of God the Father alone, relegating the Son to a subordinate position, but he still looked upon Christ as divine. In this period Arianism was the most common form of anti-Trinitarianism. Priestley was not at this time a Unitarian, but as his studies continued he was increasingly to challenge orthodox interpretation.

---

[16] Rutt, I i, 23, 24–5.
[17] Rutt, I i, 24, 25. See also Joseph Priestley, *An Examination of Dr Reid's Inquiry into the Human Mind on the Principles of Common Sense* (London, 1774), p. xix. For a full account of Priestley's debt to Collins and Hartley see Chapter 3.

PRIESTLEY'S EARLY MINISTRY: NEEDHAM
MARKET AND NANTWICH

Priestley's first ministry on leaving Daventry was at Needham Market in Suffolk, where he was invited to become assistant minister to the elderly John Meadows (1675/6–1757) in 1755. It proved to be a mistake. He was far too heterodox for his new congregation and, being Priestley, he did not conceal his advanced views. Shortly after his arrival he began a series of lectures on the theory of religion, which eventually became his *Institutes of Natural and Revealed Religion*, published in 1772–4, and which he had originally begun at Daventry. Although he generally avoided all subjects of controversy from the pulpit, many in his congregation were 'attentive to nothing but the soundness of my faith in the doctrine of the Trinity'. In this respect it was what he left out rather than what he said that demonstrated his departure from orthodoxy. When 'I came to treat of the *Unity of God*, merely as an article of religion' their suspicions were aroused. He also made no secret of his Arianism in private conversation. Meadows, the senior minister, was outraged and took a major part in the opposition against him, with the result that he was deserted by many in the congregation. As a consequence the promised salary of £40 a year was never paid, and he experienced severe financial difficulties. Attempts to undertake a school at Needham failed because of the doubts about his orthodoxy, but he was more successful in giving a series of twelve lectures on the use of the globes at half a guinea each. He was also increasingly troubled by his speech impediment which made preaching difficult, so much so that at one time he considered giving up the ministry for teaching.[18]

   He continued his theological studies, examining in particular the foundations of Christian faith. As a result he came to question orthodox doctrines further. When he left Daventry he still had 'a qualified belief' in the doctrine of atonement, that the death of Christ was a sacrifice in expiation for man's sins. At Needham he began to examine the evidence from both the Old and New Testaments.

---

[18] Rutt, I i, 30–2, 33, 41, 62. Despite efforts to improve his stammer, Priestley was still being seriously troubled in 1788; see JRUL, Lindsey Letters, volume II, no. 26, Theophilus Lindsey to William Tayleur, Shrewsbury, 29 Nov. 1788 (I owe this reference to G. M. Ditchfield).

After considering all the relevant texts, he concluded that the doctrine of atonement could not be sustained either by Scripture or reason. He published his thoughts on the subject as *The Scripture Doctrine of Remission* in 1761. This work is clearly a significant departure from Calvinism. In it he sought to demonstrate that there was no scriptural evidence to support the doctrine of atonement; on the contrary, he argued the evidence showed that salvation depended upon true repentance and moral reform. This appeal to the sufficiency of Scripture and reliance upon reason as the sole means by which to distinguish revealed truth was typical of rational dissent.[19]

Priestley was fortunate that Thomas Haynes, the minister of Upper Chapel, Sheffield, then arranged for an invitation from his former congregation at Nantwich in Cheshire. Priestley left Needham Market in September 1758. Although the congregation at Nantwich had only 60 members, it proved a much more congenial pulpit for Priestley. Many of the leading members shared his more liberal theology, the orthodox having seceded from the congregation during the previous ministry. At Nantwich Priestley set up a school, and, despite his earlier avowed distaste for teaching, he found it to be much more rewarding than he had expected. He taught about 30 boys, and in a separate room half a dozen girls, from seven in the morning until four in the afternoon, and afterwards tutored the children of a wealthy lawyer until seven in the evening. 'I had, therefore, but little leisure for reading or for improving myself in any way, except what necessarily arose from my employment' as a teacher. The demands of his congregation, however, were light, with few children to catechize or families to visit. At Nantwich, therefore, he was more teacher than preacher, even repeating the sermons previously prepared at Needham, 'where I never failed to make at least one every week'. The greater income he derived from his school enabled him to purchase books and some scientific equipment: a small air-pump and an electrical machine. The public experiments, often by the senior scholars, helped to enhance the reputation of his school, though he claimed he had only purchased the apparatus to satisfy his own curiosity. He had no leisure 'to make any original experiments until many years after'.[20] Teaching may have allowed him little time for writing, but while at

---

[19] Rutt, I i, 36–7.   [20] Rutt, I i, 42–3, 45.

Nantwich he did prepare *The Rudiments of English Grammar* (1761) for the use of his school, though it was printed too late for him 'to make trial of it' there. Published the year before Robert Lowth's *Short Introduction to English Grammar* (1762), Priestley's *English Grammar* has been seen as one of the earliest comprehensive text-books on the subject. Intended to set out 'the established principles of the English language adapted to the use of schools', it provided a detailed description of English grammar and its different components and included examples of composition drawn from the Bible and the best English authors for students to imitate. It was not his originality so much as his good sense and practical judgement that characterized the work. He rejected the approach of earlier authors who had kept rigidly to the form and structure of the Latin grammar and who used Latin definitions and terms rather than English. In turn he has been identified as one of the earliest advocates of the doctrine of usage, which forms the basis of modern scholarship. He did not attempt to establish a set of rules, arguing instead that language could only be based on usage and convention. His *English Grammar* was to go through nine editions between 1761 and 1798, including a pirated Dublin edition. It was also translated into German (1779) and French (1799).[21]

TUTOR AT WARRINGTON ACADEMY

Priestley's ministry at Nantwich was short, for in June 1761 he was invited to become tutor in languages and belles lettres at the celebrated Warrington Academy. The Academy had been founded in 1757, and Priestley, while still at Needham Market, had been proposed as tutor in classics, but the classicist John Aikin senior (1713–80), master of a school at Kibworth in Leicestershire, 'whose qualifications were superior to mine was justly preferred to me'. Priestley was to accept the invitation to succeed Aikin four years later, though 'my school promised to be more gainful to me'. He concluded,

[21] Rutt, I i, 45. See his letter to Caleb Rotheram, 18 May 1766, Rutt, I i, 64–5; Schofield, I, 79–83, 99–104; Joseph Priestley, *The Rudiments of English Grammar* (London, 1761), p. iii; A. C. Baugh and T. Cable, *A History of the English Language* (London, 1951; 5th edn., 2002), 282–5.

however, that his employment at Warrington would be 'more liberal, and less painful', in other words less demanding. 'It was also a means of extending my connexions'. Nevertheless, Priestley told the trustees who brought the invitation that he would have preferred to be tutor in mathematics and natural philosophy, 'for which I had at that time a great predilection'. Indeed, he claimed at the time he took up his duties at Warrington that he had 'no particular fondness' or partiality for the subjects he was to teach.[22]

Historians have seen the significance of Priestley's teaching at Warrington in terms of his innovation, both in the subjects he taught and the methods he used. Besides his duties as tutor in languages and belles lettres, for which he taught Latin, Greek, French, and Italian and gave lectures on the theory of language and on oratory and criticism (subjects which Aikin had previously taught), Priestley introduced lectures on history and general policy, the laws and constitutions of England, and the history of England. Priestley was led to introduce these new subjects after observing that the majority of the students he taught at Warrington were intended either for careers in business or for public life, yet the existing curriculum was designed for the learned professions, that is the ministry, the law, and medicine.[23] After a year he gave over the teaching of logic and Hebrew to Aikin and substituted lectures on civil law instead. Responsible for teaching elocution, Priestley also introduced weekly public exercises by the students, when English and Latin essays and speeches were read and even scenes from plays performed before an audience of tutors, fellow students and visitors.[24] He published the syllabus for his new lectures in 1765 as *An Essay on a Course of Liberal Education*. He had already printed, though not published, his *Lectures on the Theory of Language and Universal Grammar* (1762) for the use of his students at Warrington. The lectures show Priestley's attempts to apply scientific methods to the rules and precepts of grammar and the theory of language. His *Chart of Biography* (1765), first drawn up for use in his lectures in history 'as one of the mechanical methods of facilitating the study of that science', together with his later *Chart of History*

---

[22] Rutt, I i, 46–7, 50.
[23] Rutt, I i, 50–1; Joseph Priestley, *An Essay on a Course of Liberal Education for Civil and Active Life* ([London], 1765), pp. i–ii, 1.
[24] Rutt, I i, 51–4.

(1769), was intended to encourage a more systematic approach to the study of history. His educational philosophy clearly went beyond the preparation of textbooks and the introduction of new subjects. Ruth Watts has pointed to the influence of Locke and Hartley upon Priestley's educational theory and teaching methods, particularly his understanding of Hartley's concept of association psychology as a means of building up understanding in those being educated.[25]

Warrington has acquired the reputation as the greatest of the dissenting academies, indeed, as one of the leading education establishments in the eighteenth century, rivalling Oxford and Cambridge: a reputation which Priestley's connection as a tutor has helped to enhance. Despite the excellence of the education provided, the scholarship of the tutors, and the innovative nature of some of the teaching and curriculum as a result of the introduction of new subjects and methods of instruction, the contribution of Warrington, certainly to dissent, is more questionable. The academy's reputation was founded on its teaching of secular subjects: science, languages, and history. It educated comparatively few students for the ministry and did not match Daventry Academy either in the number of ministers it trained or in the quality of the instruction provided in theology, metaphysics, and ethics. Best described as a dissenting university, Warrington was a cheaper alternative to Oxford and Cambridge, but also one free from religious subscription. Illustrative of the best that dissent could achieve, it neither fitted the pattern of other eighteenth-century dissenting academies, nor had the broader influence on educational development so often attributed to it. With the exception of the short-lived New College, Hackney, the range of subjects and standard of education was not matched amongst dissenters until after 1803 when Manchester College moved to York.[26]

---

[25] Joseph Priestley, *A Description of a Chart of Biography with a Catalogue of all the Names Inserted in it, and the Dates Annexed to them* (Warrington, 1765), 4, n.*; Ruth Watts, 'Joseph Priestley and Education', *E&D*, 2 (1983), 87–93. See also her *Gender, Power and the Unitarians in England, 1760–1860* (London: Longman, 1998), 35–7. Edinburgh University awarded Priestley a LLD by diploma for the *Chart of Biography*. I am grateful to Professor Watts for discussing Priestley's educational philosophy with me.

[26] For a reassessment of the significance of Warrington, especially for dissent, see Wykes, 'Contribution of the Dissenting Academy', 132–4, 136. For a comparison of the educational standards at Warrington with New College, Hackney, and Manchester

While at Warrington Priestley began his early scientific experiments. In 1765, 'having composed all the lectures I had occasion to deliver, and finding myself at liberty for any undertaking', Priestley decided to embark on a history of electricity. Encouraged by the American politician and polymath Benjamin Franklin, whom he had met in London during Christmas 1764, he set about the work with astonishing energy. By the end of 1766 he had completed his 750-page *History and Present State of Electricity*. He had only intended to write 'a distinct and methodical account of all that had been done by others', and the work, as it was conceived, could easily have been seen as part of his previous historical writings, such as the *Chart of Biography* and his lectures on 'History and General Policy'. By examining points which were uncertain or in dispute he was led to experiment and test theories for himself. His history therefore included accounts of his own experiments and findings. The *History of Electricity* was his most successful scientific publication, reaching a fifth edition in 1794.[27]

Priestley was 'singularly happy' at Warrington, particularly with his fellow tutors. They were all Arians, and they shared the same opinions in religion. The only Socinian, or militant anti-Trinitarian, in the neighbourhood was John Seddon of Manchester, 'and we all wondered at him'. Although the doctrine of atonement, concerning which Aikin held 'some obscure notions', was a topic of friendly discussion amongst the tutors, when it came to the question of the Trinity none of them at this time ever 'entered into any particular examination of the subject'. Another source of contentment was his marriage. In June 1762 Priestley married Mary Wilkinson, the daughter of Isaac Wilkinson, a prosperous ironmaster near Wrexham. Besides the happiness and support she gave him, Priestley 'unexpectedly found a great resource in her two brothers, who had become wealthy, especially the elder of them'. John Wilkinson was to provide Priestley with generous assistance, particularly towards the cost of his scientific experiments.[28]

New College, see D. L. Wykes, 'Sons and Subscribers: Lay Support and the College, 1786–1840' in Barbara Smith (ed), *Truth, Liberty, Religion: Essays Celebrating Two Hundred Years of Manchester College* (Oxford: Manchester College, 1986), 31–77.

[27] Rutt, I i, 54, 56; Golinski, 78–9. See Chapter 2 below.
[28] Rutt, I i, 48–9, 58–9, 61, 217.

PRIESTLEY'S MINISTRY AT MILL HILL, LEEDS

In 1767 Priestley decided to accept the invitation to become minister of the important congregation at Mill Hill, Leeds. In his memoirs he explained his decision was chiefly influenced by the state of his wife's health, though the reasons were also financial. It proved impossible, 'even living with the greatest frugality, to make any provision for a family'. The Academy's finances were uncertain and there was little prospect of an increase in salary, but Priestley always regarded the ministry as the most important calling of all. Although there had been no requirement for him to preach at Warrington, 'wishing to keep up the character of a Dissenting minister' he had chosen to do so, and in May 1762, the month before his marriage, he had been ordained. Young ministers often delayed ordination until they were certain of their calling.[29] At Leeds, Priestley attended to his pastoral duties closely. Though he wrote few sermons, making no secret of his habit of borrowing from his friends, he paid great attention to catechizing the children and young people in the congregation. He also attempted to encourage greater attendance at the Lord's Supper, but his efforts to promote a new scheme of congregational discipline failed.[30] It was during this period that he began his experiments with gases upon which his reputation as a scientist largely rests, though his most important scientific discovery, oxygen, was made at Bowood, when he was in the employ of the Earl of Shelburne.

At Leeds he also wrote his first major political work. He had included 'Remarks on a Proposed Code of Education' in an appendix to his *Essay on a Course of Liberal Education* in response to the Anglican clergyman John Brown (1715–66), who in his *Thoughts on Civil Liberty* (1765) had advocated that the state should establish a uniform plan of public education. Priestley saw state interference as a threat to the freedom of dissenters to determine the education of their own children. He particularly feared that a state system would mean control by the established church. As a consequence, encouraged by his friends, he began to examine the subject of civil and political liberty and in 1768 he published his *Essay on the First Principles of*

---

[29] Rutt, I i, 61–2.
[30] Edward Taylor, letter to the editor, *Monthly Repository*, 13 (1818), 94.

Government, the year after he had left Warrington. This is Priestley's most significant political work and was said by Jeremy Bentham to have given rise to his dictum 'the greatest happiness of the greatest numbers'.[31] As a dissenter, deprived of full civil and political rights, Priestley was particularly sensitive to the loss of liberty. He repeated much of his earlier criticism of Brown over state interference and the rights of parents to educate their children, but he also addressed the question of religious liberty, advocating a wider toleration to include even Roman Catholics, which proved too much for some of his friends and fellow dissenters. The following year he published his *Present State of Liberty in Great Britain and her Colonies* (1769), warning against the growth of arbitrary power and government both in Britain and America and the threat to the liberty of the individual.[32]

PRIESTLEY'S ADOPTION OF UNITARIAN OPINIONS

It was while living at Leeds that in June 1769, on a visit to Archdeacon Francis Blackburne, rector of Richmond, Yorkshire, Priestley first met Theophilus Lindsey. At the time Lindsey, who had married Blackburne's step-daughter, was still vicar of Catterick, though he was soon to resign his living. It proved to be the beginning of an extraordinarily warm friendship; many of Priestley's surviving letters were written to Lindsey.[33] At Leeds Priestley returned to serious theological study and

---

[31] Rutt, I i, 52 n.†; Jeremy Bentham, *A Fragment on Government; being an Examination of what is Delivered, on the Subject of Government in General* (London, 1776), p. ii. The exact phrase is not found in Priestley's *Essay on the First Principles*. For a discussion of this attribution, see Schofield, I, 207–9; Anne Holt, *A Life of Joseph Priestley* (London: Oxford University Press, 1931), 35.

[32] Rutt, I i, 94–100, 106–7, Priestley, Leeds, to Thomas Hollis, 1 Nov. 1768, Priestley to Lindsey, 18 Jan. 1770. See Martin Fitzpatrick, 'Joseph Priestley and the Cause of Universal Toleration', *P-PN*, 1 (1977), 3–21. For a full account of the *Essay on the First Principles of Government* and Priestley's views on toleration and state interference see Chapter 4 below.

[33] Rutt, I i, 81–2. For Priestley's friendship with Lindsey, see Chapter 5 below; G. M. Ditchfield, ' "The Preceptor of Nations": Joseph Priestley and Theophilus Lindsey', *TUHS*, 23 (2004), 495–512; and *The Letters of Theophilus Lindsey*, ed. G. M. Ditchfield, Volume 1: 1747–1788, Church of England Record Society, 15 (Woodbridge: Boydell & Brewer, 2007).

there, he tells us, in consequence of 'reading with care Dr Lardner's Letter on the Logos', he became a Unitarian, some 15 or 16 years after he had originally become an Arian. As historians have pointed out, it does seem surprising that Priestley should have been influenced to change his opinions at this date by *A Letter... Concerning... the Logos* by the Biblical scholar Nathaniel Lardner (1684–1768). The work had been published in 1759, though written nearly 30 years earlier, and despite the fact that it appeared anonymously the author's name was reasonably well known. It is hard to believe that Priestley was not aware of the work before he moved to Leeds, since he was already friendly with Lardner. Indeed he visited Lardner as an old man in London in 1767. Besides Lardner, Priestley was also well acquainted with Caleb Fleming 'and several other zealous Socinians, especially my friend Mr Graham', whom he had first met when living with his aunt. He was still an Arian at the time of Lardner's death in 1769, but 'continuing my study of the scriptures, with the help of his Letters on the Logos, I at length changed my opinion', though, by his own admission, it was a long time before he came to adopt Unitarian ideas fully. Like Lardner, he became a Unitarian as a result of studying the Scriptures for himself, rather than from reading Socinian authors.[34] Perhaps it was his friendship with Lindsey that encouraged him to read, or at least re-read, Lardner's *Letter* on the Logos and to look at the arguments afresh. Certainly the friendship between Lindsey and Priestley was to prove crucial for the development of modern Unitarianism.[35]

Until the second half of the eighteenth century, as G. M. Ditchfield has shown, anti-Trinitarianism took an Arian rather than a Socinian form, and most individuals holding heterodox opinions on the Trinity were Arian. Dr Ditchfield makes the point that trinitarian speculation had long existed, especially in the Church of England, and that Socinianism, a militant anti-Trinitarianism, was not significant until championed by Priestley and Lindsey. Lindsey resigned from

---

[34] Rutt, I i, pp. 69, 37; Priestley, *Letters to Dr Horsley*, p. vi; [Nathaniel Lardner], *A Letter writ in the Year 1730, Concerning the Question, Whether the Logos Supplied the Place of a Human Soul in the Person of Jesus Christ* (London, 1759), 54–5; *The Works of Nathaniel Lardner, D.D. in Eleven Volumes: with a Life by Dr Kippis* (London, 1788), I, p. lix.
[35] Gordon, *Heads of... Unitarian History*, 109.

the Church of England in November 1773 over a point of principle, the requirement to subscribe to the Thirty-Nine Articles of Religion. After resigning his living at Catterick he established the first avowedly Unitarian congregation, at Essex Street in London, in 1774, where he attracted a remarkably fashionable congregation. They included the future evangelical William Wilberforce (for a brief time) and the Duke of Grafton, together with MPs and well connected professional men. Lindsey's correspondence demonstrates both the extent of his network of contacts and his powerful friends.

Dr Ditchfield sees 'the increasingly open avowal of Socinianism, as distinct from Arianism, and the influence in London of a strategically placed Socinian group based on Lindsey's Essex Street chapel, ... [as] decisive' in the development of Unitarianism in the final quarter of the eighteenth century.[36] By the last decade of the century a newer form of Unitarianism, with a sectarian outlook, had emerged, far different from the previous Arianism. Though often described as Socinians, Unitarians differed in refusing to address the person of Christ. The *Monthly Review* in 1792 defined Unitarianism as 'denying the Trinity' and 'maintaining the absolute unity of God' and 'proper humanity of Christ'. Priestley went further, but his humanitarian views were generally dismissed as 'necessarian' philosophy.[37]

If Lindsey provided the powerful contacts and the early organization, it was Priestley who provided the intellectual stimulus. During the 1770s and 80s, Priestley published a succession of brilliantly controversial works advancing ideas that caught up and convinced many of his readers and a generation of young ministers.[38] The *Appeal to the Serious and Candid Professors of Christianity*, in which he first expressed his newly acquired Unitarian opinions, was originally published in Leeds in 1770. Addressed to the local Calvinistic Methodists, it was the earliest and most successful of his popular tracts.[39] His *Institutes of Natural and Revealed Religion*, published in three volumes

[36] G. M. Ditchfield, 'Anti-Trinitarianism and Toleration in Late 18th-Century British Politics: The Unitarian Petition of 1792', *JEH*, 42 (1991), 46.

[37] *Monthly Review*, NS 9 (1792), 175, cited by Ditchfield, 'Anti-Trinitarianism', 48. This and the previous paragraph rely heavily on Dr Ditchfield's essay, especially 43–8.

[38] R. K. Webb, 'The Emergence of Rational Dissent' in Haakonssen, 36.

[39] Rutt, I i, 138, 139, 142; Joseph Priestley to the Revd Samuel Merivale, undated; Joseph Priestley to the Revd Theophilus Lindsey, 14 Jun. 1771; Joseph Priestley to the Revd Samuel Merivale, 23 Aug. 1771.

between 1772 and 1774, also had a popular purpose. He wrote on the constitution of the Christian church, the need for regular taking of the sacrament, and on the constitutional rights of dissenters, challenging the celebrated writer on the English constitution, William Blackstone. His polemical writings, such as his *Appeal*, though initially intended for a local audience subsequently achieved a wide circulation in a series of cheap editions with large print runs. The contentious nature of his writings made him an increasingly controversial figure. His attack on the Church of England in his *Institutes* caused a storm of anger. Because he wrote so many works, including many of a controversial nature, Priestley's connection from the mid-1760s with the bookseller and publisher Joseph Johnson (1738–1809) proved especially valuable. Johnson, one of the leading figures in the London book trade, and an early supporter of Lindsey's chapel in Essex Street, became Priestley's publisher and indeed friend, often acting as his agent in London.[40] While at Leeds Priestley also began the *Theological Repository* to publish articles of speculative theology, but it was supported by insufficient subscribers, and only three volumes were published (1769–71). It was revived when Priestley was living in Birmingham, but with no better success and given up after three further volumes (1784–88).

LIBRARIAN TO THE EARL OF SHELBURNE

In 1772 Priestley was approached by his friend the philosopher Richard Price (1723–91), minister of the Presbyterian meeting at Hackney, to become Lord Shelburne's librarian or literary companion. Priestley was attracted by the terms: £250 a year together with a house, and an annuity of £150 for life if the agreement was ended by mutual consent. He found his salary at Leeds of 100 guineas was insufficient

to defray the necessary expenses of housekeeping and much less those which my increasing connections unavoidably bring upon me; ... my philosophical

[40] Helen Braithwaite, *Romanticism, Publishing and Dissent: Joseph Johnson and the Cause of Liberty* (Basingstoke: Palgrave, 2003).

experiments, in which I have of late been exceedingly fortunate, [which] take up a great deal of my time, are necessarily very expensive and can not possibly make any return of profit. Now I think in London I should have easier access to books and instruments, and my correspondence would also be less expensive, and in several respects I should be in the way of bettering my circumstances.[41]

In June 1773 he removed to Calne in Wiltshire, near Shelburne's residence at Bowood. There he carried out his duties to provide political advice and catalogued Shelburne's books and manuscripts (now the Lansdowne manuscripts in the British Library) and his private papers. He travelled abroad with Shelburne between August and October 1774, visiting Holland, Flanders, and Germany, and spending a month in Paris, where he met many of the leading French scientists and philosophers, including Lavoisier, to whom he described some of his recent experiments on gases, as well as the discovery he had just made of 'dephlogisticated air'. Priestley's most important writings during this period were a series of metaphysical works, beginning with his hostile *Examination of Dr Reid's Inquiry* (1774), which considered the Scottish school of common sense philosophy, followed by *Hartley's Theory of the Human Mind* (1775), an abridgement of *Observations on Man* (which helped to spread Hartley's ideas in the nineteenth century), together with *Disquisitions relating to Matter and Spirit* (1777) and his *Doctrine of Philosophical Necessity* (1777). As a result of his conversations with philosophers and churchmen in Paris, he wrote *Letters to a Philosophical Unbeliever* (1780).[42]

PRIESTLEY AT BIRMINGHAM

In June 1780 Priestley left Shelburne's service and settled at Birmingham, though without any expectation of resuming his ministerial

---

[41] Rutt, I i, 197; Nottinghamshire Archives, Foljambe of Osberton MSS, DD/FJ/11/1/7/211, Priestley, Leeds, to Sir George Savile, 9–11 Nov. 1772. I am grateful to Nottinghamshire Archives for permission to quote.

[42] Rutt, I i, 197–8, 199. For Priestley's scientific and philosophical writings of this period see Chapters 2 and 3 below.

career, believing that no congregation would consider inviting someone so radical to be their minister. He chose Birmingham partly because his brother-in-law, John Wilkinson, 'wished to have us nearer to him', but also because of the advantages the town offered for his scientific and other pursuits. Within a month of his arrival at Birmingham, William Hawkes, one of the two ministers of the New Meeting congregation, resigned and Priestley received a unanimous invitation to succeed him. Priestley accepted on condition that he was allowed to limit his ministerial services to Sundays only, 'my time being much taken up with my philosophical and other studies', leaving the pastoral business of the congregation to his colleague Samuel Blyth.[43] Priestley received £100 for his ministerial duties, but his annuity from Shelburne was only about half what he had previously received, while his expenditure was twice his regular income. A number of friends led by John Fothergill raised a subscription, while others gave scientific materials, to enable Priestley to continue his experiments 'without being under the necessity of giving my time to pupils, which I must otherwise have done'. In addition, Wilkinson provided the Priestleys with a house, and William Russell, a leading member of New Meeting, met many of his household expenses. Birmingham also proved ideal in other respects. The importance of the Lunar Society in stimulating an extraordinary scientific and intellectual ferment and the benefits Priestley received have been widely recognized, but Priestley also acknowledged the advantages he received from the society of his ministerial colleagues. 'We met and drank tea together every fortnight' and they read learned papers. Priestley enjoyed the same friendly open discussion with them that he had previously enjoyed at Warrington with his fellow tutors.[44]

Priestley preached his first sermon as minister of New Meeting on 31 December 1780. His duties may have been restricted to Sundays,

[43] Rutt, I i, 338–40. There is no reference to Hawkes's resignation, or to Priestley's appointment, in the minutes of New Meeting; see BCL, Archives Department, MS UC2 [formerly MS 232]/158, 'Sketch of the New Meeting Congregation' [unfoliated].

[44] Rutt, I i, 214, 217, 338–9; R. E. Schofield, *The Lunar Society of Birmingham: A Social History of Provincial Society and Industry in Eighteenth-Century England* (Oxford: Clarendon Press, 1963). Rutt, I i, 335, Priestley, London, to Robert Scholefield, 1 Jun. 1780. Scholefield was minister of Old Meeting, Birmingham. For a list of those who assisted Priestley financially or otherwise, see Priestley's list of grateful acknowledgements, Rutt, I i, 214–17.

but he entered on them enthusiastically. He resumed the scheme he had originally introduced at Leeds of catechizing the younger children and giving lectures to the senior youths. To the latter he added the practice of expounding the Scripture lesson. Soon afterwards he told a friend that about 80 young men between the ages of 17 and 30 attended the lecture, and there were nearly 150 catechumens in all. He also added a further class. According to Lindsey in September 1783, Priestley instructed about 30 ladies, some of them married, in the principles of Christianity. 'This was the third class that had been before him that day; and this is his usual work every Sunday, added to his officiating to the whole congregation one part of it.' His lectures were so successful that the vestry meeting-room proved too small and had to be enlarged. When tensions in Birmingham between high churchmen and dissenters broke up the interdenominational Sunday schools, he readily assisted Old and New Meetings in setting up their own. He also introduced a new hymn-book and established a theological library for the use of the congregation. For Priestley these years at Birmingham were the happiest of his life, 'being highly favourable to every object I had in view, philosophical or chronological'.[45]

In 1782 Priestley published his *History of the Corruptions of Christianity*. It was perhaps his most controversial and influential book. Priestley attacked the principal elements of the Christian doctrine: the Trinity, predestination, and atonement, which in his opinion were at odds with the views of the early Christians. According to Priestley the greatest corruption was the doctrine of the Trinity. Understandably such a bold and direct attack on one of the principal doctrines of the Church and orthodox Christianity as a whole did not go unanswered. In Holland in 1785 the book was banned. In England Samuel Horsley, Archdeacon of St Albans, led the attack. Horsley ignored the principal arguments and attacked non-essentials, such as inaccuracies in Priestley's Greek translations. As a consequence Belsham remarked that while Horsley got his mitre (the bishopric of St Asaph), Priestley won the argument. Because of his published writings Priestley was already a controversial figure before he came to Birmingham. His attacks on

---

[45] BCL, Archives Department, MS UC2 [formerly MS 232]/123, s.v. 23 Jan., - Apr. 1788; MS UC2/85, pp. 11–12, 5 Mar. 1781, - Apr. 1788; MS UC2/ 158, 'Sketch of the New Meeting Congregation'; Rutt, I i, 338, 340; Priestley to Joseph Bretland, 27 Jul. 1781; Lindsey to William Turner, Wakefield, 1 Sept. 1783.

the Trinity and his rejection of original sin and atonement provoked anger, but it was the way in which he applied Hartley's materialist psychology that particularly disturbed the orthodox. His argument in *Disquisitions relating to Matter and Spirit* (1777) that the mind did not exist separate from the body and that Christ was human like us led to charges that he encouraged the growth of scepticism and atheism. For most orthodox Christians belief in the immateriality of the soul was essential to belief in the afterlife. By 1790 Priestley had become such an irritant to the orthodox that they almost came to see him as the devil incarnate. Priestley wittily reminded one opponent that if he really was so bad, then 'he should not have trodden on my cloven foot, or kicked me so near my tail, without remembering that I had horns, and he had none'.[46]

During the 1780s New Meeting was one of the leading congregations in the country actively engaging in politics and reform. Much of the leadership was provided by William Russell, but it is clear that Priestley was more involved in politics than he subsequently chose to acknowledge. From the mid-1780s he published a series of overtly political works, such as *The Importance and Extent of Free Inquiry in Matters of Religion* (1785), *Letter to the Right Honourable William Pitt* (1787), his sermon on 5 November 1789 to Old and New Meetings on *The Conduct to be Observed by Dissenters in Order to Procure the Repeal of the Corporation and Test Acts* (1789), and *Letters to the Right Honourable Edmund Burke, Occasioned by his Reflections on the Revolution in France* (1791). Historians have also detected the millenarian ideas underlying Priestley's later political and theological writing, which gave rise to his notorious reference to 'laying gunpowder, grain by grain, under the old building of error and superstition'. The American and French Revolutions convinced him that the millennium was beginning.[47]

---

[46] Thomas Belsham, *A Calm Inquiry into the Scripture Doctrine concerning the Person of Christ, Including a Brief Review of the Controversy Between Dr Horsley and Dr Priestley* (London, 1811), 439. William Hutton made a similar observation in *The Life of William Hutton, F.A.S.S., including a particular Account of the Riots at Birmingham in 1791* (London & Birmingham, 1816), 161; Joseph Priestley, *Familiar Letters, Addressed to the Inhabitants of Birmingham, in Refutation of Several Charges, Advanced against the Dissenters and Unitarians* (Birmingham, 1790), 87. For an account of *Corruptions* see Chapter 6 below.

[47] Joseph Priestley, *The Importance and Extent of Free Inquiry in Matters of Religion. A Sermon Preached before the Congregations of the Old and New Meeting at*

Priestley was also to engage in a series of public disputes with the local clergy. John Money has pointed to the long history of antagonism and conflict between high churchmen and dissenters in Birmingham, but also to a series of confrontations in the 1780s that exacerbated relations still further, involving the Birmingham Library, the Birmingham Sunday Schools, and the celebration of the centenary of the Glorious Revolution (1788), in all of which Priestley had a crucial role. The key issue, however, was the agitation over the repeal of the Test and Corporation Acts, which prevented, in principle at least, dissenters from holding crown or municipal office. The campaign was whole-heartedly supported by the members of New Meeting, and both the vestry and the principal subscribers passed a series of resolutions urging repeal and actively campaigning under the chairmanship of William Russell. Priestley himself attempted to recruit support to establish a Warwickshire Constitutional Society. For high churchmen the Test and Corporation Acts defined the relationship of the established Church to the State, with the Church seen as central to the defence of the existing order. The enthusiastic reception, initially at least, of the French Revolution by Priestley and his friends, together with the subversive nature of Priestley's attacks on the central beliefs of orthodox Christianity, convinced many churchmen that the enemies of the Church were the enemies of the state and could not be trusted with public office.[48]

PRIESTLEY AND THE BIRMINGHAM RIOTS, 1791

Priestley was to pay a high price for his radicalism and lack of popularity with the Birmingham riots in July 1791. During four days of rioting about 20 buildings in the town, including both

Birmingham, Nov. 5, 1785. To which are added, Reflections on the Present State of Free Inquiry in this Country (Birmingham, 1785), 40; Martin Fitzpatrick, 'Joseph Priestley and the Millennium' in Anderson & Lawrence, 31, 34. See Chapter 4 below.

[48] Rutt, I ii, p. 14; John Money, *Experience and Identity: Birmingham and the West Midlands, 1760–1800* (Manchester: Manchester University Press, 1977), 118 n. 10, 126–8, 142–3, 219–23; Money, 'Joseph Priestley in Cultural Context: Philosophic Spectacle, Popular Belief and Popular Politics in Eighteenth-Century Birmingham', Part One, *E&D*, 7 (1988), 60; G. M. Ditchfield, 'The Priestley Riots in Historical Perspective', *TUHS*, 20 (1991), 3–16.

Old and New Meetings and the Unitarian chapel and parsonage at
Kingswood, Priestley's house, library, and laboratory, and the houses
of the leading members of his congregation, were seriously dam-
aged or destroyed. Priestley was scarcely able to escape before the
mob arrived. Had he remained he would almost certainly have lost
his life.[49] The riots were the most dramatic event in Priestley's life,
and one which had enormous consequences for him. They clearly
destroyed more than his material possessions. They were to destroy
his sense of personal security. They also helped to turn him into a
national figure of hate. Priestley not only featured in the satires and
caricatures of James Gillray and George Cruickshank with renewed
intensity, but he was burnt in effigy with the radical writer Thomas
Paine (1737–1809), and seen by many contemporaries as the most
dangerous of all radicals.[50]

The consequences of the riots were also to be felt far beyond
Birmingham, and were to influence the development of 'Church and
King' feeling and the conservative reaction against both political and
religious radicals which emerged in the 1790s. They also indirectly
influenced the development of modern Unitarianism. They abruptly
shattered the confidence dissenters felt concerning their position
in society and the expected improvement in their civil status, thus
reversing earlier optimism over the progress of reform. By the mid-
1790s the enthusiasm with which dissenters had welcomed the French
Revolution had given way to defeat, isolation, and a deep sense of
hopelessness as war, repression, and events in France had taken an
increasingly disastrous course. Many abandoned their earlier enthusiasm for reform and radicalism, giving up politics, dissent, and in a
few cases even religion itself. Priestley's theological radicalism swept
up many in the 1780s, but the political radicalism associated with
him and the French Revolution drove many worshippers away in
the 1790s. A more militant Unitarianism was to emerge in the early
nineteenth century, replacing Arianism. In the generation following
Priestley's death Unitarianism was consolidated, and by 1820 few
Arians were left in English pulpits.

[49] For an account of the widespread impact of the riots upon Unitarians and other
radicals, see D. L. Wykes, "'The Spirit of Persecutors Exemplified": The Priestley Riots
and the Victims of the Church and King Mobs', *TUHS*, 20 (1991), 17–39.
[50] Martin Fitzpatrick, 'Priestley Caricatured', in Schwartz & McEvoy, 161–218.

HACKNEY, 1791–4

Joseph Priestley's settlement in Hackney following the Birmingham riots has generally been seen as a brief unproductive interlude before he emigrated to the United States. Although his residence in Hackney did indeed prove to be brief, lasting just over two and a half years, Priestley clearly expected his settlement to be more permanent, and it was far from being a barren, fruitless period in his life. He was to resume his ministerial career, re-establish his laboratory, and even take up teaching again. In some respects Hackney was more convenient than Birmingham. Priestley had been a regular visitor to London since the 1760s and had acquired many friends there with whom he was now able to have a more regular and closer acquaintance. He especially valued the more frequent exchanges with Lindsey, his wife Hannah, and with Thomas Belsham.[51]

Priestley did re-establish his laboratory, but as Schofield has pointed out, his most important scientific work was achieved before his move to Birmingham.[52] He also began teaching once more, offering lectures *gratis* on history and natural philosophy at New College, Hackney, replacing David Jones who had been appointed his successor as minister at New Meeting, Birmingham. New College had been established in 1786 by the supporters of rational dissent, following the closure of Hoxton Academy, to educate both lay and ministerial students on liberal principles. In terms of the students who attended and the range of subjects taught the College came to be regarded as the main successor to Warrington Academy, which was finally dissolved in 1786. New College, though, mirrored Warrington in a number of unfortunate respects. It was established on too grand a scale and much of the endowment was expended in buildings, so that financial difficulties, together with problems over student discipline, threatened the survival of the College for some years before it finally closed in 1796.[53] Priestley's teaching lacked

---

[51] D. L. Wykes, ' "We have lived very quietly and comfortably here": Joseph Priestley at Hackney, September 1791–April 1794', *TUHS*, 33 (2004), 513–27.

[52] *Scientific Autobiography,* 202–3, 267, 272.

[53] The only published account of New College remains Herbert McLachlan, 'The Old Hackney College, 1786–96', *TUHS*, 3 (1925), 185–205; though see Wykes, 'Contribution of the Dissenting Academy', 131–2. A rival academy was established

the innovation of 30 years earlier. Although his lectures on natural philosophy at the College provided a general overview of the subject, the evidence from the summary he published in 1794 reveals that he ignored new scientific advances. Nevertheless, the students he taught at Hackney included some, such as the scientist Arthur Aikin (1773–1854), who were to distinguish themselves in later life and who acknowledged Priestley's instruction as influential. The lectures he gave on history and general policy were repeated from the original lectures he had delivered at Warrington and published in 1765.[54]

The death of his friend Richard Price, minister of the Gravel Pit Meeting, Hackney, in April 1791, offered Priestley an opportunity to resume his ministerial career, though he faced opposition in the congregation to his appointment, both on doctrinal grounds, for Price had been an Arian, and from fear that his presence would attract the mob. In the first sermon he preached on becoming minister Priestley provided a detailed account of the system of catechizing he had practised with such success at Birmingham with the younger members of his congregation.[55] He was also to undertake a series of lectures on natural and revealed religion with considerable success, 'being attended by many from London'.[56] Under Priestley the religious character of the congregation changed from Arian to Unitarian. Inevitably there were losses with the withdrawal of the more orthodox members, but it is evident that through his preaching and reputation he succeeded in attracting new members, and that he left the congregation 'in a better situation than that in which I found it'. There is a rare contemporary account by two American Quakers, from the spring of 1794, of Priestley preaching: 'His mode of preaching was,

at Manchester on different principles in 1786, see Wykes, 'Sons and Subscribers' 39, 42.

[54] Joseph Priestley, *Heads of Lectures on a Course of Experimental Philosophy, Particularly Including Chemistry, Delivered at the New College in Hackney* (London, 1794); Priestley, *Essay on a Course of Liberal Education*.

[55] Joseph Priestley, *A Particular Attention to the Instruction of the Young Recommended, in a Discourse delivered at the Gravel-Pit Meeting in Hackney, Dec. 4, 1791, on Entering on the Office of Pastor to the Congregation of Protestant Dissenters Assembling in that Place* (London, 1791). See also his letter of resignation, Alan Ruston, 'Joseph Priestley at the Gravel Pit Chapel, Hackney: the Collier MS', *E&D*, 2 (1983), 115.

[56] Rutt, I ii, p. 118.

with but little action, his delivery in short sentences, distinct, fluent, and impressive'.[57]

On 21 February 1794 Priestley resigned after little over two years as minister. It is clear that immediately after the riots Priestley possessed little confidence in his long-term settlement in England and that he had seriously considered seeking refuge in France, but was dissuaded by the knowledge that 'I should have no employment of the kind to which I had been accustomed'.[58] His decision to take a house in Hackney on a long lease and to rebuild his library and laboratory is evidence of his intention to settle permanently in Hackney, but by early 1793 Priestley had determined to live in America. He made the decision for the sake of his sons, who were unable to find a settlement in England because of his reputation, though the level of abuse directed against him made his settlement increasingly uncomfortable. He and his wife left England for the New World on 8 April 1794.

CONCLUSION

Priestley's 40-year career as a minister ended in 1794 when he left for America. He never had another pulpit and in the absence of a sympathetic congregation he only preached in public again on a handful of occasions. His main ministry was at Birmingham, though he had no pastoral responsibilities beyond his duties on Sunday, but his ministries at Leeds and Hackney were also important and successful. Priestley clearly saw the instruction of younger members as some of the most important and valuable work he undertook as a minister. His reputation as a teacher, however, rests on his school at Nantwich, his work as tutor in belles lettres at Warrington Academy, and the essays he published on grammar, history, language, and educational philosophy. Either as a student or as a tutor he was associated with

---

[57] *The Records and Recollections of James Jenkins*, ed. J. W. Frost (Lewiston, N.Y.: Edwin Mellen Press, 1984), 258.

[58] BL Add MS 44,992, fo. 40r, Priestley, London, to Russell, Birmingham, 14 Sep. 1791; Joseph Priestley, *The Present State of Europe Compared with Antient Prophecies; A Sermon* [on Matt. iii. 2] *Preached... Feb. 28, 1794... the Day Appointed for a General Fast. With a Preface Containing the Reasons for the Author's Leaving England* (London, 1794), p. iv.

the three most important dissenting academies of the late eighteenth century. It was not, however, his work as a minister or a teacher but as a theologian that proved to be his lasting contribution. Priestley more than any other person, through the strength of his argument, was responsible for Unitarianism replacing Arianism as the main form of anti-Trinitarian speculation in Britain. Following an orthodox upbringing, Priestley's own religious beliefs moved rapidly from Calvinism to heterodoxy. At the age of 16 he began to have religious doubts about whether he might be saved. Within two years he was rejected by his church for having unsound doctrine. By the time he entered Daventry Academy at the age of 19 he was an Arminian, but when he left three years later he had become an Arian as a result of his studies. Surprisingly, despite his friendship with a number of Unitarians, including Lardner and William Graham, Priestley did not adopt Unitarian opinions himself until about 1769, 15 or 16 years later. By his own account he was slow to absorb these new ideas fully. From the 1770s he published a series of Unitarian works which convinced a generation of readers, but his religious views were not fully developed until later in the decade when he concluded that Christ was human like us. At Birmingham his increasing radicalism, in politics as well as religion, was to culminate in the riots of July 1791 with catastrophic results for him personally. After the achievements of the previous 40 years, the last ten years of his life in the United States can be seen as an anticlimax. By bringing his ministry to a close Priestley had retired from what he considered to be his most important work. Although he was to publish more on science in America than he had during all his years in England, his most important scientific work had been completed before he moved to Birmingham. He also continued to write on religious matters until the end of his life, though again his most important work had already been published. On the morning of Monday, 6 February 1804, the day he died, he dictated a few additions and changes to his *Doctrines of Heathen Philosophy* and said, 'That is right; I have now done.' He then closed his eyes; a short while later he was dead.[59]

[59] Rutt, I ii, 531; Schofield, II, 354, 380–401.

2

Joseph Priestley, Enlightened Experimentalist

W. H. Brock

INTRODUCTION

In their play *Oxygen*, the steroid chemist and writer Carl Djerassi and the Nobel prize winning theoretical chemist Roald Hoffmann invent a 'retrospective' Nobel prize system.[1] A jury for the retrospective chemistry prize convenes in Stockholm and quickly agrees that modern chemistry was made possible by the chemical revolution that occurred at the end of the eighteenth century and that the trigger for that revolution had been the discovery of oxygen. But who, exactly, had first discovered oxygen? And, who, therefore, deserved the retro-prize? Did Joseph Priestley deserve the award for first publishing an account of 'dephlogisticated air' in 1774? Alternatively, should it be given to the Swedish pharmacist Carl Wilhelm Scheele for his discovery of 'fire-air' in the early 1770s (though it remained unpublished until 1777)? Or should the prize go to the French lawyer Antoine Lavoisier because he was the first chemist to interpret (and name) oxygen correctly and, moreover, to use it as a lynch pin to launch the 'chemical revolution' that (unlike the conceptualizations of Scheele and Priestley) remains the basis of chemistry in the twenty-first century? The drama does not resolve the issue and adds fiction to fact to build a case for the role of women in science by supposing that

[1] Carl Djerassi and Roald Hoffman, *Oxygen: A Play in Two Acts* (Weinheim: Wiley-VCH, 2001).

Madame Lavoisier hid a letter from Scheele to her husband to ensure French priority. Djerassi and Hoffmann's Shavian play succeeds in raising an audience's understanding of what constitutes a discovery in science, the intensely competitive nature of scientific research, and how different solutions to scientific problems and observations may arise in different local contexts—in this case, England, Sweden, and France.

Priestley was a paradox to later chemists. Although he might be said to have been out-manoeuvred by Lavoisier and his followers, his reputation has lived on in the scientific community. Unusually for a man of science he was treated as a hero and commemorated as such, even though he defended a theory that proved incorrect. Until the 1970s Priestley's science was largely treated in isolation from his activities as a dissenting minister; his chemistry was seen as a self-explanatory spare time and relaxing occupation amidst his greater preoccupation with theology and politics. Chemists admired him as a British founding father of chemistry because of his work on gases, and commemorated him with a public statue in Birmingham in 1874 and at a meeting of American chemists at Northumberland, Philadelphia, the same year, which led directly to the foundation of the American Chemical Society two years later.[2] Chemists did not blame him for interpreting airs in terms of the prevailing theoretical model of phlogiston, and they accepted the logic of his phlogisticated nomenclature prior to the establishment of Lavoisier's system in 1789. What they could not understand from their later perspective was why Priestley had failed to grasp that Lavosier had developed a superior explanation, and they found his post-1800 stand against phlogiston and the arguments for the compound nature of water embarrassing and silly. While sympathizing with the problem that Priestley's confusion of hydrogen and carbon monoxide as inflammable airs posed for him and other chemists of the day, they found his refusal to accept they were different gases after William Cruickshank had demonstrated this in 1801 quite bizarre and embarrassing. Thus the

---

[2] Stephen F. Mason, 'Joseph Priestley and the Discovery of Oxygen', *Chemistry in Britain*, 10 (1974), 286–9; M. P. Crosland, 'A Practical Perspective on Priestley as a Pneumatic Chemist', *British Journal for the History of Science*, 16 (1983), 223–38; Robert G. Anderson, 'Memorializing Scientists: The Case of Joseph Priestley', in Bowden & Rosner, 30–41.

outstanding chemical historian James Riddick Partington, who has given the most complete and thorough account of Priestley's experiments on air, becomes quite angry at his obstinacy. While believing him to have been a likeable man and a great experimentalist, Partington claimed that 'his obstinate retention of theoretical (and some experimental) errors retarded the progress of chemistry'. Partington regretted that an account of Priestley's 'incorrect but influential views' was so 'dreary' though necessary in a complete history of chemistry. For Partington and other chemists, the explanation for Priestley's obduracy was that 'in science he was somewhat of an amateur, and his defective knowledge of general chemistry' exposed him to egregious mistakes.[3]

The new generation of professionally trained historians of science of the 1960s started with the assumption that such Whiggish history was quite wrong. Scientific ideas and practices had to be examined and evaluated within their social and intellectual context. Thus, as Robert E. Schofield established, Partington's view will not do. Apart from the obvious error of calling Priestley an amateur at a time when there were no professional men of science, it is clear that for someone educated in the 1750s, Priestley was adequately trained in chemistry. At Warrington he had attended a chemistry course given by the itinerant lecturer, Dr Mathew Turner of Liverpool, and Priestley was well read in the current literature. His acquaintance with the phlogiston theory had come from reading Pierre Joseph Macquer's French chemistry textbook in its English translation,[4] and this was reinforced into a total commitment following personal conversations with Henry Cavendish when the latter's first paper on 'different kinds of air' was read to the Royal Society in March 1772.[5] This is not to deny that Priestley trained himself in a different tradition of chemistry from Lavoisier. Unlike the latter, who was brought up in the French pharmaceutical investigative tradition of affinity tables and the formation of salts from acids and bases, Priestley was not. In this sense, Partington was correct in reflecting that some knowledge of and sympathy

[3] James R. Partington, *A History of Chemistry*, 4 vols (London: Macmillan, 1962), III, preface, p. v and chapter 7 (devoted to Priestley), 237–301.
[4] Pierre Joseph Macquer, *Elements of the Theory and Practice of Chymistry*, trans. Andrew Reid, 2 vols. (London, 1758; 2nd edn. 1764).
[5] Schofield, I, 259–69, esp. 268.

with this continental material might have saved him from mistakes and confusion. At the end of the day, whatever Priestley's theoretical position was, it was his observations and experiments that enabled others to interpret nature in a new way. This chapter will review these observations and experiments before turning to the ways recent historians have interpreted Priestley's scientific activities in the context of his theological, educational, and political activities. Finally, it will re-examine the question of Priestley's attitude towards Lavoisier and his continuing support for a phlogistic world view.

ELECTROSTATICS

In modern disciplinary terms, Priestley made contributions to physics, chemistry, and botany through his investigations of electricity, optics, gases, and photosynthesis. He published six papers on electricity in the five years before 1772, when his attention moved to chemistry, and summarized his knowledge in a large and influential book in 1767, *The History and Present State of Electricity,* and a much shorter primer in 1768, *Familiar Introduction to the Study of Electricity.* The study of electrostatics had become one of the most popular of the Newtonian sciences during the first half of the eighteenth century. Apart from offering absorbing intellectual puzzles, it had the advantage for itinerant lecturers that it could be demonstrated by spectacular experiments that guaranteed large fee-paying audiences. Priestley would have seen such demonstrations as a youth and demonstrated them himself at Nantwich and Warrington. Electricity, the power asserted by certain substances like amber to attract small objects to it when rubbed, had been distinguished from magnetism by William Gilbert at the beginning of the seventeenth century. Later investigators explained this property by imagining that rubbing ejected subtle effluvia from ordinary matter and that neighbouring light objects were swept along by air rushing to fill the spaces left. Such ideas had led to the building of powerful mechanical machines for producing electrified bodies by friction. In 1747 the Dutch Newtonian experimentalist Petrus van Musschenbroek of Leyden had tried to trap the effluvial electricity in a bottle half filled with water and found that the

'Leyden jar' could be used to administer very powerful shocks. When the instrument was combined with Stephen Gray's demonstration that the electric power could be conducted large distances through appropriate materials (conductors), the stage was set for exciting theatrical demonstrations of electricity. In the 1750s, Benjamin Franklin and Franz Aepinus developed a powerful new theory and language that argued that electrification consisted in the redistribution of the electrical effluvia to and from matter. Bodies became positively electrified when the effluvium was attracted to matter, and negatively electrified when the effluvium was drained from matter. The theory elegantly explained why positive and negative bodies possessed repulsive powers with respect to their own kind but, like magnets, were mutually attractive.[6]

Enlightenment historians followed David Hume in agreeing that the progress of the arts and sciences depended upon social and political factors and not solely on individual genius. At Warrington, where among other things Priestley taught history, he came to see human history as a story of an erratic but constant progress and the betterment of human knowledge. Knowledge of nature had increased in step with human progress and been an integral part of that progress. The history of science, like political history, could not, he wrote, 'but animate us in our attempts to advance still further'.[7] Because electricity was the most popular and exciting of the sciences in the 1760s, Priestley conceived the idea of writing about its progress since antiquity and thereby illustrating human progress vividly.

Priestley's historical charts published in the 1760s had tended to stress the role of particular individuals in history. A series of works on the history of science would also demonstrate this but show as well how scientific progress needed the participation of many investigators, meaning that science was accessible to everyone. Electrostatics was all the rage, and by contacting experimentalists Priestley hoped to make the first of the planned science histories, *The History and Present*

---

[6] John L. Heilbron, *Electricity in the Seventeenth and Eighteenth Centuries* (Berkeley, CA: University of California Press, 1979).

[7] Joseph Priestley, *The History and Present State of Electricity, with Original Experiments* (London, 1767), p. ii; John G. McEvoy, 'Electricity, Knowledge, and the Nature of Progress in Priestley's Thought', *British Journal for the History of Science*, 12 (1979), 1–30.

State of Electricity, as interesting and as up to date as possible. John Canton, with whom Priestley stayed in London in 1765, proved a true friend and introduced him to other electricians such as Benjamin Franklin (then in London acting as Pennsylvania's colonial agent), and William Watson (who had remodelled the Leyden jar to make it a more effective instrument). The London electricians not only encouraged Priestley's writing project but also supplied him with primary sources, contacts with London instrument makers and, most importantly, suggested that his rapport with and understanding of the subject would be increased if he repeated some of their observations. It was in this way that the book, published in 1767, came to contain several original findings, such as the effect of air pressure on electrification, and the fact that the non-metal charcoal was a conductor. Besides offering an analytical history of the subject that is still valuable 250 years later, like Kepler's account of his exhausting struggle with planetary data to deduce the three planetary laws, Priestley provided a blow by blow account of his experiments whether illuminating or not. He was astutely aware that sales of the book might be increased if he were a Fellow of the Royal Society, and the coterie of London electricians duly obliged by promoting his election in June 1766. The experience of composing the *History* also led him in the direction of commerce when Priestley persuaded his brother Timothy to help him construct a large machine for the production of frictional electricity. Following the publication of the book the two brothers constructed several of these machines for purchase by readers of Priestley's *History* who were attracted to making their own experiments. To this end, the book contained a great deal of advice concerning workshop tools and the construction of apparatus, and drawing perspective diagrams of experimental situations.

Reading between the lines of his text we can see that Priestley had already begun to be interested in fundamental issues such as the maintenance of life on earth. In fact the discovery of charcoal's conducting power came from wondering whether it was possible to 'restore' the life-giving properties of spoiled (or mephitic) air released from an animal's lungs or from the burning of cinders (charcoal). In this context he made his first reference 'to what the chymists call *phlogiston*'.[8] Obviously this question concerned the economy and

---

[8] Priestley, *History of Electricity*, 600.

balance of nature and what, today, we call the carbon or oxygen cycle. It was while testing whether an electric charge might restore the respiratory quality of air that he discovered that charcoal was an excellent conductor. From this observation he was led to a general exploration of the conductive power of different materials, including ice, metals, acids and salts. Again, when testing the conductivity of a metallic cup, he discovered that only the outer surface retained a charge; there was no charge on the inner surface. This observation allowed him to speculate that, like Newton's gravitating bodies, charged bodies attracted one another according to an inverse square law. This was demonstrated formally by Charles Coulomb in France some 20 years later using a delicate torsion balance.

The History of Electricity, for which Priestley made his own drawings, was an outstanding success in terms of sales, monetary return, and the reputation it brought him both at home and abroad. Two further editions were called for in the next decade (1769, 1775), and Priestley also published *A Familiar Introduction to the Study of Electricity* in 1768, a concise primer for tyro electricians, which also passed through another three editions in the next 20 years. Commitment to revisions of his work meant that Priestley never entirely abandoned his interest in electricity when engaged in pneumatics. During the 1770s, for example, he published a number of papers recording new electrical phenomena such as discharge patterns, and comparisons of the resistances to conduction and strengths of electrical discharges of different substances. Many of these observations remained mysterious and were not properly understood until the emergence of the electronic theory of matter in the twentieth century. The electrical writings and observations also led him into correspondence with continental electricians, in particular with Alessandro Volta in Italy.

OPTICS

Encouraged by the success of his *Electricity*, Priestley set to work to create a similar history of man's exploration of optical phenomena. This proved a much more difficult task. There were no small groups of researchers actively engaged in the study of light willing to help him, and much of the subject, even when he was describing the experimental properties of mirrors and lenses, involved the use of and understanding of mathematics. However, he succeeded in producing a thorough and workmanlike account of the subject, including discussions of the nature of vision that owed much to his reading of David Hartley's *Observations on Man*, and evidence that light was particulate in nature. In the case of the latter Priestley was indebted to another Yorkshire clergyman, John Michell of Thornhill, who had ingeniously 'weighed' a beam of light by measuring the momentum induced on a copper foil resting on a needle point by sunlight focused from a concave mirror. *The History and Present State of Discoveries Relating to Vision, Light, and Colours* (1772) was, however, written in haste, and the errata sheets suggest that he had not completely mastered the subject. Although there was a German translation in 1774, there was never any call for further English editions.

Unlike the book on electricity, for which he received payment from his publisher, Joseph Johnson, Priestley was forced to publish his account of work on vision, light, and colours by subscription, making himself out of pocket in the process.[9] This experience put paid to his previously announced intention to write histories 'of all the other branches of experimental philosophy upon the same extensive plan' as electricity and optics.[10] He had, in any case, become much more interested in the properties of 'air', and it was for this subject that his name was to be remembered by chemists. Making his own experiments and publishing the results in book form would be cheaper than purchasing and reviewing other people's work— though we should not underestimate the expense and sophistication of Priestley's apparatus. It was not just candles, mice, and equipment borrowed from the kitchen and laundry.[11] Priestley had chosen an area of natural philosophy that was soluble by the simple investigative procedures that the Newtonian divine, Stephen Hales, had pioneered in his *Vegetable Staticks* in 1727. Moreover, the results of making

[9] Joseph Priestley, *The History and Present State of Discoveries Relating to Vision, Light, and Colours*, 2 vols (London, 1772). See discussion in Schofield, I, 241–9.

[10] Priestley, *Vision*, I, p. xi; F. W. Gibbs, *Joseph Priestley: Adventurer in Science and Champion of Truth* (London: Nelson, 1965), 50–1.

[11] R. G. W. Anderson, 'Priestley Displayed' in Anderson & Lawrence, 91–6; Bowden & Rosner, 42–71 (illustrations).

further investigations of the air had practical uses, as in artificial spa waters and tests for the goodness of air that had medical and hygienic potential, as well as theological significance for the improvement of mankind physically and morally.

PNEUMATIC CHEMISTRY

In his *Memoirs* Priestley attributed his interest in airs to the fact that when in Leeds he lived next door to a brewery whose fermenting vats produced an abundance of fixed or mephitic air (carbon dioxide).[12] But his interest in the cosmic balance between breathable and vitiated air dated long before he arrived in Leeds. He was well aware, for example, of the views of the Irish surgeon David Macbride on fermentation and putrefaction. Macbride had shown that fixed air was generated from rotting animal carcases, but arrested or inhibited the decay of a freshly killed animal. From this he had drawn the conclusion that fixed air played a vital role in living processes and that scurvy, seen as a putrefactive disease, might be prevented by the eating of fixed-air-rich vegetables.[13] What the Leeds brewery provided was an opportunity for Priestley to experiment with fixed air, and it was while doing so that he stumbled upon the fact that it acidulated and sweetened ordinary water. He recalled this phenomenon in 1772 when dining with the Duke of Northumberland in London. His host produced a bottle of distilled water that was being recommended as suitable for use in ships. The diners found the water tasted distinctly flat, leading Priestley to recall how water could be sweetened with fixed air. Perhaps such acidulated water would also prevent scurvy, as Macbride had speculated? Rapidly and ingeniously Priestley had within a few days rigged up an apparatus (adapted from one devised by Macbride) whereby domestic water could be impregnated with fixed air. The device was shown to the College of Physicians and to

---

[12] For Priestley's *Memoirs* see Rutt I i; and the abridged edition by Robert E. Schofield, *Scientific Autobiography*.

[13] David Macbride, *Experimental Essays* (London, 1767). See Partington, *Chemistry*, III, 143; Schofield, I, 257; Christopher Lawrence, 'Priestley in Tahiti. The Medical Interests of a Dissenting Chemist' in Anderson & Lawrence, 1–10.

the Admiralty and subsequently tested on Captain Cook's 1772 voyages. Priestley also quickly published instructions on how to prepare artificial 'Pyrmont' waters, making his name widely known both in Britain and on the continent.[14] Others, such as John Mervin Nooth and Jacob Schweppe made improvements to the gas–water mixing mechanism and gave birth to the soda and mineral water industry.[15] It was the physician John Pringle who, as President of the Royal Society, persuaded the Royal Society to award Priestley its Copley medal in 1772 for his supposed demonstration of the anti-scorbutic value of soda water.

As Priestley had already indicated in his optical work, he planned to extend the work of Stephen Hales on the study of the air liberated from heating solid bodies, but it was only in the summer of 1772 that he began serious investigations. He used Hales's apparatus, which had been improved by other students of airs such as the Whitehaven physician William Brownrigg and the London natural philosopher Henry Cavendish. Brownrigg had devised a platform (the beehive shelf) whereby mephitic airs could be collected in glass vessels under water, and Cavendish, by collecting soluble airs over mercury instead of water, had extended knowledge of fixed air (carbon dioxide) and differentiated inflammable air (hydrogen) from ordinary air.[16] The use of mercury enabled Priestley to identify the water-soluble gases, sulphur dioxide, ammonia, and hydrogen chloride. The pneumatic apparatus had a significant role in the later development of chemistry; for example, it was used in school teaching demonstrations until the middle of the twentieth century.

Priestley's first original and significant discovery came in June 1772 when, following one of Hales's hints, he investigated the action of nitric acid on a number of metals, generating a 'nitrous air' that formed brown fumes when mixed with ordinary air. If the mixing was done over water, 'about one-fifth of the common air, and as much

[14] Joseph Priestley, *Directions for Impregnating Water with Fixed Air, in Order to Communicate to it the Peculiar Spirit of Pyrmont Water, and Other Mineral Waters of a Similar Nature* (London, 1772). See Gibbs, *Priestley*, 57–60; Lawrence, 'Priestley in Tahiti', in Anderson & Lawrence; Schofield, I, 250–9.

[15] For Nooth and Schweppe, see *Oxford DNB*.

[16] Partington, *Chemistry*, III, 124–5 (on Brownrigg); Joseph Priestley, *Experiments and Observations on Different Kinds of Air* (London, 1774), 6; John Parascandola and Aaron J. Ihde, 'History of the Pneumatic Trough', *Isis*, 60 (1969), 351–61.

of the nitrous air as is necessary to produce that effect' disappeared. This felicitous discovery, which attracted much attention in Paris,[17] formed the basis of the quantitative test that Priestley recommended for assessing the salubrity of air. The test played a vital role in the differentiation of dephlogisticated air two years later. Meanwhile, he found that when nitrous air was stood over a paste of iron filings and water it lost some of its phlogiston because the salubrity test showed that the water diminished by a quarter rather than a fifth. This 'dephlogisticated nitrous air' was later termed 'laughing gas' or 'nitrous oxide'. Another discovery of 1772 was a 'marine acid air' (hydrogen chloride) formed when adding metals to hydrochloric acid instead of nitric acid.

The comedy of errors and corrections concerning Priestley's and Lavoisier's discovery and understanding of dephlogisticated air (oxygen) is well known and need not be rehearsed again here.[18] It suffices to say that Priestley initially believed he had generated dephlogisticated nitrous air by heating the calx of mercury (mercuric oxide) with the large burning glass presented to him by the London instrument maker Parker in August 1774, and he reported this to Lavoisier personally on his only visit to Paris with Lord Shelburne in the same month. It was only in March 1775, when Priestley performed the nitrous air test of salubrity, that he realized that it was a different air completely, and one that was more salubrious than any previously tested sample of atmospheric air. It was for this reason that he termed it dephlogisticated air. He took pleasure in correcting Lavoisier, who meanwhile had gone into print identifying the gaseous product of the combustion of mercury calx as fixed air.

Priestley himself was never clear in his own mind about what he had identified, and in later writings he seems to have believed that his purest air was a combination of 'spirit of nitre and earth' together with phlogiston, rather than, as Lavoisier believed, an element

---

[17] Henry Guerlac, 'Joseph Priestley's First Papers on Gases and their Reception in France', *Journal of the History of Medicine*, 12 (1957), 1–12.

[18] James B. Conant, 'The Overthrow of the Phlogiston Theory. The Chemical Revolution of 1775–1789', *Harvard Case Histories in Experimental Science*, 2 vols (Cambridge, MA: Harvard University Press, 1957), I, 68–115.; W. H. Brock, *The Fontana History of Chemistry* (London: Fontana HarperCollins, 1992), 87–127 and bibliography 682–4.

physically combined with caloric (heat) to form a gaseous material. Priestley had no concept of a gas, and like most of his English pneumatic predecessors, and as the running title of his publications on gases implies, he seems to have perceived each of the factitious airs he prepared and investigated as ordinary air in different states of purity. Different airs resulted from the admixture of acidic materials to which phlogiston was either added or subtracted. Possibly, if Priestley had discovered either acrid green chlorine or the brown fumes of bromine gas he would have thought differently. As it happened, only one of the gases he prepared, brown nitrogen dioxide, possessed both colour and smell and possibly for this reason he referred to it as nitrous vapour. Priestley's exciting investigations were written up as an uninterrupted account of preparations and observations in a series of six volumes published between 1772 and 1790.[19] (See the table at p. 61 for a summary of Priestley's 'different kinds of air'.) Although there was nothing disorderly about his experiments, because they were published in the order they were carried out, revisions, additions, and corrections had to be given in later volumes, to the disgust of French investigators who preferred to write their results up synthetically rather than what Priestley termed 'analytically and ingeniously'.

Historians have frequently commented on the fact that Lavoisier's apparatus was both extensive and expensive in comparison with Priestley's. In fact, however, Priestley's own collection of apparatus before the Birmingham riots was equally impressive. In his claims for compensation his laboratory and apparatus were valued at one-sixth of the wordly goods that had been lost. In today's values this means his scientific collections were worth about £60,000.[20] Their loss must have been devastating, as his comment in the *History of Electricity* years before suggests:

---

[19] Joseph Priestley, *Experiments and Observations on Different Kinds of Air*, 3 vols (London, 1774, 1775, 1777); revised eds, I (1775 and 1781); II (1776 and 1784). *Experiments and Observations Relating to Various Branches of Natural Philosophy*, 3 vols. (London and Birmingham, 1779, 1781, 1786); all six vols revised and abridged as *Experiments and Observations on Different Kinds of Air and Other Branches of Natural Philosophy*, 3 vols (Birmingham, 1790).

[20] Anderson, 'Joseph Priestley: Public Intellectual' in Bowden & Rosner, 11–16 at 15.

TABLE Priestley's 'Different Kinds of Air'

Priestley's name	Modern name	Colour	Smell	Preparation
Dephlogisticated air (1774)	Oxygen	None	None	Action of heat on calx of mercury, or potassium nitrate.
Phlogisticated air (1772)	Nitrogen	None	None	Heat iron, tin or lead in air.
Nitrous air (1772)	Nitric oxide	None	None	Dissolve copper in dilute nitric acid.
Nitrous vapour (1772)	Nitrogen dioxide	Brown	None	Mix nitrous air with air or dephlogisticated air.
Dephlogisticated nitrous air (1774)	Nitrous oxide	None	Sweet	Mix nitrous air with iron filings or potassium sulphide.
Fixed, or mephitic air (1771)	Carbon dioxide	None	None	(1) Hydrochloric acid on chalk; (2) nitric acid on charcoal; (3) heat limestone powder in gun barrel.
Inflammable air (1772)	Carbon monoxide	None	None	(1) Heat iron oxide with charcoal; (2) pass electric discharge through fixed air.
	Hydrogen	None	None	Action of dilute acids on iron filings.
Vitriolic acid air (1774)	Sulphur dioxide	None	Pungent	Add mercury to hot concentrated oil of vitriol (sulphuric acid).
Marine acid air (1772)	Hydrogen chloride	None	Pungent	Heat marine acid (hydrochloric acid) or common salt with oil of vitriol (sulphuric acid).
Alkaline air (1774)	Ammonia	None	Pungent	Heat slaked lime (calcium hydroxide) with sal ammoniac (ammonium chloride).
Fluor acid air (1775)	Silicon tetrafluoride	None	None	Heat Derbyshire spa (calcium fluoride) with silica and oil of vitriol (sulphuric acid).

The instructions we are able to get from books is, comparatively, soon exhausted; but philosophical instruments are an endless fund of knowledge. By philosophical instruments, however, I do not mean here the globes, the orrery, and others, which are only the means which ingenious men have hit upon to explain their own conceptions of things to others; but such as the air pump, condensing engine, pyrometer, &c. (with which electrical machines are to be ranked) and which exhibit the operations of nature, that is of the God of nature himself, which are infinitely various. By the help of these machines, we are able to put an endless variety of things into an endless variety of situations, while nature herself is the agent that shows the result. Hereby the laws of action are observed, and the most important discoveries may be made; such as those who first contrived the instrument could have no idea of.[21]

PHOTOSYNTHESIS

The hydrological cycle, or the continuous circulation of water from seas and rivers into the atmosphere by evaporation and its condensation as rain, frost, and snow, was conceived and understood by most early societies. Its extension to other cycles, whereby through a series of physical and chemical changes materials return to a starting point, proved a fruitful concept and seemed to confirm elegantly that the economy of nature had been designed by a wise and powerful deity. In the seventeenth century, the German physician and chemist Georg Stahl suggested that a fatty material he and other chemists called *phlogiston* (from the Greek for fire or flame) that was released during burning and putrefaction was recycled by plants and animals. This view must have been absorbed by Priestley during his studies at the academy at Daventry. From his close study of the work of Stephen Hales in the 1770s, Priestley also believed that plants breathed like animals, deriving much of their nutrition from the absorption of air and water. Hales asserted that plants imbibed or 'fixed' atmospheric air at night, and 'perspired' it during the day. Further studies by the Cumberland physician William Brownrigg and many others had

---

[21] Priestley, *Electricity*, p. xi.

shown that Hales's fixed air was stale or vitiated and unable to support animal life.

In 1771 Priestley observed that vitiated air (whether polluted by combustion, respiration, or the putrefaction of calcinations) was restored by green plants, such as sprigs of mint, if they were grown in the atmosphere for several days. Such restored air was fully capable of supporting the burning of a candle or the life of a mouse. Like Stahl, Priestley explained his finding in terms of a phlogiston cycle: chemical processes involving combustion, calcinations, respiration, and putrefaction all discharged phlogiston into the atmosphere; plants recycled this vital substance by absorbing it into their systems, and so into the bodies of animals via the feeding habits of herbivores and carnivores. Priestley speculated that phlogiston was the animating principle and was possibly converted into animal electricity in the brain and distributed in the blood stream. Foods not containing phlogiston or materials in which it was inseparable would not nourish an animal. After discharging its function, phlogiston was exhaled from the lungs into the atmosphere.[22]

The discovery of dephlogisticated air in 1774–5 merely led to a slight change in this view of the phlogiston cycle in nature. Plants removed phlogiston from the air and returned it to the atmosphere as dephlogisticated air. Priestley saw that the cycle would be validated if he could collect samples of the air respired by plants. This was a tricky proposition until, in 1778, he observed that sprigs of mint when immersed in water gave off bubbles. He ingeniously collected these air bubbles and, using the usual combustion and eudiometric tests, showed that the air was, indeed, dephlogisticated air. In a further surprising twist, he observed that the air bubbles were emitted more abundantly in light.[23] These observations and experiments were carefully repeated and extended by the Anglo-Dutch physician Jan Ingen-housz and reported in English.[24] It was Ingen-housz who

[22] Joseph Priestley, 'Observations on Different Kinds of Air', *Philosophical Transactions of the Royal Society*, 62 (1772), 147–264, esp. 166.

[23] Joseph Priestley, 'On the Spontaneous Emission of Dephlogisticated Air from Water in Certain Circumstances', *Experiments and Observations Relating to Various Branches of Natural Philosophy*, I (1779), 335–60; II (1781), 16–52. Schofield, II, 153–7.

[24] Jan Ingen-housz, *Experiments Upon Vegetables, Discovering their Great Power of Purifying the Common Air in the Sunshine* (London, 1779).

demonstrated that light was essential to the process we now know as photosynthesis (the term only dates from 1893), and that it was only the green parts of plants that emitted dephlogisticated air. The roots, flowers, and tree branches always emitted a 'phlogisticated' air, as did the leaves and green parts of plants in the dark. The Swiss chemist, botanist, and theologian Jean Senebier suggested that the dephlogisticated air emitted from green plants in the light was quantitatively balanced by the amount of fixed air (carbon dioxide) absorbed in the dark, though he found this extremely difficult to demonstrate quantitatively. Like Priestley, Senebier saw the phlogiston cycle and its connection with light and darkness as a wonderful demonstration of God's benevolence and design.[25] Priestley also lived long enough to see another Swiss botanist, Nicholas-Théodore de Saussure, quantify the gaseous and water exchanges between plants and the atmosphere and, following Lavoisier, transform the phlogiston cycle into the oxygen cycle (or what, today, is usually called the 'carbon cycle' in deference to the role of carbonic acid in photosynthesis).

INTERPRETING PRIESTLEY'S SCIENCE

So far we have considered Priestley solely as an empirical investigator and writer. Apart from optics, in each case we have seen him make contact with a specific audience or community of scholars interested in the same subjects as he was. In the case of electricity, he was in personal contact with a group of London electricians and, later, with Volta and other Italian electrical investigators, as well as with instrument makers. The making of artificial waters brought him into contact with the navy and with members of the medical profession as well as, once again, instrument makers. Work on airs again brought him into contact with medical men interested in issues concerned

---

[25] Jean Senebier, *Mémoires Physico-Chymiques sur l'Influence de la Lumière Solaire*, 3 vols (Geneva, 1782). The best account of the early history of photosynthesis remains Leonard K. Nash, 'Plants and the Atmosphere' in J. B. Conant (ed.), *Harvard Case Histories in Experimental Science*, II (Harvard University Press: Cambridge, MA, 1950), 326–436. Strangely, scientists have only recently discovered (2006) that plants also emit huge quantities of methane.

with public health,[26] as well as with the French school of chemists led by Antoine Lavoisier. Contextualization studies have changed the way history of science is practised in recent years. Gone is the view, much favoured by scientists when examining their discipline's historical roots, that past science can only be understood in the context of the present culture in which a 'scientific fact' is used. Instead, the historical, social, political, and cultural contexts are believed actually to govern the emergence of scientific knowledge. The circulation and diffusion of science from and between different cultural contexts result in conflict, argument, and bargaining, from which a more or less universal consensus emerges.[27] Social negotiation and, it must be said, making things work better, determine what is held as truth by a majority within a research discipline. Contextualization provides a helpful explanation and rationalization of the conflict between Lavoisier's oxygen-centred and Priestley's phlogiston-centred chemistry.

In the wake of debate concerning Thomas Kuhn's *Structure of Scientific Revolutions* in the 1970s, several sociologists of science adapted the views of the German sociologist Jürgen Habermas to identify the 'interests' held by individual or groups of natural philosophers. These interests were then used to explain the choices made in selecting a paradigm or a designated pathway of experimental and observational investigation (Kuhn's 'normal science'). Habermas's work on the emergence of knowledge during the Enlightenment also laid stress upon the emergence of the 'public sphere' of knowledge generation, as opposed to the older sphere in which power and opinion was directed solely by the state. As defined by the literary scholar Robert Holub, 'the public sphere is a realm in which individuals gather to participate in open discussion',[28] and is ideally unconstrained by external pressures. It is the arena which mediates between society and the state, and provides the means for expressing a public

[26] Lawrence, 'Priestley in Tahiti', in Anderson & Lawrence, 3–4.

[27] David N. Livingstone, *Putting Science in its Place: Geographies of Scientific Knowledge* (Chicago: University of Chicago Press, 2003); Golinski. For a good review, see Paul Elliott, 'Origins of the "Creative Class": Provincial Urban Society, Scientific Culture and Socio-Political Marginality in Britain in the Eighteenth and Nineteenth Centuries', *Social History*, 28 (2003), 361–7.

[28] Robert C. Holub, *Jürgen Habermas. Critic in the Public Sphere* (London: Routledge, 1991), 3.

opinion about society. This public sphere model has been applied to Enlightenment science with particular success by historians of science such as Jan Golinski, Larry Stewart, and others.[29] Golinski demonstrates how in the eighteenth century natural philosophers promoted public discourse about their work and how ideals concerning Enlightenment influenced its practice and presentation. For Priestley in particular, scientific knowledge was the engine of social progress and moral reform. Private laboratory experiments only become public when they are communicated, whether by replicated visual demonstration, by written accounts, or by assimilation into textbooks and teaching. For this to happen, audiences (whether of scientific peers, aristocrats, or laypersons) have to be persuaded to become involved. Priestley's practice was to write literary 'cookery books' that encouraged everyone to participate, urging that by repeating or conducting their own experiments, men and women could draw their own conclusions rather than having conclusions handed down to them by specialists and experts. Circumstantial accounts of experiments were more persuasive than reconstructed accounts that dispensed with the historical record. Priestley's 'candour' was, however, sometimes seen as mere verbosity—the angry and frustrated London lecturer Brian Higgins, for example, accused Priestley of plagiarism and of wrapping well-known phenomena in a bombast of 'accidents', 'surprises', and irrelevant digressions.[30] Nevertheless, through his work on airs, Priestley succeeded in popularizing chemistry—a subject that had hitherto figured little in itinerant lecturers' patter and been largely confined to the medical profession. Judging by his popularity or lack of it, his candidature for caricature and ridicule, and his posthumous claims for public commemoration, Anderson has rightly called Priestley a 'public intellectual'.[31]

Golinski noted that the problem for historians has always been to find an overarching link connecting Priestley's science with his

[29] Jürgen Habermas, *The Structural Transformation of the Public Sphere* [1962], trans. Thomas Burger (Oxford: Polity Press, 1989); Golinski; Larry Stewart, *The Rise of Public Science: Rhetoric, Technology, and Natural Philosophy in Newtonian Britain, 1660–1750* (Cambridge & New York: CUP, 1992).

[30] Golinski, 88–90; Schofield, II, 124–9. Priestley rebutted Higgins's charges in *Philosophical Empiricism* (London, 1775).

[31] Anderson, 'Priestley, Public Intellectual' and 'Memorializing Scientists', in Bowden & Rosner, 11–16, 30–41.

theology, metaphysics, and political views and actions. In his book *Mechanism and Materialism* (1970), Robert E. Schofield, the future biographer of Priestley, developed the thesis that Newtonian natural philosophy generated two competing styles of interpreting nature. On the one hand, 'mechanism' saw reality in terms of particles that exerted forces of attraction and repulsion and sought mathematical and quantitative explanations for the phenomena of nature; on the other hand, 'materialism' sought explanations in terms of properties carried by imponderable fluids such as ether, electricity, and caloric. For Schofield the overarching link in Priestley's scientific output was his views concerning the nature of matter (the 'nut shell' atom) and the Newtonian tradition of mechanism.[32] Schofield was particularly struck by the idea that Priestley fell under the spell of the Croatian divine and natural philosopher, Roger Boscovich, and his mathematical idea that matter could be reduced to points that exerted short-range forces of attraction and repulsion. This model had obvious resonance with Priestley's theological dissolution of the matter–spirit dichotomy.

Schofield's thesis was scotched by John McEvoy, Edward McGuire, and others on the grounds that there were only particular instances and contexts in which Priestley invoked Boscovich's model and that there was no evidence that he was guided by it over the 40-odd years of his scientific investigations and theological thinking. We must always remember that Priestley 'composed, edited and interpreted texts selectively for his own polemical [and didactic] purposes'.[33] In any case, it was pointed out, mechanism and materialism were never mutually exclusive ways of interpreting nature in the eighteenth century. For Priestley, forces and fluids were not alternatives; rather,

[32] Arnold Thackray, *Atoms and Powers: An Essay on Newtonian Matter Theory and the Development of Chemistry* (Oxford: Oxford University Press, 1970); R. E. Schofield, *Mechanism and Materialism: British Natural Philosophy in an Age of Reason* (Princeton: Princeton University Press, 1970); R. E. Schofield, 'Joseph Priestley and the Physicalist Tradition in British Chemistry' in Lester Kieft and Bennett R. Willeford Jr. (eds), *Joseph Priestley. Scientist, Theologian, and Metaphysician* (Cranbury, NJ: Bucknell University Press/Associated University Presses, 1980), 92–117. Cf. Erwin N. Hiebert, 'The Integration of Revealed Religion and Scientific Materialism in the Thought of Joseph Priestley' in the same volume, 27–61.

[33] Simon Schaffer, 'Priestley's Questions: An Historiographical Survey', *History of Science*, 22 (1984), 151–83, at 172.

fluids such as electricity, magnetism, and phlogiston were the seat of various powers that mediated the direct action of God's power.[34] Schofield was clearly impressed by McEvoy's critique and alternative explanation. While he continued to believe that Priestley did speculate about an underlying physical matter theory from time to time, Boscovich and short-range forces are not in the foreground of his later two-volume biography of Priestley or in his most recent thoughts (2004) on the subject.[35]

Expanding upon a view first proposed by the veteran chemical historian Philip Hartog in the 1940s, McEvoy himself has argued that it was the metaphysical and theological components that made up Priestley's commitment to rational dissent, and that this in turn underlay his commitment to scientific investigations. Viewed in this light there is a 'synoptic unity of epistemological, metaphysical, methodological, theological, and strictly scientific parameters in his thinking'.[36] Priestley was committed to the belief that God continually provided 'life and happiness' to the world and that nature was a 'deterministic system of benevolence'. Thus, the laws of nature that natural philosophers unveiled in their investigations were so structured as to make their discoverers awed and happy, as he repeatedly noted in his *Electricity*. Nature was fecund and inexhaustible and the evil in the world only apparent in the short term. Such deterministic theism had the consequence that much evil and immorality would cease if man strove to moral perfection through the study of nature. Civil history revealed man's slow growth towards this moral perfection while the study of the history of the sciences had an especial

[34] J. G. McEvoy, 'Joseph Priestley, Natural Philosopher: Some Comments on Professor Schofield's Views', *Ambix*, 15 (1968), 115–23; J. G. McEvoy and J. E. McGuire, 'God and Nature: Priestley's Way of Rational Dissent', *Historical Studies in the Physical Sciences*, 6 (1975), 325–404; J. G. McEvoy, 'Joseph Priestley, "Aerial Philosopher": Metaphysics and Methodology in Priestley's Chemical Thought, from 1772 to 1781', *Ambix*, 25 (1978), 1–55, 93–116, 153–75, and 26 (1979), 16–38; Simon Schaffer, 'Priestley and the Politics of Spirit', in Anderson & Lawrence, 39–53.

[35] Schofield, I and II; Schofield, 'Joseph Priestley, Natural Philosopher', *Bulletin History of Chemistry*, 30 (2005), 57–62, a paper given at the bicentennial celebration of Priestley's life held by the American Chemical Society in August 2004.

[36] McEvoy, 'Electricity', 2; McEvoy, 'Causes and Laws, Powers and Principles: The Metaphysical Foundations of Priestley's Concept of Phlogiston', in Anderson & Lawrence, 55–71; Philip J. Hartog, 'Newer Views of Priestley and Lavoisier', *Annals of Science*, 5 (1941), 1–56.

advantage in demonstrating the power and wisdom of God and the progress of man. As we have seen, the latter was the stimulus for Priestley's entry into a history and investigation of electricity.

As is well known, Priestley followed David Hartley in extending Locke's empiricism in rejecting innate ideas for a mind whose properties were solely a function of sensations and the associations of ideas. It followed that every individual was determined by the environmental circumstances of his or her life. The mind was entirely governed by what went on in the external world. Any judgements or hypotheses about nature were due to the mechanical associations of ideas, albeit these could be weighed and tested by environmental feedback. It was the task of the philosopher to judge whether these mechanical associations were 'real knowledge' or 'mere opinion', the judgement resting upon the idiosyncrasies of the person's education. Priestley knew that one had to distinguish prejudices that arose from false associations of ideas from real knowledge that associated the 'necessary nature of things'. Priestley's thesis guaranteed or generated philosophical necessity since all phenomena were ultimately determined by the intricate play of or association of God's laws. A theory was 'a system of principles to which all the facts may be reduced'.[37] Hypotheses, by contrast, involved propositions that had not been or could not be proved or linked into a causal chain of general principles. McEvoy sees this distinction as a basic weapon in Priestley's methodological armory and demonstrated its use in an analysis of Priestley's *History of Electricity*.[38] This work, McEvoy argued, is a cornerstone for understanding Priestley's scientific work and especially for explaining his critical attitude towards Lavoisier.

While finding McEvoy's severely epistemological approach helpful at an intellectual level, Golinski, following Simon Schaffer and his student John Money, takes a more sociological view by setting Priestley's publications in the context of the interest groups with whom Priestley was seeking audience and, as Maurice Crosland shrewdly observed, financial support, rational recreation, and a haven from theological disputation.[39] These approaches have the advantage of avoiding

---

[37] Joseph Priestley, *Experiments and Observations*, III (1786), p. xxii.

[38] McEvoy, 'Electricity', esp. 10–19.

[39] Schaffer, 'Priestley's Questions', 151–83; 'Priestley and the Politics of Spirit', 39–53; John Money, 'Joseph Priestley in Cultural Context: Philosophic Spectacle,

labelling Priestley as a 'chemist' (as later practising scientists have
inevitably done), and seeing him instead as a natural philosopher
tailoring his investigations to suit different audiences within the public realm, who repaid in kind by subscribing to his publications,
giving him instruments and chemicals, or generally patronizing
his work disinterestedly.

He made personal links with numerous people who could help him, mostly
those whom he could repay in some respect with his work. He also made connections of a different kind with the more diffuse and distant audience that
he reached through his published works. Priestley's vision of a public culture
of science was extrapolated from the social and political circumstances in
which he worked through the 1760s to the 1790s.[40]

Thus we find him targeting electricians in the 1760s, soliciting Fellows
of the Royal Society and members of the medical profession interested
in public health during the 1770s, and (while living in Birmingham)
cultivating members of the Lunar Society, a Midlands club which he
saw as an ideal example of how public science should be conducted.
By looking at book reviews, records of library borrowings, and lists of
subscribers, Golinski established that Priestley succeeded in reaching
a broad and well dispersed readership. His greatest success, at least
until the 1790s, was in stimulating a widespread interest in gases and
in encouraging others to work in this field.

When considering the clients for Priestley's work we can see that it
was of interest and use to itinerant lecturers, fellow natural philosophers, the medical profession, and instrument makers. Lecturers such
as John Waltire, John Banks, and Adam Walker added Priestley's
pneumatics to their repertoire, frequently seeking his advice on
the skills needed for a reliable repetition and reproduction of an
experiment. Natural philosophers such as Henry Cavendish, Richard
Kirwan, and, above all, Antoine Lavoisier were indebted to Priestley
for opening up the third dimension of chemistry—the study of gases
as opposed to that of just solids and liquids. Aspiring medical reformers and environmentalists such as John Pringle and David Macbride,
who had already speculated about the deleterious effects of vitiated

Popular Belief and Popular Politics in Eighteenth-Century Birmingham', *E&D*, 7
(1988), 57–81 and 8 (1989), 69–89. Crosland, 'A Practical Perspective'.

[40] Golinski, 66.

or mephitic air on the health of urban societies, seized first upon Priestley's evidence that fixed air dissolved in water might be an antidote to scurvy, and upon dephlogisticated air as a cure for many physical ailments. In Italy Priestley's eudiometry (the volumetric analysis of gaseous reactions) led Felice Fontana and Marsilio Landriani to influential public health campaigns concerning the goodness of air, while in England it prompted Erasmus Darwin, James Watt, and Thomas Beddoes to an investigation of whether inhaling the different species of factitious airs that Priestley and others had identified was an antidote for tuberculosis. It was at Beddoes's pneumatic hospital in Bristol that the young Humphry Davy cut his chemical teeth as Priestley's heir.[41] Such investigations of air quality (eudiometry) and pneumatic properties also significantly involved instrument makers in making and improving the designs of eudiometers, apparatus for making soda water, and devices for the preparation and transfer of gases in bulk.

The case of eudiometry has interested a number of scholars. It is pointed out that the analysis of the quality of air as devised by Priestley built the phlogiston theory into the design of the instrument (just as today when physical theories are 'black boxed' into laboratory machines). Ironically, the eudiometer could, however, be adapted into an instrument for measuring the amount of oxygen in an air sample, though the method fell out of favour during Priestley's and Lavoisier's lifetimes because it involved too many sources of error. It was Jean Senebier who pointed out in 1783 that Priestley's eudiometry was vitiated by the fact that most gases were slightly soluble in water over time and that, therefore, it was not possible to standardize the technique. By then Volta had introduced a different method of igniting an air sample with inflammable air (hydrogen) by an electric spark, and it was this instrumental method (and not Priestley's less accurate 'goodness of air' test) that Lavoisier used to demonstrate the decomposition of water in 1784. Quite apart from its failure as an accurate instrument, Golinski provides a convincing

[41] Simon Schaffer, 'Measuring Virtue: Eudiometry, Enlightenment and Pneumatic Medicine', in Andrew Cunningham and Roger French (eds), *The Medical Enlightenment of the Eighteenth Century* (Cambridge & New York: CUP, 1990), 281–318; Brian Dollan, 'Conservative Politicians, Radical Philosophers and the Aerial Remedy for the Diseases of Civilization', *History of the Human Sciences*, 15 (2002), 35–54.

case that Priestley's eudiometry ultimately failed because Priestley failed to establish a network of expert practitioners on the grounds that if the method was made more complicated to avoid errors it would defeat his aim of making science available to all. By deliberately not standardizing a methodology that took into account sources of error, in the long term his goodness of air programme failed to work.[42]

Schaffer has intriguingly suggested that a contextual approach explains the paradox of Priestley being at one and the same time revolutionary in his political and theological thought yet seemingly conservative in his science. In fact, Priestley's contemporaries saw linkages between Priestley's science and political revolution. Schaffer's solution is to see Priestley's scientific 'discoveries' as resources for making new forms of natural knowledge. For example,

in pneumatics, Priestley's work could be deployed as part of a model system of physiological-medical knowledge and control, in which no event was terrifying and all natural phenomena, if well understood, were to be displayed as ultimately purposive.[43]

In this new natural theology in which the universe became a laboratory, earthquakes, for example, were no longer to be viewed as punishments, but part of a divine scientific system which reinvigorated the atmosphere and earth to keep them fit for vegetable, animal, and human existence. The radical implication of this was that imperfect and corrupt states ignored the system of natural laws at their peril and that perfection would come about by working with God's system.

THE PHLOGISTON PROBLEM

The exact nature of the Chemical Revolution concerning which Priestley and Lavoisier represented a 'before and after' image is still argued about by historians as Djerassi's and Hoffmann's drama

---

[42] Golinski, ch. 4; Schaffer, 'Priestley's Questions', 168–9; Schaffer, 'Priestley and the Politics of Spirit', in Anderson & Lawrence, 39–53.

[43] Schaffer, 'Priestley and the Politics of Spirit', in Anderson & Lawrence, 50.

portrays. Simplistically it had to do with the replacement of phlogistic explanations of combustion and calcinations by one that involved the gas oxygen. Combustion was not caused by the loss of a phlogistic principle but by a combination with the oxygen of the air, with a corresponding accompaniment of an increase in weight. However, much more was involved in the eighteenth-century transformation of chemistry, including the postulation of a new category of physical matter, the gaseous state. The nature of acids and acidity (oxygen was after all Lavoisier's principle of acidity) was also redefined, as were the formation of salts, and the mechanism of respiration. New ideas about composition and the naming of chemical constituents were introduced, together with the introduction of standards of measurement that involved precise quantitative assays. More recently, historians have also suggested that it is also necessary to re-examine the alchemical corpuscular tradition upheld and exploited by seventeenth- and early eighteenth-century alchymists, such as Joan Baptista van Helmont and Wilhelm Homberg, which Lavoisier, but not Priestley, inherited and in which he was trained.[44]

All historians of science are agreed, however, that what counted most in the reconstruction of chemistry was the superior persuasive and rhetorical powers of Lavoisier and his followers. Here the principal trick was to insist upon a new chemical nomenclature that forced the user to speak the language of the new French chemistry. Priestley was caught in this bind, forced in his later writings to repeatedly 'translate' his phlogistic terminology of phlogisticated and dephlogisticated airs into the new oxygen-centred language whenever he sought to raise an experimental objection to the French chemistry. As Beretta has observed:

It was the difference in the terminology that Priestley and Lavoisier employed that made it difficult to translate and reconcile their empirical observations.... Their different philosophies of language, Priestley's skepticism concerning any systematic and speculative reform of chemical language illustrates the strength of the British philosophy of language outlined by

---

[44] William R. Newman and Lawrence M. Principe, *Alchemy Tried in the Fire: Starkey, Boyle, and the Fate of Helmontian Chymistry* (Chicago: Chicago University Press, 2002).

Bacon and Locke, who warned of the metaphysical danger inherent in the introduction of neologisms and stressed the primacy of facts and experience over words.[45]

Priestley was never clear in his own mind what phlogiston was, and the opinions he expressed are all contradictory. Sometimes, for example in 1774, he implied that it was light or electricity and different from, though the cause of, heat, which he explained as a vibration of the constituent parts of a material; at others, as in 1783, he agreed with Richard Kirwan and Henry Cavendish that it was probably inflammable air, though in practice he persistently confused carbon monoxide with hydrogen, both of which burn with a blue flame in the presence of oxygen. That phlogiston was not simply the principle of combustion was clearly demonstrated to Priestley by the fact that phlogisticated air (nitrogen) was nonflammable and noncombustible even though rich in phlogiston. The presence of phlogiston was a necessary but not sufficient condition for combustibility, and this fact implied to Priestley that a substance's properties depended upon subtle questions connected with composition and power of affinity. Ironically, this was in line with contemporary chemical thinking, and it should be noted that Lavoisier's *calorique* played a similar role in differentiating gases from the solid and liquid states.

Priestley was certain that phlogiston, not Lavoisier's misplaced caloric, played a vital role in the transformations that chemists studied, as well as in living processes such as respiration, and that it was not registered by the balance pan (an imponderable body).[46] However, as Partington and Schofield, the only historians to pay close attention to Priestley's final scientific writings, point out, at the end of his life he was far less dogmatic and sceptical about phlogiston than the challenging title, *The Doctrine of Phlogiston Established* (1800), might suggest. Nevertheless, totally confused by undifferentiated inflammable airs and unable to replicate Lavoisier's decomposition of water quantitatively, even when using Volta's new electric

[45] Marco Beretta, *The Enlightenment of Matter: The Definition of Chemistry from Agricola to Lavoisier* (Canton, MA: Science History Publications, 1993), p. xiv, 171–8.

[46] Joseph Priestley, 'Observations on Respiration, and the Use of the Blood', *Philosophical Transactions of the Royal Society*, 66 (1776), 226, reprinted in *Experiments and Observations on Different Kinds of Air*, III (1777), 55–84; Partington, *Chemistry*, III, 268–9.

pile (the electric battery), he dug himself into a morass that left him isolated from mainstream chemical philosophy at the beginning of the nineteenth century.

As we can see from our 'post-Lavoisian' position, Priestley's objections to Lavoisier's chemistry were often, indeed, usually, perfectly valid. For example, Priestley objected that not all acids contained oxygen. In repeating Lavoisier's iconic demonstration of phlogiston-free conservation of matter in which a weighed proportion of mercuric oxide when heated decomposed into quantities of mercury and oxygen, he found they did not exactly match the original weight of calx as Lavoisier had claimed. The same claimed congruity failed when Priestley passed a weighed amount of water over hot iron as steam; it decomposed into proportions of hydrogen and oxygen that did not quite match the original weight of water. Priestley constantly urged that in Lavosier's quantitative decompositions and syntheses the proportions were never as exact as an algebraic equation. For example, in the decomposition of mercuric oxide Priestley consistently got less mercury back than he started with. In any case, he observed, Lavoisier's pretence of measuring to four or five places of decimal was pure window dressing. To this Lavoisier replied that expensive and superior apparatus was needed to achieve precision which, of course, was anathema to Priestley's democratic approach to chemical experimentation.

As McEvoy observed, from Priestley's point of view Lavoisier's doctrine was too bound up with a false judgment that elaborate instruments were more reliable than simple ones.[47] From Priestley's viewpoint phlogiston had proved useful and adaptable in differentiating the airs he had discovered, but at the cost of relating them to each other rather than relating them to their origins in solid and liquid substances. Crosland also points out that because his chemical investigations involved the gaseous state exclusively, Priestley naturally thought and dealt in volumes rather than in *weights*, thus differing completely from the admittedly more difficult gravimetric direction that chemistry was to take from Lavoisier and Dalton.[48]

---

[47] John G. McEvoy, 'Continuity and Discontinuity in the Chemical Revolution', *Osiris*, 2nd series, 4 (1988), 195–213, at 204.

[48] Crosland, 'A Practical Perspective', 235; McEvoy, 'Priestley, Natural Philosopher', 121.

Priestley's 'objections' were perfectly valid from a philosophical point of view, and are interesting insofar as they demonstrate that new scientific theories become adopted, not because experimental data 'prove' one thing or another, but because the new explanation is more persuasive and productive of new ideas and practices. Lavoisier and his converts were well aware of anomalies in the new theory, but they were content for these to be explained at a later time as part of what Kuhn suggested constituted normal science. Meanwhile, the new paradigm gave a wonderfully consistent shape to the chemistry of elements, acids, bases, and salts and promised new insights into the mysteries of animal and vegetable chemistry.

Although Priestley openly confessed that he saw the merits of the new French theory and admitted that he would, like his former phlogiston allies Richard Kirwan and William Nicholson, willingly convert to the oxygen theory, he refused while certain of his observations remained impossible to interpret by that theory. Chief among these were Lavoisier's failure to acknowledge that his 'synthesis' of water from its supposed elements also produced nitrous acid. Priestley saw this as evidence, not of contamination of oxygen by nitric oxide (as Lavoisier implicitly believed), but that water was already present in inflammable and dephlogisticated airs and that the nitrous acid was produced from the ponderable bases of the gases after phlogiston had escaped. Although Priestley was 'right' that nitrous acid was produced, it was for the wrong reasons, and it was left to Humphry Davy to show by rigorous application of purification and careful analysis that the acid was a by-product of contamination. As previously mentioned, another significant issue was 'inflammable air' which, as hydrogen in the new system, supposedly originated from the water when a metal was dissolved in an acid solution.

metal + acid in water solution = metal oxide + hydrogen
[non-metal oxide + water]

But, Priestley objected, it was possible to make inflammable air (meaning Lavosier's hydrogen) without the presence of any water, as when air was passed over a heated mixture of charcoal and the calx of iron (iron oxide). Lavoisier's disciples could not explain this experiment until 1801 when William Cruickshank showed that the inflammable air produced in this instance was not hydrogen at all, but the gas, carbon monoxide, which ironically Priestley himself had first prepared in 1772.

By 1801 Priestley was living in isolation in a remote corner of Pennsylvania and with no local person to offer helpful criticism. He rejected Cruickshank's explanation in his usual vigorous manner.[49] As Schofield and Verbruggen have demonstrated, most of Priestley's criticisms have valid explanations today: chemical reactions never proceed in the ideal manner represented by a simple equation. There are always side products, and varying the conditions of temperature and pressure alters product yields. Priestley lacked the analyst's tacit knowledge of what to ignore in a chemical reaction. For Priestley, observational facts were more important than proposing simplifying and dogmatic hypotheses that could come and go— as he accused the French chemists of doing. Such a dogmatic and dictatorial approach to chemistry restricted its public availability as knowledge and took the power of decision making from everyman.[50] Nevertheless, authoritative simplification has proved the backbone of scientific progress.

CONCLUSION

For followers of Karl Popper's philosophy of science Priestley's experience shows that theories can never be proved, only falsified: Lavoisier falsified the phlogiston theory, whereas Priestley, equally Popperian, clung to observations that, to him, falsified the anti-phlogistian theory.[51] To Kuhnians, Priestley's case demonstrates the role of anomalies both in disproving theories or paradigms and in bolstering them. For sociologists, for whom successful scientific knowledge and

[49] Joseph Priestley, *The Doctrine of Phlogiston Established and that of the Composition of Water Refuted*, 2nd edn. (Northumberland and Philadelphia, 1803).

[50] Schofield, 'Priestley, Natural Philosopher'; Freddy Verbruggen, 'How to Explain Priestley's Defense of Phlogiston', *Janus*, 59 (1972), 47–69; Golinski, 148; Michael F. Conlin, 'Joseph Priestley's American Defense of Phlogiston Reconsidered', *Ambix*, 43 (1996), 129–45.

[51] Karl Popper, *Conjectures and Refutations* (New York: Basic Books, 1963).

practice need public demonstration and display, Priestley shows the importance of scientific networks and the origins of explanations in local contexts and how theories collide because of resistance to universalization of particular explanations. There was no local person or group in America who was a convinced anti-phlogistonist who might have dissuaded Priestley from his continuing commitment to phlogiston.

We may well agree with McEvoy's conclusion regarding the 'synoptic nature of Priestley's mind by revealing the intelligibility of his electrical [and pneumatic] thought on philosophical principles that encompass the totality of reality'.[52] However, Priestley's adherence to Hartleian associationism placed him out of sympathy with any kind of Platonism. Consequently he was unable to 'idealize' chemical reactions and see them in a simple form (or in a simplified explanation). When science idealizes, it leaves anomalies for later followers to add explanations such as 'side reactions', the presence of impurities, altered physical conditions, etc. But, as examples from the past repeatedly show (e.g. Kepler's construction of planetary laws from a mass of raw data whose inaccuracy hid the planetary perturbations from sight), simplification is a necessary feature of scientific progress and the first step towards advancing knowledge. Perhaps by its very nature democratic public science is bound to fail because it inevitably fails to simplify.

Yet, despite the failure of Priestley's campaign for a truly public science, the scientist and historian cannot fail to be moved by Priestley's insight into the nature of experimentation and scientific progress as he expressed it in his *Electricity*:

It may be said, that I ought, at least, to have waited till I had seen the connection of my new experiments with those that were made before, and have shown that they were agreeable to some general theory of electricity. But when the facts are before the public, others are as capable of showing that connection, and of deducing a general theory from them as myself. If but the most inconsiderable part, of the temple of science be well laid out, or a single stone proper for, and belonging to it be collected; though at present it be ever so much detached from the rest of the building, its connection and relative importance will appear in due time, when the intermediate parts shall be completed. Every *fact* has a real, though unseen connection with every other fact: and when all the facts belonging to any branch of science are collected, the system will form itself. In the mean time, our guessing at the system may be some guide to us in the discovery of the facts; but, at present, let us pay no attention to the system in any other view; and let us mutually communicate every new fact we discover, without troubling ourselves about the system to which it may be reduced.[53]

[53] Priestley, *Electricity*, 579–80; quoted McEvoy, 'Electricity', 24.

3

Joseph Priestley, Metaphysician and Philosopher of Religion

James Dybikowski

INTRODUCTION

What ties Priestley's philosophical thought together and makes it distinctive is his sustained determination to repatriate for Christianity metaphysical and epistemological positions that other Christian thinkers rejected as dangerous and tantamount to infidelity and atheism. On the one hand, he saw that many contemporaries who engaged in natural investigation rejected the Christian revelation, the promise of a future life, and, indeed, God's existence.[1] On the other, he recognized that some articles of Christianity such as the doctrine of the Trinity, as well as commonly accepted metaphysical commitments such as the dualism of matter and spirit, encouraged the view that Christianity is not supportable by the same methods, principles of enquiry, or standards of evidence demanded of natural investigation, whether of physical or psychological phenomena. Priestley's solution was to strip Christianity of the features that made it unattractive to those committed to such investigation by showing them to be corruptions. A purified rational religion, he argues, is not only compatible with philosophy, but also provides resources to beat off sceptical doubt, whether about the external world, causality, morals,

[1] Joseph Priestley, *Letters to a Philosophical Unbeliever, Part I* (2nd edn., Birmingham, 1787), pp.[iii]–xi. This reference is to a dedication that appeared in the second edition. Other references are to this edition as the earliest edition available in ECCO.

or a future state of rewards and punishments. A related resource for coping with the sceptic, he identifies, is to lower expectations by displacing the demand for absolute certainty with the acceptance of probability, related because for Priestley rational religion, whether natural or revealed, rests for the most part not on demonstration, but on probability.[2]

The main metaphysical and epistemological ideas that characterize Priestley's mature philosophical thought are:

1. The association of ideas, which, he argues, explains all mental states, including reasoning and moral ideas.

2. The doctrine of necessity, which holds all human actions to be caused and, by virtue of that, necessitated, and which, far from constituting a threat to morality, helps us to better understand it.

3. Materialism.

For him, each of these doctrines is not only individually defensible, but also contributes to a coherent system fully consistent with natural investigation and its extension to human and animal minds. The significance of their individual defensibility is that while Priestley believes materialism and the association of ideas both entail the doctrine of necessity, that doctrine can be shown to be true even if they were to be rejected. A theme that runs through all these doctrines is the notion that an understanding of causes and effects is key to understanding the natural world, psychological phenomena included. It is at the foundation of the association of ideas, the doctrine of necessity, materialism, and, indeed, natural religion.

Priestley concedes that he adopted many of these positions from others: the association of ideas, for example, from David Hartley (1705–57), and the doctrine of necessity from Anthony Collins (1676–1729) and Hartley. His adoption of materialism traces back to ideas about unconventional ways of conceiving matter he encountered through Father Roger Joseph Boscovich (1711–87) and John Michell (1724–93). These ideas, he believed, overcame inveterate

---

[2] Joseph Priestley, *Institutes of Natural and Revealed Religion* (2nd edn., Birmingham, 1782), II, pt. III, 147–50. References are to this edition as the earliest edition available online in ECCO.

prejudices about the nature of matter, although they needed a longer gestation period before he developed them into a full-blown monistic materialism. Boscovich, indeed, was offended by Priestley's praise since he had no wish to lend comfort to materialists.[3]

Priestley's originality turns less on the components of his system than on the system itself as combined with a primitive, rational Christianity that pre-dates its corruption by the 'Oriental' doctrine of a separate soul, which he views as the foundation of the beliefs of Christ's preexistence and deification. His attractiveness as a philosopher arises from his spirited and unflinching defence of these ideas against determined opposition. As he remarks about his commitment to the doctrine of philosophical necessity: 'We all see *some things* in so clear and strong a light, that, without having any high opinion of our own understandings, we think we may challenge all the world upon them.'[4] Challenge he certainly did. His skill as a controversialist ensured that the ideas he championed reached a far wider audience than they had when expressed by, say, a Hartley.

Given Priestley's project, it is not surprising that he should remark: 'Let us then study the *Scriptures, Ecclesiastical History*, and the *Theory of the Human Mind*, in conjunction; being satisfied, that from the nature of the things, they must, in time, throw a great and new light upon each other.'[5] Materialism, for example, offers a basis for viewing Christ as human rather than as a being that, in virtue of an immaterial soul, must have existed prior to his birth. It also provides a basis for Priestley's attempt to justify the doctrine of the resurrection promised by Christian revelation. Priestley's manner of mingling these and related enquiries is a feature of his writing that makes reading him difficult for the modern reader, who expects them to be more decisively demarcated. His methodology, however, is part and parcel of the project of tying philosophy and religion more closely together.

[3] *Scientific Autobiography,* Priestley to Boscovich, 19 Aug. 1778; Boscovich to Priestley, 17 Oct. 1778. For Boscovich and Michell and their influence on Priestley, see John W. Yolton, *Thinking Matter: Materialism in Eighteenth-Century Britain* (Minneapolis: University of Minnesota Press, 1983), 109 ff.

[4] Joseph Priestley, *A Letter to the Rev. Mr. John Palmer, in Defense of the Illustrations of Philosophical Necessity* (Bath, 1779), 91.

[5] Joseph Priestley, *The Doctrine of Philosophical Necessity Illustrated* (London, 1777), p. xvi.

THE GENESIS OF PRIESTLEY'S IDEAS

Priestley entered Daventry Academy at the age of 19, after a hiatus that followed his earlier schooling when he was left largely to his own devices. By his own account he had previously been educated 'in the very straitest principles of *reputed orthodoxy*'.[6] At Daventry he enjoyed his first sustained social experience of free enquiry. On key questions, his fellow students divided nearly equally as did his tutors: 'We were permitted to ask whatever questions, and to make whatever remarks we pleased; and we did it with the greatest, but without any offensive, freedom'. He later attempted to produce such an atmosphere as a teacher at Warrington Academy.[7] This experience was replicated once more, albeit all too unusually, in his great debate on liberty and materialism with his philosophical contemporary Richard Price, with whom he profoundly disagreed, but whom he held in the greatest respect. It stands out as a model of civility in debate.

At Daventry Priestley came to embrace, as he describes it, 'the heterodox side of almost every question'.[8] A reference in a lecture to David Hartley's *Observations on Man* led him to read the work.[9] Priestley was not only convinced by Hartley's account of the mind based solely on the association of ideas derived from sensory experience, but was also confirmed in his commitment to the doctrine of necessity.[10] Of this last, Priestley remarks: 'There is no truth of which I have less doubt, and of the ground of which I am more fully satisfied. Indeed, there is no absurdity more glaring to my understanding than the notion of Philosophical Liberty.'[11] For Priestley, philosophical liberty, or the power to initiate motion or to act in a certain way or otherwise while the circumstances are the same, is a philosophical fantasy that bears no real relation to what we ordinarily mean or should mean by 'liberty'.

The conception of philosophical liberty Priestley mocks is one he had earlier embraced. The first philosophical exchange he recalls

---

[6] Joseph Priestley, *Disquisitions relating to Matter and Spirit* (London, 1777), p. v.
[7] Rutt, I i, 50–51, n*.   [8] Rutt, I i, 25.   [9] Rutt, I i, 24.
[10] For Hartley, see Richard C. Allen, *David Hartley on Human Nature* (Albany, NY: State University of New York Press, 1999).
[11] Priestley, *Doctrine of Philosophical Necessity*, p. xxii.

in his memoirs occurred between himself and the freethinker Peter Annet around 1749–51.[12] Priestley had learned Annet's system of shorthand and wrote to suggest improvements. Their correspondence broadened into a debate over philosophical liberty and necessity: Priestley defended philosophical liberty while Annet's efforts to dislodge him from that view failed. He was later pleased that he rejected Annet's offer to publish their correspondence because where Annet failed to convince him, the reading of Anthony Collins's *Philosophical Inquiry concerning Human Liberty* soon thereafter did.[13] Of Collins's little book Priestley remarks: 'This treatise is concise and methodical, and is, in my opinion, sufficient to give intire satisfaction to every unprejudiced person'.[14] He later oversaw its republication in 1790, adding a critical preface.[15] His own debate on this and related issues with Richard Price mirrors Collins's debates with Samuel Clarke (1675–1729), England's great rationalist metaphysician, earlier in the century.[16]

If reading Collins first persuaded Priestley of the doctrine of philosophical necessity, his reading of Hartley confirmed him in that view. What impressed Priestley about Hartley's defence of the doctrine is that he too arrived at it contrary to his previous disposition and that he was a Christian, whereas Collins was reputedly an unbeliever and one of the most daunting challengers of the evidence for Christian revelation. For Priestley, unlike Hartley, however, the adoption of the doctrine of necessity preceded that of the association of ideas.

If Priestley was a convinced necessitarian in the 1750s, he did not commit himself to materialism until the 1770s. Once again he found

---

[12] Rutt, I i, 19. For Annet, see James A. Herrick, *The Radical Rhetoric of the English Deists: The Discourse of Skepticism, 1680–1750* (Columbia, SC: University of South Carolina Press, 1997), 125–44. For the timing of the exchange with Annet, see Schofield, I, 57.

[13] Rutt, I i, 24.   [14] Priestley, *Doctrine of Philosophical Necessity*, p. xxx.

[15] *Philosophical Inquiry concerning Human Liberty. By Anthony Collins, Esq. Republished with a Preface by Joseph Priestley* (Birmingham, 1790). For Collins, see James O'Higgins, S.J., *Anthony Collins: The Man and his Works* (The Hague: Martinus Nijhoff, 1970) and, for a very different account, David Berman, *A History of Atheism in Britain from Hobbes to Russell* (London and New York: Routledge, 1988).

[16] For Richard Price, see D. O. Thomas, *The Honest Mind: The Thought and Work of Richard Price* (Oxford: Clarendon Press, 1977); for Samuel Clarke, see J. P. Ferguson, *Dr Samuel Clarke: An Eighteenth Century Heretic* (Kineton: The Roundwood Press, 1976); and Samuel Clarke: Special Issue, *E&D* 16 (1997).

himself rejecting a conventional orthodoxy, the dualism of matter and spirit, he had previously accepted. He embraced materialism gingerly at first and then with full commitment in a string of publications that mostly appeared while he was in the employ of Lord Shelburne as his librarian. The high water mark of this commitment was the publication of *Disquisitions relating to Matter and Spirit* (1777), which with its annex, the *Doctrine of Philosophical Necessity Illustrated*, is his most significant philosophical work. He openly entertained materialism in the introductory essays to his edition of Hartley's *Theory of the Human Mind* (1775) and had broadly suggested it in his *Examination of Reid's Inquiry* (1774). Hartley was no materialist, but Priestley found materialism to be a natural development from his account of the human mind.[17] The strength of his commitment to materialism owed a great deal to the close attention he paid to the doctrine following the ferocious criticism to which he was subjected on simply entertaining it in print.[18] He was not a man to back down in the face of attack.

Equally notable about Priestley's conversion to materialism is that it followed an extended journey with Lord Shelburne to the continent, which included a stay in Paris. There he met materialists, but also at the same time 'unbelievers in Christianity, and even professed Atheists'.[19] These included the Baron d'Holbach (1723–89), whose house Priestley visited in Shelburne's company.[20] While Priestley was sympathetic to many of the philosophical opinions he encountered, he regarded the fashionable rejection of Christianity as arising from prejudice and a false view of the positions to which it was supposedly committed. As he remarks in the preface to his book on Reid's philosophy, 'the true interest of christianity is promoted no less by throwing down weak and rotten supports, than by supplying it with firm and good ones'.[21] Thoroughly pursued, philosophy supports natural and

---

[17] Joseph Priestley (ed.), *Hartley's Theory of the Human Mind, on the Principle of the Association of Ideas; with Essays relating to the Subject of it* (London, 1775), p. xix.

[18] Rutt, I i, 203. For an account of the criticism, see Yolton, *Thinking Matter*, 115–25.

[19] Rutt, I i, 199.

[20] See Alan Charles Kors, *D'Holbach's Coterie: An Enlightenment in Paris* (Princeton: Princeton University Press, 1976), 105.

[21] Joseph Priestley, *An Examination of Dr Reid's Inquiry into the Human Mind on the Principles of Common Sense, Dr Beattie's Essay on the Nature and Immutability of*

revealed religion, while Christianity, rationally interpreted, is in keeping with the doctrines of philosophical necessity and materialism. Key to his advocacy of these last, however, is the removal of false views and ancient prejudices: the association with ancient fatalism and modern Calvinism in the case of the former, and the deeply held view that matter of its nature is passive, inert, and impenetrable in the case of the latter. Matter's supposed possession of these properties rendered it ineligible as a subject that could think or perceive.

Priestley's development of this system of ideas spans a relatively brief period from 1774 until about 1780. Some parts appeared in print beforehand, most notably in his *Institutes of Natural and Revealed Religion* (1772–4), where he systematically sets out his approach to natural and revealed religion, but after 1780, this intensely creative philosophical period was largely over. With the exception of the association of ideas, he had had his say. Alas, the manuscript he was preparing to illustrate Hartley's doctrine was lost in the Birmingham riots in 1791.[22]

SCOTTISH COMMON SENSE AND HARTLEY

One of the first philosophical works Priestley read as a young man was Locke's *Essay concerning Human Understanding* (first published 1690).[23] It repeatedly surfaces in his philosophical writings as a marker against which he defines his positions, favourably at times because its general approach to human knowledge provides 'the corner stone of all just and rational knowledge of ourselves', but critically at others because its views on the sources of knowledge, on liberty and on the possibility of thinking matter are either too unclear or too timid.[24]

When Priestley encountered the critique of Locke's empiricism made by Thomas Reid (1710–96) in his *Inquiry into the Human Mind, on the Principles of Common Sense* (1764), he found Reid's 'notions of

Truth, and Dr Oswald's Appeal to Common Sense in behalf of Religion (London, 1774), p. xxviii.

[22] Rutt, I ii, 6n*.   [23] Rutt, I i, 13.

[24] Priestley, *Examination of Dr Reid's Inquiry*, 5.

human nature [to be] the very reverse of those which I had learned from Mr. Locke and Dr Hartley (in which I thought I had sufficient reason to acquiesce)'.[25] When he later published his critical examination of Reid's common sense philosophy, he included attacks on other Scottish philosophers influenced by him, notably James Beattie (1735–1803) and his *Essay on the Nature and Immutability of Truth; in opposition to Sophistry and Scepticism* (1770) as well as James Oswald (1715–69) and his *Appeal to Common Sense in behalf of Religion* (1766). They appealed to common sense to shore up the foundations of morality and religion, as Reid had for knowledge of the external world. For these philosophers, common sense is the view that there are certain beliefs, based neither on education nor on habit, that we cannot help having because of our common human nature. Beattie, for example, claimed that common sense rules out the doctrine of philosophical necessity as absurd. Part of Priestley's argument to disarm common sense philosophy is to show how easily it multiplies the phenomena it claims are only explainable by resorting to a variety of seemingly disconnected instinctive principles. It thereby abandons the simplicity he views as a hallmark of a correct metaphysical picture of the natural world and our place within it. In morality and religion especially, he argues that common sense threatens to displace the proper role of reason.

For Reid, common sense philosophy answers the scepticism of Hume and the idealism of Berkeley, but it identifies Locke as opening the door to both, whatever his intentions. For if ideas are not images of external objects and if we perceive ideas rather than external objects, ideas cannot be a source of knowledge about the external world and are compatible with its nonexistence.[26] Reid accepts this sceptical argument, but rejects the theory of ideas that generates it. His response is that there are first principles forming part of our natural constitution that make belief in an external world instinctive and its denial absurd.

---

[25] Priestley, *Examination of Dr Reid's Inquiry*, p. vii. Two useful collections of articles on various aspects of Reid's philosophy are: Melvin Dalgarno and Eric Matthews (eds), *The Philosophy of Thomas Reid* (Dordrecht: Kluwer Academic Publishers, 1989) and Terence Cuneo and René Van Woudenberg (eds), *The Cambridge Companion to Thomas Reid* (Cambridge: CUP, 2004). The former collection in particular deals with his relation with Priestley.

[26] Priestley, *Examination of Dr Reid's Inquiry*, 28–36.

Typically Priestley's critique of Reid is read now to see how well he grasps Reid's philosophical intentions and how effectively his critique answers him. The general verdict is that he has mixed success at best.[27] Indeed, when Reid published his later and philosophically most significant works, Priestley paid no heed. For our purposes, it is more illuminating to consider how Priestley's critique, right or wrong, contributes to the development of his philosophical outlook.

Unlike Reid, Priestley displays a robust immunity to the problem of scepticism. He rejects Reid's solution to scepticism about an external world as motivated by a false problem. For him, it is unreasonable to expect to silence all doubt of its existence as absurd. Such doubt ought to be acknowledged as possible, but scepticism is not its inevitable consequence. 'It is quite sufficient', he argues,

if the supposition [of an external world] be the easiest hypothesis for explaining the origin of our ideas. The evidence of it is such that we allow it to be barely possible to doubt of it; but that it is as certain as that two and two make four, we do not pretend.[28]

Its existence is the most *probable* explanation of experience because 'it exhibits *particular appearances*, as arising from *general laws*, which is agreeable to the analogy of every thing else that we observe'.[29] Berkeley's idealism offers an alternative explanation, holding God to be the direct cause of ideas in our minds, but it is far less probable because it fails to give a good explanation for the existence of general laws. While ideas are the immediate objects of thought, we properly infer and reason about external objects to which these ideas relate as representational signs, although not as images.[30] If philosophers in the ideas tradition sometimes talk about them that way, it is a mistake to construe their talk as anything but figurative.[31]

[27] See, for example, Alan P. F. Sell, 'Priestley's Polemic against Reid', *P-PN*, 3 (1979), 41–52.

[28] Priestley, *Examination of Dr Reid's Inquiry*, 58. Locke also addresses and dismisses sceptical doubt about the external world. See John Locke, *Essay concerning Human Understanding*, IV, 2, §14, ed. Peter H. Nidditch (Oxford: Clarendon Press, 1975, based on Locke's 4th edn., 1700), 536–8.

[29] Priestley, *Examination of Dr Reid's Inquiry*, p. lix.

[30] Ibid. 57. For Berkeley, see David Berman, *George Berkeley: Idealism and the Man* (Oxford: Clarendon Press, 1994).

[31] Priestley, *Examination of Dr Reid's Inquiry*, 30.

For Priestley, the attraction of the way of ideas is that it opens the way to natural enquiry into the mind as illustrated in the work of Hartley. Priestley's basic objection to Reid is that his appeal to common sense effectively 'checks all farther inquiry, and is therefore of great disservice in philosophy'.[32] In the hands of Beattie and Oswald, it becomes 'exceedingly dangerous and alarming; setting aside all reasoning about the fundamental principles of religion, and making way for all the extravagancies of credulity, enthusiasm, and mysticism'.[33] Nor are its damaging effects limited to religion because they can just as easily be used to support conservatism in politics as well.[34] For Priestley, common sense's appeal to nature is too facile. It attributes to nature phenomena such as the dread of fire, which, for him, are clearly learned by associating ideas.[35] It also attributes to custom what results from reason, such as the belief that the future will be like the past. For Priestley, we know that the future will be like the past because it always has been.

On the distinctively physiological approach Priestley adopts from Hartley, sensations, caused by external objects, are conveyed through the nerves to the brain. He admits that we are presently ignorant of what sensations and the ideas they generate in the mind are, but for him this is not a reason to reject Hartley's causal approach, his theory of vibrations in particular striking Priestley as the most plausible available account of how sensations are transmitted to the brain. Given that vibrations can differ from each other in degree, kind, place, and so on, corresponding to the variety of sensations and ideas as well as their associations, the theory offers a rich and more compelling model than the classical picture of the mind as a tablet on which sensations are impressed and registered.

Priestley confronts what he takes as Reid's central objection to this kind of theory, that even if ideas are conveyed to the mind, it, as an unextended and indivisible substance, could not be affected by them, since they would share no common property. Priestley's moral is that: 'If then we wish to preserve this external world, which is very convenient for many purposes, we must take care to entertain

---

[32] Ibid. 22.   [33] Ibid. 160–1.

[34] See, for example, Paul B. Wood, 'Thomas Reid's Critique of Joseph Priestley: Context and Chronology', *Man and Nature*, 4 (1985), 29–45.

[35] Priestley, *Examination of Dr Reid's Inquiry*, 90.

notions of mind and ideas more compatible with it.'[36] Priestley pursues this hint in his essays on Hartley. Given how much Hartley's theory explains by reference to matter and material properties right up to perception itself, would it not make sense to explain perception likewise?[37] He suggests: 'I rather think that the whole man is of some *uniform composition*, and that the property of *perception*, as well as the other powers that are termed *mental*, is the result (whether necessary or not) of such an organical structure as that of the brain.'[38] The suggestion occasioned a storm of controversy, but Priestley, far from backing down, fully embraced it and in embracing it, he concluded that perception must indeed be a necessary result of that structure.

For Priestley, Hartley's improvement on Locke is that his theory accounts for *all* thought by the association of ideas, not just some, including reasoning, the passions, volitions and moral ideas. This last is a point that others believed had to be explained by reference to something like a moral sense or innate ideas.[39] When Priestley comments on Hartley's account, he focuses, as Hartley had, on the development of moral ideas from early childhood and on that development in the context of acquiring skills in action.[40] A child stretches its hand and grasps without any particular intention in response to some stimulus. Its muscles contract involuntarily. When a toy, for example, is placed in its hand later, the child learns to grasp it and reach out even when the toy is at a distance. Thus an original involuntary automatic action by means of association becomes a voluntary action, still performed mechanically, although Priestley would later caution that one should not be misled by the negative associations of such language into supposing that he was reducing human action to the movements of 'a common clock, or a fulling-mill'.[41] For Priestley, this analysis is even more compelling when one considers how the action comes to be performed habitually without reflection in a 'secondarily automatic' manner. For if the initial and

---

[36] Priestley, *Examination of Dr Reid's Inquiry*, 59–60.
[37] Priestley, *Hartley's Theory of the Human Mind*, pp. xix–xxi.
[38] Ibid. p. xx.   [39] Ibid. p. xxiii.   [40] Ibid. pp. xxvii ff.
[41] Priestley, *A Letter to the Rev. Mr. John Palmer*, 83.

end stages are mechanical, so likewise should be the middle.[42] The moral is that 'voluntary' contrasts not with 'necessitated', but with 'involuntary'.

Similarly, ideas of moral right and wrong are acquired as a child has the experience of being checked by a greater power. Initially the child yields to that greater power. As its understanding develops, it distinguishes between parents and its relation to them and the way its peer group relates to parents. The commands of parents as not to be resisted or disputed transform into ones that *ought* not to be resisted, and transferred from that context to other authorities, external and internal. The basis of the transformation from 'must' to 'ought' is the discovery that there are reasons for some actions and against others.[43] What these reasons are and the basis for paying them heed Priestley develops in his writings on natural and revealed religion. He is prepared to continue using the language of 'moral sense', but it is to be understood as shorthand for this process learned by association.[44] Earlier philosophers who use the phrase, such as the Earl of Shaftesbury and Francis Hutcheson, intend to signify that our ability to distinguish right and wrong, virtue and vice, has a natural basis in our constitution as well as our natural affections and dispositions.[45]

PHILOSOPHICAL NECESSITY

For Priestley, both materialism and the association of ideas entail mechanism and hence the doctrine of necessity.[46] That said, Priestley originally adopted the doctrine from reading Anthony Collins, who relies on neither materialism nor the association of ideas, as well as Hartley, who rejects materialism. Collins insists that the necessity

---

[42] Priestley, *Doctrine of Philosophical Necessity*, 42–3.

[43] Priestley, *Institutes of Natural and Revealed Religion*, I, pt. I, 77.

[44] Priestley, *Letters to a Philosophical Unbeliever, Part I*, 225.

[45] See Rivers, II, index references to 'sense, moral'.

[46] Priestley, *Doctrine of Philosophical Necessity*, pp. xix–xx; 36; *A Free Discussion of the Doctrines of Materialism and Philosophical Necessity, in a Correspondence between Dr Price and Dr Priestley* (London, 1778), 241.

he defends is moral necessity, not 'absolute, physical, *or* mechanical necessity…as is in clocks, watches' and the like.[47] Nevertheless an agent's actions are determined by *causes* such as willings, volitions, and choices.[48]

Collins's use of the expression 'moral necessity' struck dualists like Samuel Clarke as brazen. When Clarke used it, he did so in an inverted commas sense. Clarke agrees that stones, clocks, and watches *move* by physical necessity, but reasons and motives only incline; they do not necessitate. Even if it is certain that a strongly motivated action will be performed, that is a far cry from saying that the motive causes or determines the agent to act.[49] For Clarke, the agent with reasons has the power or liberty to act otherwise, but chooses not to do so. Certainty is one thing: necessity, quite another. Necessity applies to physical objects that are passive and moved, not to beings that act. Like Collins, Priestley accepts that 'moral' differs from 'physical necessity' only in its sphere of application. Both necessities are equally real. As he had for Collins, the figure of Samuel Clarke looms behind Priestley's account as the defender of philosophical liberty he seeks to disarm. Most objections he encountered, whether from Richard Price or others, were variants of arguments advanced by Clarke.

For Priestley, philosophical necessity is a modern doctrine, which, he claims, Hobbes, whom he admires, was the first to formulate.[50] It should not be confused with the ancient doctrine of fate or the doctrine of predestination. While fate claims the inevitability of outcomes such as Oedipus' killing of his father and sleeping with his mother, it has no view of how these outcomes will be produced and in particular how the motives of human agents, whether or not they are aware of them, determine choices through a chain of causes and effects ultimately tracing back to God.[51] So likewise for Calvinism where, as Priestley puts it, 'the work of conversion [is] wholly of

[47] Anthony Collins, *A Philosophical Inquiry concerning Human Liberty* (London, 1717), p. iii.

[48] Ibid. 48–50.

[49] Samuel Clarke, *Remarks upon a Book, entituled, A Philosophical Enquiry concerning Human Liberty* (London, 1717), 15–18.

[50] Thomas Hobbes, *Leviathan, or the Matter, Forme, & Power of a Common-Wealth Ecclesiaticall and Civill* (London, 1651), pt. II, 21, ed. C. B. Macpherson (Harmondsworth: Penguin Books, 1968), esp. 261–3.

[51] Priestley, *Doctrine of Philosophical Necessity*, p. xxv.

God's free and sovereign grace, independent of every thing in the person thus regenerated or renovated, and to which he cannot in the least contribute'.[52] For Priestley, many objections to philosophical necessity, such as that it renders human activity irrelevant or insignificant, apply only to these other doctrines from which he distinguishes philosophical necessity.

One factor inhibiting the acceptance of philosophical necessity for Priestley is the common misconception that liberty and necessity are incompatible. This the Hobbist tradition denies, provided that liberty is defined as simply a power of doing whatever one wills or pleases, without being prevented by an alien cause.[53] If only this is required, actions can be free because unimpeded by anything external to the agent while still determined by the agent's antecedent motivations and desires. According to Priestley, this is all that most intend by 'liberty' when they are uninfluenced by larger philosophical and religious agendas. Part of Priestley's purpose in defending the doctrine of necessity, accordingly, is to show how well it matches up with commonly held pre-philosophical notions. When the implications of this conception of liberty are spelled out, however, people are 'alarmed and staggered' and, as a result, disown their pre-philosophical view, supposing their experiences must really be different from what they had supposed.[54] For Priestley, the obstacles that prevent acceptance of the doctrine of necessity have less to do with philosophical argument than with the unpalatable consequences that are thought to follow from it, whether they touch on morality or God. His aim, accordingly, is to defuse these reactions. As he remarks in his editor's preface to his edition of Collins's *Philosophical Inquiry concerning Human Liberty*: 'If persons have strength of mind not to be frightened by names, and be capable of attending to things only, the strongest objections to the doctrine of necessity will not affect them'.[55]

For Priestley, philosophical necessity is supported by an absolutely general and compelling argument from the nature of cause and effect. As such, it relies on the truth neither of the association of ideas nor of materialism. Whether one considers inanimate bodies, such as a

---

[52] Priestley, *Letter to the Rev. Mr. John Palmer*, 71.
[53] Priestley, *Doctrine of Philosophical Necessity*, pp. xxvii–xxix.
[54] Ibid. 104.
[55] Collins, *Philosophical Inquiry*, ed. Priestley, p. vii.

balance, or mental phenomena, the same circumstances—states of mind and views of things—invariably result in the same effect. Given the invariability of the effect, the only reasonable conclusion is 'that there must be a sufficient reason in the nature of the things, why it should be produced in these circumstances'.[56] For Priestley, this is to say that human actions, as much as the movements of bodies, are governed by laws of nature ordained by God.

The claim that we often cannot predict what an agent will do in certain circumstances is a product of ignorance rather than an objection to the argument. Were it possible for there to be opposed outcomes in indistinguishable circumstances, there would be effects without causes, a consequence Priestley says that even defenders of philosophical liberty would find unacceptable. Indeed, if there could be effects without causes, the most compelling argument for God's existence, at least in Priestley's view, would be undermined. For it would be possible for the material universe to come into existence without a being distinct from it as its cause. But since defenders of philosophical liberty concede that the motives of agents align with their actions, they grant, according to Priestley, the premise of his argument, even though they reject its conclusion.

Priestley is well aware of the counter that while it may be *certain* how agents will act in view of their motives, those motives do not necessitate actions as physical causes do. Motives only incline and provide reasons or ends of action, but their role is not causal or, if causal, then only in the sense of final causes, not necessitating ones. Priestley's reply is that the best evidence we possess for physical causes is allowed by the objection in the moral case, the certainty of the effect. 'If my mind be as *constantly* determined by the influence of motives, as a stone is determined to fall to the ground by the influence of gravity, I am constrained to conclude, that the *cause* in one case acts as necessarily as that in the other.'[57] True, Priestley allows, the expression 'moral certainty' is sometimes used to imply nothing more than a high degree of probability. Such a use of the notion can be traced

---

[56] Priestley, *Doctrine of Philosophical Necessity*, 10. See James A. Harris, 'Joseph Priestley and "the Proper Doctrine of Philosophical Necessity"', *E&D*, 20 (2001), 23–44, and *Of Liberty and Necessity: The Free Will Debate in Eighteenth-Century British Philosophy* (Oxford: OUP, 2005), 167–78.

[57] Priestley, *Doctrine of Philosophical Necessity*, 18.

back at least to Descartes where it means nothing stronger than a certainty sufficient for the conduct of life.[58] That, however, is not the issue here.[59] Nor would there be any reason to treat wrongdoers differently, he maintains, even if it were possible to distinguish what was certain from what was necessary.[60] The attempt to distinguish physical from moral necessity by anything other than subject matter fails. Each is as law-governed and necessary as the other.

Neither does he accept the argument that human action is caused, but only by a mind itself in abstraction, independently of motives and not itself determined.[61] For exclusive of motives, the mind has no reason to choose one course of action over another and thus lacks the capacity to serve as the cause of its own determinations. The proposal is one Priestley regards as 'chimerical': 'the will cannot properly determine *itself*, but is always determined by *motives*.'[62]

Many proponents of liberty, however, were not satisfied. For those like Samuel Clarke and Richard Price, an action necessitated by the agent's reasons or motives would not only not be free, but not be an action at all, since the person's movements would be merely passive as effects of causes. While it may be morally certain that an agent who has particular reasons and motives will act on them, certainty of outcome does not establish necessity, a point strongly reinforced by the consciousness agents possess of their own freedom. Unless it were possible for a person to act otherwise even though the person chooses not to do so, moreover, the person's actions would fall outside the scope of virtue and morality. For if they were necessitated by a causal chain that leads back to God, those actions would be neither praiseworthy as virtuous nor blameworthy as vicious any more than they would be if the agent had been compelled to act by force. Their necessary occurrence due to a causal chain that agents are not at liberty to break or interrupt at the time of choice removes them from the scope of morality, which requires a robust philosophical liberty, not the anaemic liberty of spontaneity Priestley offers instead. The objection, in sum, is that Priestley has no sufficiently robust account

---

[58] I owe this point to an unpublished paper by Charles Wolfe.
[59] Priestley, *Letter to the Rev. Mr. John Palmer*, 26–7.   [60] Ibid. 27–30.
[61] Price and Priestley, *Free Discussion*, 291–6.
[62] Priestley, *Doctrine of Philosophical Necessity*, 72.

of human agency to support virtue and morality. On his view, the real causes of actions become agents' motives rather than agents in their own right, but motives of themselves cannot cause anything.[63]

Priestley rejects this account of agency. As for the consciousness we are said to have of our liberty, the characterization of the experience is ambiguous, for it depends on just what that liberty is that we are said to have a consciousness of. He argues that all we really can claim to be conscious of is the absence of any impediment to choosing whatever seems preferable on balance or not making a choice, if indeed that should appear preferable.[64] That the deliberating agent may make rapid changes of preference in no way undermines the position. Were it possible to act altogether independently of motive, he sees neither anything praiseworthy about it nor reason to attribute it to the agent, since it would be mysterious how the action would have been produced.[65] For Priestley, to act from a motive is for the *person* to act from a cause within, rather than because of some foreign cause. If this still falls short of the supposed requirements for action, so be it, but these are not requirements either of agency or of moral judgement.

For Priestley, the argument that morality and virtue require philosophical liberty fails. On the contrary, 'Whatever it is *within a man* that leads him to virtue, and that will certainly and necessarily incline him to act right ... they deem to be a *virtuous principle*, to be the *foundation of merit*, and to *intitle to reward*.'[66] That the person possesses such a disposition as a result of early parental training or natural temper does not diminish that claim: 'Men are charmed with a virtuous conduct, with the principle that was the cause of it, with the principle that was the cause of that principle, and so on, as far as you please to go.'[67] The stronger the disposition—and for Priestley virtue turns on habituation and disposition—the more automatic, easy, and mechanical the person's actions. This in no way diminishes the person's accountability or the propriety of praise or blame for the actions that flow from that state of mind, provided these notions are properly understood. On the contrary, praise and reward for virtue function

---

[63] Price and Priestley, *Free Discussion*, 136–40.
[64] Priestley, *Doctrine of Philosophical Necessity*, 47–8.
[65] Ibid. 72.   [66] Ibid. 67.   [67] Ibid. 67–8.

to reinforce the disposition while blame and punishment for wrong-doing serve as correctives through the application of causal force on the agent and others. If praise and blame, reward and punishment were inefficacious, they would not be rationally defensible. Contrary to the objection, the doctrine of necessity provides a foundation for accountability because it ensures that rewards and punishment have their 'fullest effect' whereas the doctrine of philosophical liberty, he claims, does not.

For the purposes of philosophy, however, Priestley is prepared to discard the language of 'responsibility', 'merit' and 'demerit', 'praise' and 'blame'. 'Every thing that really corresponds to them', he says, 'may be clearly expressed in different language.'[68] All too commonly these expressions are defined in a way that assumes the truth of the doctrine of philosophical liberty. For him, the crucial issue is whether a moral governor concerned with the good of his subjects would treat them as his theory maintains. In his view, the answer is plainly 'yes'. A causal influence on future action would be effective for voluntary actions. To refute his theory, Priestley argues, the objector needs to show not the incompatibility of his language with contrived concepts of responsibility and the rest, but with what a concerned moral governor would do.

As Priestley acknowledges, the potential impact of his view for many common attitudes would be significant. Attitudes of self-congratulation and self-reproach, shame, guilt, remorse, and pardon would have no place for a fully convinced believer in the doctrine of necessity. He is particularly attentive to the example of remorse. He grants that this attitude implies the belief that one could have acted otherwise in the circumstances of action. For Priestley, however, this belief is false. The reality is that one would act no differently if one were faced with the same circumstances, but when one learns from one's mistakes, one approaches the circumstances of action with an altered disposition. Change in conduct does not need to be motivated by remorse, accordingly, and hence the capacity for it is not required for morality to function.

---

[68] Price and Priestley, *Free Discussion*, 149; Priestley, *Letter to the Rev. Mr. John Palmer*, 79–81.

It is clear from the references to moral government that Priestley ties his approach towards necessity to theology and religion, in which he closely follows his mentor Hartley.[69] For on his view, to succeed in fully adopting the doctrine of necessity and living one's life as far as is deliberately possible in accordance with it depends on our success in cultivating a philosophical state in which we see ourselves as God's instruments and God as the true author of our actions. Such a perspective is transformational even if it may not be sustainable for lengthy periods. Our ordinary attitudes are displaced by humility, the love of God, and the view of other human beings as part of one family.[70] This gives Priestley all the more reason to question Hume's rejection of humility as a 'monkish' virtue that is a product of superstition and false religion rather than the natural judgement of unprejudiced reason.[71]

We realize that in view of God's goodness, there can be no absolute evil. For what evil there is must only exist to promote the overall sum of good and, as a result, to be '*annihilated*'. This consoling view serves as 'the only *sure anchor of the soul* in a time of adversity and distress'.[72] While we are in awe of God, we cannot and should not attempt to imitate him. In particular, human beings are not sanctioned to do evil so that good can come of it. Their path, lacking God's knowledge, must be that of a virtue that is *rule governed*, even if acting differently were to contribute to the overall good. What is significant for our view of the world in such a state is that we stand in communion with God's will, not that we should imitate what God alone can do. Patently the effects of the doctrine of necessity would look rather different if this theology were to be rejected.

However, if all human actions are ultimately ascribable to God, whose instruments we are, God must be the sole ultimate cause of evil, whether moral or natural. Priestley does not shy away from this conclusion, but argues that while God may be the cause of evil, it does not follow that God is evil. For that conclusion to follow,

---

[69] See Harris, *Of Liberty and Necessity*, 161–4.

[70] Priestley, *Doctrine of Philosophical Necessity*, 108–9.

[71] See David Hume, *An Enquiry concerning the Principles of Morals* (London, 1751), sect. ix; ed. with an introduction by J. B. Schneewind (Indianapolis: Hackett, 1983), 73–4.

[72] Priestley, *Doctrine of Philosophical Necessity*, 110.

the production of sin and evil must have been God's intention or purpose, which it is not. Since God's overriding aim and achievement is the happiness of his creatures, God is virtuous because his actions arise from a calculation of and a motivation to produce *'general utility'*.[73] Evil is not part of God's design except as it promotes the general good. It follows that the means chosen by God must be necessary to achieve this end.

Here Priestley once again sharply disagrees with Hume.[74] For Hume, if God is good, human actions arising from God's causality cannot be evil. For if they were, so likewise must God be. One cannot have it both ways. Priestley disagrees. The evil done by God and the evil done by humans is very different. God may have created humans with evil dispositions, making them vicious and subject to reproach and punishment, but God's object was the general good. Indeed, according to Priestley, 'if [God] prefers that scheme in which there is the greatest prevalence of virtue and happiness, we have all the evidence that can be given of his being infinitely holy and benevolent, notwithstanding the mixture of vice and misery there may be in it.'[75]

In his *Dialogues concerning Natural Religion* (1779), Hume challenges the claim that we are in a position to draw this inference from experience.[76] For how do we know that God could not have done better unless we are independently convinced of God's infinite benevolence? But the only evidence we have for this proposition is the world we know from experience. For all we know on this basis, the being that produced such a world may have been a bumbling, apprentice designer, however good its intentions. Priestley's contrast between the basis for judging God and for judging men, however, depends on the perfection of the former as against the imperfection of the latter.

---

[73] Ibid. 120.

[74] David Hume, *An Enquiry concerning Human Understanding*; originally published as *Philosophical Essays concerning Human Understanding* (London, 1748), sect. viii, pt. ii; ed. Charles Hendel (Indianapolis: Bobbs Merrill, 1955), 108–11.

[75] Priestley, *Doctrine of Philosophical Necessity*, 124.

[76] For responses to Hume's philosophy of religion, see James Fieser (ed.), *Early Responses to Hume's Writings on Religion* (Bristol: Thoemmes Press, 2001). These constitute vols. V and VI of *Early Responses to Hume*.

MATERIALISM

There are two keys to Priestley's materialism. The first is a pair of
methodological principles he adapts from Newton of not multiplying
causes to explain appearances beyond necessity as well as assigning
similar causes to similar effects.[77] As he sees it, the consistent application of these principles places the dualism of matter and spirit on
the defensive. For him, dualism is a philosophical invention burdened
with the insuperable difficulty of explaining the relation between
matter and spirit. Everything dualism purports to explain, he argues,
can be better explained by monism, the monism of matter in particular. For Priestley, what really counts is monism, not whether one
characterizes it as materialism. For him, the desired result is a single
subject capable of possessing both material and mental attributes,
whatever the real nature of these proves to be. About this last Priestley
does not pretend to know.

The second point is that from Priestley's perspective modern philosophers, notably those influenced by Descartes and the
Cartesian tradition, have adopted dualism because they mistakenly
attribute to matter solidity or impenetrability as well as passivity. For
many dualists matter and spirit share no common property, although
Clarke and Price are exceptions because they believe spirit to be
extended. For the dualist of either stripe, however, perception and
thought are not attributable to a material being. But once properties
like impenetrability and passivity are no longer seen to be essential to
matter, according to Priestley, the case for materialism can be viewed
in a new light with the principal objections to it falling away.[78] Far
from being impenetrable or inert, matter of its nature is anything but
solid and consists of physical points that possess powers of attraction and repulsion that are exercised within spheres of influence.
According to Priestley, the effect of these powers had been confused
with impenetrability in the philosophical tradition. If some do not
recognize what they take to be matter in this description, so be it.
The consequence is that nothing stands in the way any longer of

---

[77] See Harris, 'Joseph Priestley and "the Proper Doctrine of Philosophical Necessity" ', 32–4, who notes that Priestley's formulation of the first of Newton's principles
departs from Newton's script.

[78] Priestley, *Disquisitions Relating to Matter and Spirit*, 81.

attributing perception and thought to matter so conceived and, more particularly, to material systems.[79]

Priestley also attempts to deflect other lines of philosophical objection that turn on the difference between thought or perception and other known properties of matter. He argues that they neither support immaterialism nor rule out materialism, but reflect ignorance: 'we have no more conception of how the powers of sensation and thought can inhere in an *immaterial*, than in a *material* substance'.[80]

One objection on which Priestley lavishes special attention turns on the unity of consciousness, which requires the power of thought to be simple and indivisible, where matter, by contrast, is divisible. In that case the argument is that consciousness would necessarily be a property of the parts, and rather than a single consciousness there would be indefinitely many. But if consciousness does not belong to the particles of, say, the brain, neither can it belong to the brain as a whole.[81] Samuel Clarke developed this objection in his celebrated controversy with Anthony Collins on the natural immortality of the soul.[82] Priestley's response is the same as Collins's: consciousness is a property of systems of matter and need not be a property of that system's parts any more than the parts of a sphere need themselves be circles. Priestley and Collins, accordingly, defend the possibility of emergent properties that belong to systems although not to their divisible parts, where Clarke and others reject it.

For Priestley, perception and thought are properties that necessarily arise from material or corporeal organization in living beings, even though in the current state of knowledge we may not be able to explain their real nature.[83] To begin with, human perception and thought are never found in experience apart from, and are plainly dependent on, organized systems of matter.[84] That this should be our invariable experience warrants concluding that there is a necessary

---

[79] Priestley, *Disquisitions Relating to Matter and Spirit*, p. xxxviii.
[80] Ibid. 82.   [81] Ibid. 86–90.
[82] Samuel Clarke, *A Defense of an Argument made use of in a Letter to Mr Dodwel, to Prove the Immateriality and Natural Immortality of the Soul* (London, 1707), 8–15. The whole controversy is conveniently collected in *The Works of Samuel Clarke*, 4 vols (London, 1738; rpt. New York: Garland Press, 1978), III, 721–913.
[83] Priestley, *Disquisitions Relating to Matter and Spirit*, 28.
[84] Ibid. 28.

connection between the two. Priestley parts company with Locke who, while he sees nothing incompatible with the hypothesis that thinking could be superadded as a property of matter by the power of God, nevertheless maintains it to be more likely that the soul is immaterial. According to Priestley, Locke should have concluded that there is no reason to attribute thought to anything but matter.[85] For Priestley, the foundation for an immaterial soul is the belief that only such an entity can survive death and possess the power of perception and thought in such a state.[86] For from the soul's immateriality and its claimed indivisibility, the natural immortality of the soul was inferred, as it had been since Plato.

In the ancient world and with the Epicureans in particular, materialism was associated with the view that death puts an end to our existence and that even if the same atoms that constitute our bodies were reassembled, the reassembled being would not be identical with the being that died.[87] The dispersal of the atoms constitutes an irreparable break in identity. For Priestley, a major challenge is to reconcile materialism, as he understands it, with the possibility of a future life rendered certain by the evidence of revelation, with rewards and punishments distributed for the way we live our lives. In the ancient world this possibility was associated with the survival of an immaterial soul with powers of thought serving as the bearer of personal identity. But classically, on such a view, the immaterial soul at death is finally freed from the impediment of the body, which, for Priestley, does not combine well with the Christian doctrine of the resurrection. For those like Price who agree with Priestley about the shortcomings of the classical doctrine for Christianity, the immaterial soul survives separation from the body in an inactive state until the resurrection. Unless an immaterial soul does so, there could be no resurrection because whatever might be brought together at such a time would have no claim on our interest as being us, even if it claimed to have the same memories and states of consciousness we once had while living.[88] At best, it would only be like us and

[85] Priestley, *Disquisitions Relating to Matter and Spirit*, 73. See Locke, *Essay*, IV, 3, §6.

[86] Priestley, *Disquisitions Relating to Matter and Spirit*, 81.

[87] See Lucretius, *De Rerum Natura* (*On the Nature of the Universe*), bk. III.

[88] Price and Priestley, *Free Discussion*, 107–8.

hence not a proper subject to experience the rewards and punishments merited as a result of the conduct of our lives. If so, the motive for virtue provided by the doctrine of resurrection would disappear.

In order to defend the doctrine of the resurrection, Priestley distinguishes the identity of the man from the identity of the person.[89] The difficulty is that following death the parts of the human body are dispersed and may become parts of other bodies. But, Priestley argues, this happens even during life when the material parts that constitute us—the identity of the man—change over time, while the person remains the same, irrespective of the pace of change. Projecting these changes into the future, we feel concern for our future selves, since what matters for personal identity is 'the *sameness and continuity of consciousness*'.[90] In its absence, the propriety of rational reward and punishment disappears. If, however, we can project and imagine ourselves knowing each other and conversing again in a resurrected state, the requirement for personal identity would be satisfied. While there is no need on Priestley's view to preserve bodily identity or continuity, he believes that the body will in fact be reconstituted at the resurrection, not the whole of it, but the particles constituting 'the *germ* of the organical body'.[91] So while the man's capacity for consciousness and thought ceases, those particles can be reconstituted by the power of God and revived.

Price challenged Priestley's claims. Among other things, he argues that Priestley needs the resurrection of the same body with the same material parts to defend his claims. If thinking arises simply from the arrangement of parts of matter that disperse at death and if the same arrangement were subsequently produced with different matter, that would constitute another person. Otherwise, Price, Priestley, and whomever else one might care to consider could be one and the same if they happened to possess the same arrangement and, by virtue of that, the same consciousness. Priestley's answer is that while their minds would be 'exactly *similar*', they would be '*numerically different*'.[92] Death does not entail the loss of existence of the man, but the

---

[89] Priestley, *Disquisitions Relating to Matter and Spirit*, 155–65; Price and Priestley, *Free Discussion*, 75.

[90] Priestley, *Disquisitions Relating to Matter and Spirit*, 159.   [91] Ibid. 161.

[92] Price and Priestley, *Free Discussion*, 76–8.

loss of that man's powers to think and perceive. If so, Price counters, the restoration of personal identity at the resurrection depends on the reconstitution of the matter that constituted the man. But if death does not entail loss of existence of the man following the dissolution of the body, the man must also have existed prior to birth because the matter that constitutes the man existed then as well. For Priestley, however, the times before birth and after death are asymmetrical. Only the matter that would constitute Christ existed before his birth and not Christ himself.

Priestley, however, devotes the lion's share of attention to countering the objections to materialism that purport to make it incompatible with God's being and nature and with Christianity in particular. Traditionally God had been represented as immaterial and, indeed, Priestley himself before his adoption of materialism had had no qualms in doing so.[93] Yet if materialism were true, critics argued, God too might be material.[94] Priestley answers that we know so little of God's essence that we have no proper idea of it in view of the evident differences between God's powers and ours. Hence there is no inference from human materiality to divine materiality. That said, he has no special difficulty with the representation of God as immaterial so long as 'immaterial' is not taken to mean having no common attributes with matter.[95] For a God who shares no common attribute with matter would not be able to act on the creation. Such a God would be as remote from the universe as the Epicurean gods who, while material, could neither affect nor be affected by anything else. But while Priestley would prefer to be noncommittal about God's nature, the sting is removed from representing God as material once matter's nature is properly understood.[96] He notes that the arguments founded in natural religion for God's being as an intelligent first cause distinct from its creation and its attributes—its wisdom, power, and goodness— are unaffected, if the creation be held to be material. The charge that materialism is tantamount to atheism, accordingly, is without foundation.

---

[93] Priestley, *Institutes of Natural and Revealed Religion*, I, pt. I, 37.
[94] Priestley, *Disquisitions Relating to Matter and Spirit*, 103–13.
[95] Ibid. 108.   [96] Ibid. 108–9.

NATURAL AND REVEALED RELIGION AND MORALITY

In his *Institutes of Natural and Revealed Religion* (1772–4) Priestley systematically sets out the basic principles of natural and revealed religion for the benefit of young members of Christian congregations.[97] His later *Letters to a Philosophical Unbeliever* (1780), by contrast, while incorporating his earlier argument, is written more informally as a series of letters that focus on the challenge to Christianity of unbelievers like David Hume (1711–76) and the Baron d'Holbach, whose anonymously published *Système de la nature* (1770) articulates an aggressive atheism.[98]

Like many Christian apologists, Priestley maintains that while natural religion turns on what can be justified by natural reason, its principles would not have been discovered without the benefit of revelation.[99] Moreover, natural religion leaves so much undecided that he gives greater weight to revelation, notwithstanding his conviction that God's being, benevolence, and providence can all be satisfactorily established by reason. In view of his empiricist outlook, it is not surprising that he rejects the methods by which rationalists, like Samuel Clarke, tried to establish these propositions. Where Clarke argues that God's existence as a self-existent being can be demonstrated *a priori* because rejecting it entails a contradiction, Priestley starts from the existing universe as we know it from experience and argues from it that there must be a self-existent being as its ultimate cause.[100] That said, some of his arguments, such as his defence of a single God because it would be contradictory to suppose there were two or more infinite beings of the same kind, owe a debt to Clarke and the rationalist tradition.[101]

[97] Priestley, *Institutes of Natural and Revealed Religion*, I, pt. I, [p. i].

[98] Priestley, *Letters to a Philosophical Unbeliever, Part I*, 160–74. For the Baron d'Holbach's view, see Alan Charles Kors, 'The Atheism of d'Holbach and Naigeon' in Michael Hunter and David Wotton (eds), *Atheism from the Reformation to the Enlightenment* (Oxford: Clarendon Press, 1992), 273–300.

[99] Priestley, *Institutes of Natural and Revealed Religion*, I, pt. I, 3; Priestley, *Letters to a Philosophical Unbeliever, Part I*, pp. xvii–xviii.

[100] Priestley, *Letters to a Philosophical Unbeliever, Part I*, 182–95. Clarke's argument is to be found in *A Demonstration of the Being and Attributes of God* (London, 1705). See Samuel Clarke, *A Demonstration of the Being and Attributes of God and Other Writings*, ed. Ezio Lailati (Cambridge: CUP, 1998), Introduction.

[101] Priestley, *Letters to a Philosophical Unbeliever, Part I*, 65–6.

For Priestley, there must be a self-existing first cause, since otherwise it would be impossible to account for appearances. What are commonly designated causes are not really such, since they do not fully explain their own or any other being's existence. If they did, there would be no need to refer to a prior or superior cause.[102] In *Letters to a Philosophical Unbeliever*, he additionally claims that the idea of a cause 'implies not only something prior to itself or at least cotemporary with itself, but something capable at least of comprehending what it produces.'[103] He recognized from the first that Hume's scepticism about causality constituted a challenge to this argument. He finally turned to disarm it in *Letters to a Philosophical Unbeliever*.[104]

For God's intelligence, power, benevolence, and moral governance, Priestley relies on the argument from design. He argues that as it is evident from experience that a chair, say, is initially produced by a designer distinct from itself and capable of comprehending its nature and uses, so wherever there is a fitness or correspondence of one thing to another, there must be a cause capable of grasping and designing that fitness. Human beings make tables, but there must be a superior cause, God, who designed and produced human beings.[105]

The attributes to which Priestley devotes the lion's share of attention are God's goodness and benevolence. For him, benevolence is inferred from God's evident intention to promote the happiness of his creatures, an objective which, he claims, can be seen to be achieved from an examination of God's creatures and reflection on the progressive improvement of the state of the world over time, most evidently over the previous century. Even war, he observes, is 'unspeakably less dreadful than formerly'—a consideration that has not worn well.[106]

For Priestley, if there is a difficulty, it lies with the inference to the infinity of God's benevolence. Given that infinite happiness is

[102] Priestley, *Institutes of Natural and Revealed Religion*, I, pt. I, 5–7.

[103] Priestley, *Letters to a Philosophical Unbeliever*, Part I, 41.

[104] Priestley, *Institutes of Natural and Revealed Religion*, I, pt. II, 208; Priestley, *Letters to a Philosophical Unbeliever*, Part I, 196–201. Hume, *Enquiry concerning Human Understanding*, sects. iv–v.

[105] See Robert H. Hurlbutt, *Hume, Newton, and the Design Argument*, revised edn. (Lincoln, NE: University of Nebraska Press, 1985).

[106] Priestley, *Letters to a Philosophical Unbeliever*, Part I, 82.

impossible for finite beings, God appears to have done the best that could be done for his creation, notwithstanding the existence of pain, disease, and death. For even these evils contribute to God's purpose, whether that be the welfare of individuals or the overall sum of happiness through the course of time, since, he claims, a succession of creatures enhances the overall sum of happiness more than the continuance of the same creatures. He acknowledges that if God is infinitely benevolent, resourceful, and powerful, it is arguable that human nature might have been constructed without mixing good and evil. His answer is that since everything appears for the best for us, so too it is reasonable to suppose this is so for the whole, some appearances notwithstanding.

In his arguments Priestley opposes Hume, whose *Dialogues concerning Natural Religion* systematically seeks to dismantle such reasoning. Priestley, who had never been impressed by Hume's philosophical ability, clearly sees this to be his real intention when he notes that while Philo, the sceptic, awards the palm of victory to Cleanthes, the champion of the argument from design, Hume gives Philo the best of the argument.[107] Priestley dismisses Hume's arguments out of hand, although most readers judge them to be far more powerful than he credits.

Priestley was not content to leave his dismissal of Hume at that. He also engaged with other aspects of his philosophy as well as with inferences Christians characteristically drew from it. One discussion of special interest is of Hume's account of causation based on the observation of constant conjunction.[108] Hume's analysis poses two central difficulties for Priestley. The first is that Hume claims that anything may produce anything. If so, it would be entirely possible for the universe to come into existence or to have existed from eternity without a cause. One Christian response was to reject the principle that apparently leads to this conclusion by looking for a source of the idea of causation outside sensory experience. This is not a lead Priestley, given his empiricist commitments, can follow. His reply is simply that on the basis of experience 'it is indelibly impressed upon the minds of all men, that all events whatever, and all productions

107 Ibid. 127.
108 Hume, *Enquiry Concerning Human Understanding*, sect. vii.

whatever, must have a necessary and adequate cause; so that "nothing can come to be without a cause foreign to itself".[109] Hume denies that experience can show this to be true of the universe.

Unlike Hume, Priestley views causation as a highly complex abstract idea based on a very large number of different sensory impressions and the association of ideas. True, when we see the behaviour of iron near a magnet, we cannot give a satisfactory explanation *why* this should be. Yet invariable experience and knowledge of the circumstances warrants concluding that magnets necessarily have such an effect. There is in short '*some* real and sufficient cause in all such conjunctions.'[110] Priestley notes in his *Examination of Reid* that when

the same events never fail to take place in the same circumstances, the *expectation* of the same consequences from the same previous circumstances is necessarily generated in our minds, and we can have no more suspicion of a different event, than we can separate the idea of *whiteness* from that of the other properties of *milk*.[111]

This is a point about the mind and does not itself justify the view that there is a real necessitating cause present when there are such conjunctions. For Priestley, however, there is more to it than that. For it is not just any constant conjunction that justifies the supposition that necessity is in play, but ones that explain *how* the cause comes to have such an effect. One of Priestley's examples is how it is that the sounding of one string on a musical instrument causes a second string in unison with the first to vibrate. That explanation arises from coming to know that sound is a vibratory motion of the air that produces the vibration of the second string. Thus to say causes necessitate effects is to say that their relation is governed by a law of nature, and there could not be a cause without an effect unless this law were violated. But violated he believes it can be by miracles. Putting this last to the side, Priestley's reply is still problematic because Hume denies there is a secure empirical foundation that the

---

[109] Priestley, *Letters to a Philosophical Unbeliever, Part I*, 199.

[110] Ibid. 199. See Richard Popkin, *The High Road to Pyrrhonism* (San Diego, CA: Austin Hill Press, 1980), 213–26.

[111] Priestley, *Examination of Dr Reid's Inquiry*, pp. xl–xli.

future will be like the past. James Harris has recently suggested the most plausible explanation why Priestley does not appear bothered by Hume's argument is that he regards the laws of nature as expressions 'of the unchanging will of God'.[112] But if that is the explanation, it must be based, as Harris observes, on something other than experimental reasoning.

According to Priestley, one can derive all God's other moral perfections including justice, mercy, and truth from his benevolence.[113] God's benevolence is expressed as an impartial regard for the general happiness of the totality of his creatures and mankind in particular. This impartial regard, he argues, is consistent with the unequal distribution of happiness so long as inequality promotes a greater degree and sum of happiness.[114] This standard is the basis for the 'rule' of right and wrong.[115] In general, for Priestley, human virtue turns on observing rules. God is not so bound in showing mercy, for example, because he knows 'the secrets of [our] hearts'.[116] It is only exceptionally that departures from rules designed to promote virtue can be justified because such deviations are liable to produce more harm than good.

The highest order rules for right and wrong, however, are not intended as direct guides to human conduct. The first is regard for the happiness of others, which Priestley takes as equivalent to obedience to God's will; the second, regard for our own *real* happiness, so long as it does not come at the expense of others.[117] The difficulty in applying the first rule is that very little good would result if one did.[118] Unlike God, human benevolence is limited and not subject to strict impartiality, for the greatest good to others is promoted if humans prefer those closest to them, not only marriage partners and children, but also their country.[119] Self-interest, moreover, is best promoted when it is not our direct aim. There may be prudence, but not virtue unless other motives are also at play. Real self-interest entails that we heed God and do good to others as well as heeding conscience, which

---

[112] Harris, 'Joseph Priestley and "The Proper Doctrine of Philosophical Necessity"', 41–4.
[113] Priestley, *Institutes of Natural and Revealed Religion*, I, pt. I, 52–5.
[114] Ibid. 43.   [115] Ibid. 61.   [116] Ibid. 54.
[117] Ibid. 61–3.   [118] Ibid. 93.   [119] Ibid. 114–17.

Priestley analyses as the psychological internalization of these rules, which allows us to act when there is no time for deliberation.[120] Self-interest is promoted through regard for the good of others, within the constraints Priestley identifies. Whatever failure there is in rewarding virtue in this life will be rectified in the after life. That this is so cannot be established with certainty by natural religion, although he maintains there is some evidence from the analogy of nature, including the improving state of things in the world.

Like Locke in *The Reasonableness of Christianity* (1695), however, Priestley claims it is necessary to look to revelation for a complete, perspicuous, and fully authoritative system of ethics as well as for stronger assurance of the motives for virtue.[121] Natural religion, by itself, is too abstract and general. He reviews the ethical systems of those who preceded Christianity, who generally did not connect religion and morality, as well as deists who reject revelation and atheists.[122] The contrast, he argues, can be seen in the difference between Christians and non-Christians on a host of issues, including the propriety of suicide and the status of chastity and humility as virtues and of fornication and sodomy as vices. Where Priestley in so many domains is anything but a conventional thinker, when it comes to the content of morals, he comes across as quite conservative. For him, it is possible in some restricted sense to be a virtuous atheist, but the knowledge of morality's full scope and the strongest motives for acting morally depend on God.[123] The way that life is viewed and its significance are entirely different, Priestley argues, as between a believer and an atheist. In one of his late American works, *Socrates and Jesus Compared*, Priestley, who takes Socrates as embodying the best the non-Christian world has to offer, compares him adversely to Christ and attributes the unfavourable comparison to the inferiority of Socrates' knowledge 'concerning God, providence and a future state'.[124]

---

[120] Priestley, *Institutes of Natural and Revealed Religion*, I, pt. I, 63, 124.

[121] Ibid., pt. II, 173–4. For Locke's view, see the particularly useful edition of John C. Higgins Biddle, *The Reasonableness of Christianity as Delivered in the Scriptures* (Oxford: OUP, 1999), ch. 14.

[122] Priestley, *Institutes of Natural and Revealed Religion*, I, pt. II, 196–7.

[123] Priestley, *Letters to a Philosophical Unbeliever, Part I*, p. vi.

[124] Joseph Priestley, *Socrates and Jesus Compared* (Philadelphia, 1803), 40.

CONCLUSION

Priestley's chief importance as a philosophical theorist lies in keeping alive, clarifying, and deepening lines of thought under threat of being marginalized as the exclusive preserve of unbelievers. His forthright and lucid championing of the cause of necessity, most notably, made it easier to entertain such a view impartially and more difficult to dismiss it out of hand. His spirited defence of the doctrines of necessity and materialism has been singled out for praise by the likes of the Victorian scientist T. H. Huxley, who found his 'among the most powerful, clear, and unflinching expositions of materialism and necessarianism which exist in the English language'.[125] That praise is now dated, but it is clear that he exercised a strong influence for some time to come for just these reasons. As James Harris observes, Priestley's formulation of the doctrine of necessity became the point of departure for defenders of necessity for the next 40 years in Britain, particularly among dissenters, as Thomas Reid's libertarianism did on the other side of the debate.[126] He did not enjoy such an influence in the formulation of materialism. As John Yolton has observed, most failed to take on board what was distinctive and original in his version of the doctrine.[127] As for his third major philosophical interest, the association of ideas, he served as a champion of Hartley through his edition, but the loss of his manuscript during the Birmingham riots meant that this potential legacy was left unrealized.

Priestley has not enjoyed the same attention from contemporary philosophers as many whom he opposed, such as Reid, Clarke, or Price, or, for that matter, many who influenced him, such as Hartley, Collins, or Locke. His account of religion, natural and revealed, is the exception.[128] Unlike any of these other thinkers, there is no contemporary book dedicated to his philosophical thought generally, as there should be. He appears more prominently in histories of the development of ideas in the eighteenth century, notably of materialism,

---

[125] T. H. Huxley, *Science and Education: Essays* (New York: D. Appleton and Company, 1899), 22.

[126] Harris, *Of Liberty and Necessity*, 17.   [127] Yolton, *Thinking Matter*, 200.

[128] For Priestley on natural religion, see Schofield, I, ch. 7, and Schofield, II, ch. 2.

necessitarianism, and notions of personal identity.[129] Valuable as they are, such accounts ignore the systematic quality of Priestley's philosophical thought to which he attaches so much weight.

[129] His contribution to eighteenth-century materialism is canvassed by Yolton, *Thinking Matter*; to necessitarianism by Harris, *Of Liberty and Necessity*; and to personal identity by Raymond Martin and John Barresi, *Naturalization of the Soul: Self and Personal Identity in the Eighteenth Century* (London and New York: Routledge, 2000).

4

Joseph Priestley, Political Philosopher*

Martin Fitzpatrick

INTRODUCTION

In his own day, Joseph Priestley's fame as a scientist was matched by his infamy as a politician and political philosopher. One caricature depicted him as 'Docter Phlogiston', punningly subtitled, 'The Priestley Politician or the Political Priest'.[1] Later generations tended to remember Priestley for his fame and not for his notoriety. In forgetting the Priestley viewed in his time as a dangerous radical, we forget an important aspect of his contribution to the thought of the day. If one studies his political philosophy it is not possible to separate his contribution to political thought from his challenge to the status quo.

By the standards of the time, Priestley was not an active politician. He claimed not to be involved in any political organizations. On the eve of leaving Britain for America in 1794, he wrote to the *Morning Chronicle*, 'I am not, nor ever was, a member of any political society whatever.'[2] That may be strictly true, but it is not

---

* I am indebted to James Dybikowski for comments on an earlier version of this chapter.

[1] Martin Fitzpatrick, 'Priestley Caricatured', in Schwartz & McEvoy, 161–218, plate 1.

[2] Gay Hill, 'Gunpowder Joe: Priestley's Religious Radicalism' in Malcom Dick (ed.), *Joseph Priestley and Birmingham* (Studely, Warwickshire: Brewin Books, 2005), 21–30 at 22. See also Joseph Priestley, *The Present State of Europe compared to Ancient Prophecies* (1794), in Rutt, XV, 524–5.

the whole truth.[3] Although he was not a member of the Society for Constitutional Information, unlike several dissenting ministers,[4] in the period just before the Birmingham riots of 1791 he was trying to persuade two fellow members of the Lunar Society, Matthew Boulton (1728–1809), manufacturer and entrepreneur, and his partner James Watt (1736–1819), the engineer, to join a local branch of the society.[5] The merchant William Russell (1740–1818), another close friend, was chairman of the local committee for the abolition of the Test and Corporation Acts, which Priestley supported even if he was not a member. In 1787 he was a member of the local committee in Birmingham formed that year for the abolition of the slave trade.[6] Priestley was not, however, a political activist in the manner of Dr John Jebb (1736–86), the inveterate campaigner for civil and religious liberty, or Dr Joseph Towers (1737–99), a leading light in the Society for Constitutional Information. His radical reputation rested on his many publications, which ranged from major works on political philosophy, philosophy, theology, and science to occasional sermons and pamphlets. He claimed that his only concern was to use persuasion, to 'enlighten the minds of the people'.[7] His forthright arguments and incautious words were such that some friends as well as many adversaries wished that he would put his pen down.[8] His more considered works posed a challenge to current ways of thinking, and several were written before he became embroiled in political controversy. His teaching days at Warrington Academy were particularly

[3] The case for Priestley's political involvement has been made with some vigour by Jenny Graham in 'Revolutionary Philosopher', parts one and two.

[4] Ministers who were members include Richard Price and George Walker (founder members), Andrew Kippis, Joseph Towers, Robert Robinson, John Jebb (a former cleric and founder member). PRO, TSP, 11/1133.

[5] Hill, 'Gunpowder Joe: Priestley's Religious Radicalism', 22.

[6] Malcom Dick, 'Joseph Priestley, the Lunar Society and Anti-Slavery', in Dick (ed.), *Joseph Priestley and Birmingham*, 65–80 at 68–9.

[7] Joseph Priestley, *A Letter to the Right Honourable William Pitt... on the Subjects of Toleration and Church Establishments*, 2nd edn., corr. & enlarged (London, 1787), 21–2.

[8] This charge was levelled at him quite early in his career; see Joseph Priestley, *Letters to the Author of Remarks on Several Late Publications relative to the Dissenters, in a Letter to Dr Priestley* (London, 1770), Letter 1, 4. For Priestley's dissenting pamphleteering see R. E. Richey, 'Joseph Priestley: Worship and Theology (Part I)', *TUHS*, 15 (1972), 52, n.2.

fruitful in this respect, for there he had time to read and reflect, and the opportunity to exchange ideas with fellow tutors. During this period he produced notable works on education, grammar, history, and natural and political philosophy. Of these the most important for his political philosophy were his *Essay on a Course of Liberal Education for Civil and Active Life* (1765), which also contained his syllabus of lectures on history and general policy, lectures which were finally published in a developed form in 1788, and, shortly after he left Warrington, his *Essay on the First Principles of Government, and on the Nature of Political, Civil and Religious Liberty* (1768). In 1790 he referred to the lectures and essay as the key sources for his political ideas in order to counter his critics who were accusing him of subversion.[9] Even if one acquits him of that charge, he did set out to unsettle conventional truths and with the publication of the *Essay* his reputation as a radical political philosopher was established.

NATURAL RIGHTS AND SOVEREIGNTY

With the exception of Priestley scholars, it is fair to say that until the latter part of the twentieth century for students of political ideas Priestley was not much more than a footnote to the development of Jeremy Bentham's utilitarianism. However, with the publication in 1977 of H. T. Dickinson's groundbreaking study, *Liberty and Property*,[10] Priestley was placed fully within the context of the politics and political thought of the time. That work explored in detail the dimensions of radical and conservative thought in the late eighteenth century. Dickinson sees Priestley as a representative of the radicalization of Lockeian political theory. His view has particular merit in that Priestley himself recognized his indebtedness to Locke but

[9] Joseph Priestley, *Familiar Letters, Addressed to the Inhabitants of Birmingham in Refutation of Several Charges, Advanced Against the Dissenters and Unitarians*, 2nd edn (Birmingham, 1790), 13, 88.

[10] H. T. Dickinson, *Liberty and Property, Political Ideology in Eighteenth-Century Britain* (London: Weidenfeld & Nicolson, 1977), 197–9.

believed that his ideas needed to be developed further. Locke had argued that God had endowed men and women with certain natural rights, to life, liberty, and property, and men and women had entered into civil society and created political institutions in order to preserve those rights.[11] Late eighteenth-century radicals were not content with Locke's notion of the supremacy of the legislature once government was formed, for they believed that women's and men's natural rights were not sufficiently guaranteed if they were only embodied in the notion of government as a trusteeship for their preservation, a trusteeship which could only be revoked by revolution. Natural rights could only be preserved if citizens played a positive role in the political life of the community. Whereas for Locke the sovereignty of the people was passive, for the radicals it was, or at least should be, active. Natural rights needed to be translated into civil liberties in order that they could be exercised. Indeed there were two slightly contradictory elements in radical thought. On the one hand there was the demand for the people's right to exercise their liberties, which in effect led to the programme for parliamentary reform, embodying demands for a more democratic franchise, for a re-organization of the representation, and for shorter parliaments. This found its most extreme expression in the programme emanating from the report on the state of the representation of the Westminster subcommittee in 1780, which contained all the elements of the People's Charter of 1838.[12] On the other hand there was a reassertion of the right to resist those who abused power. The one was a concern for reform and inclusion, the other embodied a deep suspicion of those in power and something of the old Country suspicion of the power of the state. Both these currents flowed strongly in the first three decades of George III's reign.

Priestley was undoubtedly interested in reform, but his main contribution was on the side of those who were suspicious of the power of the state and the behaviour of the governors. These were clearly articulated in the work central to his political philosophy, his *Essay on Government* of 1768. In a key passage Priestley declared:

[11] John Locke, *The Second Treatise of Government* (1690), ed. J. W. Gough (Oxford: Basil Blackwell, 1956), 43–5, § 87–9.

[12] See E. C. Black, *The Association: British Extra-Parliamentary Organization, 1769–1793* (Cambridge, MA: Harvard University Press, 1963), 59–61.

if the abuses of government should, at any time be great and manifest; if the servants of the people, forgetting their *masters*, and their masters' interest, should pursue a separate one of their own; if, instead of considering that they are made for the people, they should consider the people as made for them; if the oppressions and violations of right should be great, flagrant, and universally resented; if the tyrannical governors should have no friends but a few sycophants, who had long preyed upon the vitals of their fellow citizens, and who might be expected to desert a government, whenever their interests should be detached from it: if, in consequence of these circumstances, it should become manifest, that the risque, which would be run in attempting a revolution would be trifling, and the evils which might be apprehended from it, were far less than those which were actually suffered, and which were daily increasing; in the name of God, I ask, what principles are those, which ought to restrain an injured and insulted people from asserting their natural rights, and from changing, or even punishing their governors, that is their *servants*, who had abused their trust; or from altering the whole form of their government, if it appeared to be of a structure so liable to abuse?[13]

It should be pointed out that Priestley prefixed this passage by saying that it referred to the 'largest states', although it is clear that Britain came within that category. Indeed, he followed up this radical affirmation of the right of resistance with a disquisition relating mainly to seventeenth-century history in which he makes it clear that the people have the right to punish their governors for the abuse of power. In this context he was not afraid to mention Charles I and justify his execution.[14] As Dickinson has noted, the radicals went beyond Locke in allowing the people to sit in judgement on their governors, to dissolve a government which did not protect their political rights, and erect a new one in its place.[15] This represents a radicalization of Locke rather than a departure from his thinking. With Priestley there is undoubtedly a difference of emphasis as well as of tone, but it is worth noting that it was Locke who wrote,

---

[13] Joseph Priestley, *An Essay on the First Principles of Government*, 2nd edn. (London, 1771), 24–5. References are to this edition unless otherwise stated. This passage is cited in Dickinson, *Liberty and Property*, 197–8.

[14] Priestley, *Essay on Government*, 33–40, esp. 38–40. Joseph Priestley, *Lectures on History and General Policy, to which is prefixed, an Essay on a Course of Liberal Education for Civil and Active Life*, 2 vols (1788, 2nd edn. London, 1793), II, Lecture xxxvi, 30.

[15] Dickinson, *Liberty and Property*, 199.

When a King has dethroned himself and put himself in a state of war with his people, what shall hinder them from prosecuting him who is no king, as they would any other man who has put himself into a state of war with them.[16]

Dissenters were willing to acknowledge the role they had played in the development of liberty through their resistance to Charles I, though less keen to be remembered as regicides.[17] When Priestley published his *Lectures on History and General Policy* in 1788 he drew attention to David Hume's verdict that 'the precious sparks of liberty were kindled and preserved by the puritans in England, and that "it is to this sect, whose principles appear so frivolous, and whose habits so ridiculous, that the English owe the whole freedom of their constitution" '. Priestley added, 'We shall take the compliment, and despise the reflection.'[18]

The essence of Priestley's position was that a king ought to be treated as any other man who broke the law. He was not setting out to justify republican government. He described the period after the dissolution of the monarchy as one of 'absolute anarchy and confusion'.[19] Less contentious in the public memory than the revolution of the mid-seventeenth century was the Glorious Revolution of 1688/9. It also provided a better example of the right to resist a government which abused its trust, for the resistance to James II was broadly based in the political community and the nation at large.[20] The dissenting interpretation of the revolution was famously encapsulated in the formula which Richard Price expressed in his *Discourse on the Love of Our Country* (1789). In this sermon preached to celebrate the centenary of the revolution, Price, while critical of the *status quo*, argued that the Revolution had established the constitution on the basis of firm principles. It recognized 'the right to liberty of conscience in religious matters', 'the right to resist power when abused', and 'the right to chuse our own governors; to cashier them for misconduct;

---

[16] Locke, *The Second Treatise of Government*, 120, § 239.

[17] See John Seed, 'History and Narrative Identity: Religious Dissent and the Politics of Memory in Eighteenth-Century England', *JBS*, 44 (2005), 46–63 at 55–7.

[18] Priestley, *History and General Policy*, I, Lecture lvi, 296.

[19] Priestley, *Essay on Government*, 38–40; Priestley, *History and General Policy*, II, Lecture xxxvi, 30.

[20] See Bradley, 146.

and to frame a government for ourselves'.[21] In so doing, Price was reiterating the principles of the Society for Commemorating the Glorious Revolution, which had invited him to preach his sermon and which consisted largely of dissenters. The dissenting principles and preoccupations were manifest in Price's demand for the liberty of conscience, and his assertion that in respect of toleration the Glorious Revolution was incomplete.

POLITICAL AND CIVIL LIBERTY

Generally speaking the success of the Glorious Revolution and the development of toleration for the dissenters, imperfect as it was, meant that, although in theory they emphasized the right to resist power when abused, in practice, at least in the domestic context, their main orientation was to reform. Priestley's distinction between political liberty and civil liberty indicates his own priorities and contained the potential to clarify contemporary thinking about reform.[22] He defined political liberty as 'the power, which the members of the state reserve to themselves of arriving at the public offices, or at least, of having votes in the nomination of those who fill them'.[23] If, unlike other radicals, he was not preoccupied with developing a detailed programme for political reform, the democratic *tendency* of his ideas is clear, for he argued that a state in which political liberty had the most perfect expression was one in which 'every member enjoys an equal power of directing the strength and sentiments of the whole community'.[24] He distinguished such liberty from civil liberty, defined as 'that power over their own actions, which members

---

[21] Richard Price, *A Discourse on the Love of Our Country*, 6th edn with additions (London, 1790), 34.

[22] J. A. W. Gunn, *Beyond Liberty and Property: The Process of Self-Recognition in Eighteenth-Century Political Thought* (Kingston and Montreal: McGill-Queens University Press, 1983), 244.

[23] Priestley, *Essay on Government*, 9.

[24] Ibid. 11. Priestley offered a fairly typical programme of reform in his *The Present State of Liberty in Great Britain and Her Colonies, By an Englishman* (new edn. corr., London, 1769), 19.

of the state reserve to themselves, and which their officers must not infringe.'[25]

Priestley's distinction was shared by few contemporary radicals, of whom Richard Price was more typical.[26] He encompassed all forms of liberty, including political liberty, under the concept of civil liberty and implied that Priestley should have used a more confined term for his notion of civil liberty.[27] For Price political liberty was inseparable from civil liberty, which he understood in the broadest terms.[28] It embodied the political freedom of individuals to act as their own legislator, the moral freedom to act as one chooses, and the religious freedom to follow one's own conscience. The only proviso was that one should not invade the rights of others.[29] Although there was room in Price's thought for practical, pragmatic considerations, his notion of civil liberty was essentially *a priori*, deriving its thrust from his moral philosophy. In Priestley's case, his attitude to liberty was derived from a more empirical approach to politics. Political liberty was distinct because it did not exist in a state of nature: civil liberties existed 'in full force' in a pre-social state, whereas political liberty was gained in civil society. It was derived from the natural right to control one's own destiny, but it existed in different degrees. It was what man 'may or may not acquire in the compensation he received' for the loss of some civil liberty.[30]

Indeed, in many states political liberty was imperfect. More interestingly, Priestley accepted that the right to political liberty could be, or might have been, alienated. True, he argued the actions of one

[25] Priestley, *Essay on Government*, 9. See also John A. Passmore (ed.), *Priestley's Writings on Philosophy Science and Politics* (London: Collier-Macmillan, 1965), 27.

[26] An important exception to this was David Williams. See James Dybikowski, 'David Williams and the Eighteenth Century Distinction between Civil and Political Liberty', *E&D*, 3 (1984), 15–40.

[27] Richard Price, *Additional Observations on the Nature and Value of Civil Liberty and the War with America* (1777), in Bernard Peach, *Richard Price and the Ethical Foundations of the American Revolution* (Durham, NC: Duke University Press, 1979), 141–2, n. 'm'.

[28] *Price: Political Writings*, ed. D. O. Thomas (Cambridge: CUP, 1991), Introduction, p. xviii; D. O. Thomas, 'Progress, Liberty and Utility: The Political Philosophy of Joseph Priestley', in Andersen & Lawrence, 73–9, at 78.

[29] Price, *Additional Observations*, 140–1.

[30] Priestley, *Essay on Government*, 10.

generation in alienating their right could not be binding on subsequent generations, but this contrasts with Price's belief that 'a people will never oppress themselves or invade their own rights'.[31]

Theorizing about the nature of liberty on the basis of the assumption that at some time in the past men moved from a pre-social state to a state of civil society undoubtedly has its limitations. In reality all government had originated to some degree in oppression.[32] Nonetheless, the hypothesis was useful in thinking about the way civil society *ought* to be formed, for it provided a reminder of the essential purpose of government which Priestley believed had been ignored by so many 'of our great writers'.[33] It was commonplace to adjudge the values of specific legislation in terms of its contribution to the public good, but few in discussing 'the first principles of society, and the subject of civil and religious liberty' had placed the public good at the heart of their considerations.[34] For Priestley that was not only an important consideration, it was the *only* consideration. He spelt this out in a passage which reminds us of how his political philosophy was dependent upon his theology and metaphysics, and of how he was prepared to declare his position with a stark clarity:

To a mind not warped by theological and metaphysical subtilties, the divine being appears to be actuated by no other views than the noblest we can conceive, the happiness of his creatures. Virtue, and right conduct consist in those affections and actions which terminate in the public good; justice and veracity, for instance, have nothing intrinsically excellent in them, separate from their relation to the happiness of mankind; and the whole system of right to power, property and everything else in society must be regulated by the same consideration: the decisive question, when any of these subjects are examined, being, What is it that the good of the community requires?[35]

It is no surprise that Bentham attributed the principle of the happiness of the greatest number to a reading of Priestley's essay.[36] Subsequently scholars have sought in vain to find that formulation in his work, and there are many alternative potential sources for

---

[31] Price, *Additional Observations*, 143.
[32] Priestley, *Essay on Government*, 12.
[33] Ibid. 13.   [34] Ibid. 14.   [35] Ibid. 14.
[36] Roy Porter, *Enlightenment: Britain and the Creation of the Modern World* (Harmondsworth: Allen Lane, The Penguin Press, 2000), 412.

Bentham's felicific calculus.[37] However, as the above passage demonstrates, Priestley was prepared to state in the most explicit manner
the subordination of all ends and virtues to the principle of the
pursuit of happiness. The age in which he lived was preoccupied
with happiness, and the 'self-evident' right to pursue it was drafted
into the American Declaration of Independence by Priestley's friend
Thomas Jefferson.[38] The declaration reflected a re-orientation of
thought away from original sin and the depravity of man towards
man's potential for earthly fulfilment. There is much in Priestley's
thought to encourage that trend, but the happiness which he sought
was ultimately religious. He believed that God had so designed us that
the pursuit of happiness would lead to our own good and the general
good. Individual self-interest and the good of the community were
essentially in harmony. The natural rights of the individual would
not conflict with calculations about the good of the community.
Natural rights and utility were broadly consonant. Yet this did not
mean that Priestley gave priority to political liberty in which the
people through participation could maximize the happiness of all.
Indeed, late eighteenth-century radicals were no doubt disappointed
to read that he did not believe that 'the good of mankind requires
a state of the most perfect political liberty'. He thought that that
was only possible in small republics, although he did not favour
their creation, for he thought that larger states would find such
states easy prey.[39] His solution in relation to political liberty was
pragmatic.

The first aspect of his solution was to suggest that there should
be gradations of political participation according to one's means, on
the common assumption that only the better off were sufficiently
educated to be qualified for full participation and that the more
property individuals owned the more they had a stake in 'the fate
of their country'. He added a qualification to this view in the second

[37] See Robert Shackleton, 'The Greatest Happiness of the Greatest Number: the
History of Bentham's Phrase', *Studies on Voltaire and the Eighteenth Century*, 90
(1972), 1461–82; Schofield, I, 207–8.

[38] Darrin McMahon, *Happiness: A History* (New York: Atlantic Monthly Press,
2006), 312–31.

[39] Priestley, *Essay on Government*, 15–16; see also Priestley, *History and General
Policy*, II, Lecture xxxviii, 45, and xliii, 121.

edition of his *Essay*, in which he stated that he was referring to those of '*moderate* fortune' rather than the really affluent, for such people were 'generally better educated, have, consequently, more enlarged minds, and are, in all respects, more truly *independent*, than those who are born to great opulence'.[40] The most important group in society were the middle class who were both propertied and educated, and, so Priestley believed, were in the ideal situation to act in the interests of the whole community.[41] The logic of his argument would appear to favour the idea of elective monarchy, but he thought that the elective principle should stop short of monarchy which 'ought to be, in some measure, hereditary'. Elective monarchies were generally unstable, being 'the theatres of cabal, confusion, and misery'.[42]

The second aspect of the solution was to confine the role of the state as much as possible and to privilege civil over political liberty. Here Priestley was more in line with the thinking of fellow radicals, who tended to view the state with distrust. In this respect, although they were inheritors of the Country tradition of suspicion of Westminster, they formulated their suspicion in general terms. It was Thomas Paine, often regarded as a proto-socialist thinker, who wrote at the beginning of his *Common Sense* (1776) that 'Society in every state is a blessing, but government, even in its best state, is but a necessary evil; in its worst state an intolerable one.'[43] Later, in part two of his *Rights of Man* (1792), which worried moderate reformers such as Christopher Wyvill (1740–1822) for its suggestion of a scheme of assistance for the poor, Paine still took the view that 'the more perfect civilisation is, the less occasion for government'.[44] Priestley was, therefore, not unusual in believing that civil society was more important than the state which protected it and that civil liberty was more important than political liberty. For him the crucial importance

[40] Priestley, *Essay on Government*, 16–17.
[41] Priestley, *History and General Policy*, II, Lecture xli, 95. See also Priestley, *The Present State of Liberty in Great Britain and Her Colonies*, 10.
[42] Priestley, *Essay on Government*, 18; a similar point was made by James Burgh, *Political Disquisitions: or, an Enquiry into Public Errors, Defects, and Abuses*, 3 vols (London, 1774–75), I, p. xi.
[43] Thomas Paine, *Rights of Man, Common Sense and Other Political Writings*, ed. Mark Philp (Oxford and New York: OUP, 1995), 5.
[44] Paine, *Rights of Man*, ed. Philp, 216, 300.

of political liberty was as a guarantor for civil liberty. He was not opposed to strong government, and indeed spoke so favourably of government that he could be misinterpreted. In the opening pages of his *Essay on Government* he expressed the view that 'whatever was the beginning of this world, the end will be glorious and paradisiacal, beyond what our imaginations can now conceive'. He then described government as 'the great instrument of this progress of the human species'.[45] One could be forgiven for thinking that he was in tune with the idea, increasingly prevalent in the Enlightenment, that government was a moralizing agency and that the well-being of the people could be improved in a whole variety of ways through legislation. Indeed, the utilitarian in Priestley could not entirely rule out the development of the role of government for improving the lives of individuals, and the empiricist in him favoured experimentation in government. Others, such as the radical dissenting minister Joseph Towers, followed Priestley in arguing that 'the best system' of politics was that which would 'promote the happiness of the greatest number of individuals',[46] but that still begged the question as to what was best for individuals.

CIVIL LIBERTY

In his definition of civil liberty—'that power over their own actions, which members of the state reserve to themselves, and which their officers must not infringe'—Priestley's emphasis was on the freedom of the individual, for he believed that it was best for individuals to help themselves. This he thought was in accord with history and experience and was indicative of the intention of divine government, which was that man should be self-taught.[47] He accepted that in the course of early education the parent or teacher reinforced good associations and tried to exclude the bad. Such a system of pains and penalties had both political and theological dimensions, for he

[45] Priestley, *Essay on Government*, 4–5.
[46] Joseph Towers, *A Vindication of the Political Principles of Mr. Locke in Answer to the Objections of… Dr Tucker, Dean of Gloucester* (London, 1782), 212.
[47] Priestley, *Essay on Government*, 263.

believed when a child reached maturity ideas of '*moral right*, and *moral obligation*...are easily transferred from the commands of a parent to those of a magistrate, of God, and of conscience'.[48] Government, through the enforcement of law, tried to ensure that citizens were well behaved. But government for the most part should not engage in positive action to enhance individual happiness, or, to put it another way, the purpose of government was to create a framework of security in which individuals could enjoy personal liberty. It should confine itself to those things which it can do best for the good of the whole. Apart from ensuring the security of the citizens from external aggression and administering justice, the remaining role was in the 'erecting some public works, and forming public institutions, useful to the whole and posterity'.[49] He did not spell out what these were, but it is clear that he was wary of encouraging the development of the use of the power of the state for the supposed positive advantages of all, for, in trying to ensure the good of all, governments were prone to endanger, at least for some, the very advantages for which they had entered into society, namely security and freedom from oppression. Society was such a complex thing that the best way for it to be served was by allowing individuals to pursue their own interests: 'it is most adviseable to leave every man at perfect liberty to serve himself till some actual inconvenience be found to result from it'.[50] Although Priestley conceded that the precise boundaries of 'civil government' were difficult to fix, he was clear enough that for the government to take action there needed to be compelling arguments that legislation would further the public good more effectively than individual initiative. He accepted that 'experiments only can determine how far this power of legislation ought to extend', while counselling strongly that

it becomes the wisdom of the civil magistracy to take as little upon its hands as possible, and never to interfere, without the greatest caution, in things that do not immediately affect the lives, liberty, or property of members of the community.[51]

[48] Joseph Priestley, *Hartley's Theory of the Human Mind on the Principle of the Association of Ideas; with Essays relating to the Subject of It* (London, 1775), pp. xlii–xliii. Priestley, *History and General Policy*, II, Lecture xlvii, 159–79.
[49] Priestley, *History and General Policy*, II, Lecture xxxviii, 47.   [50] Ibid.
[51] Priestley, *Essay on Government*, 58–9.

Priestley believed that individual liberty was essential for all those areas of society which involved the progress of truth and the development of knowledge, and included collective scientific endeavour within the parameters of individual truth seeking.[52] If there were other areas of state activity with potential utilitarian value, he still needed much convincing. Since Elizabethan times the poor had been supported by relief from their parishes. Priestley was not impressed and believed that it would have been better if the government had never taken action on their behalf.[53] He accepted that the poor had been disadvantaged under all forms of government,[54] yet he also accepted that inequality was part of the divine scheme of things. It created the need for society and encouraged the virtues of humility, patience, and gratitude amongst the disadvantaged and strengthened 'the principle of benevolence' amongst the more fortunate. Although he believed that one was 'in duty bound' to 'lessen the evils' which necessarily arise from inequality, and was not above reminding manufacturers that they might be responsible for some of them,[55] he was strongly opposed to assistance which could be claimed as of right. In an argument which has a modern ring to it, he suggested that 'the more poor of any kind you provide for in this way, the more you will create'.[56] Yet his stance was not entirely negative; he suggested something like a compulsory national insurance scheme for the poor, but it was only for the poor. His attitude appears extremely harsh today, but insofar as it can be justified, it arose from the view that poor relief was actually harmful to 'the most deserving' poor. Moreover, his argument that taxing the poor for their future relief would have the effect of increasing wage levels has some plausibility.[57] In contrast, contemporary attempts to assist the poor by topping up their wages only succeeded in driving down wage levels. Priestley generally

[52] Priestley, *Essay on Government*, 54–5.

[53] Priestley, *History and General Policy*, II, Lecture xxxviii, 57–8.

[54] Priestley, *Essay on Government*, 50.

[55] Joseph Priestley, *A Sermon on Behalf of the Leeds Infirmary Preached at Mill Hill Chapel Leeds in the Autumn of 1768* (Leeds: Jackson, 1910), 21.

[56] *The Case of Poor Emigrants recommended in a Discourse Delivered at the University Hall in Philadelphia, on Sunday, February 19, 1797*, Rutt, XVI, 504–5.

[57] Priestley, *History and General Policy*, II, Lecture xxxviii, 58–9.

favoured a free market economy, but justified his insurance proposals on the grounds that 'out of a number of evils, [we] must choose the least'.[58]

Priestley's severest strictures against state interference were in relation to the progress of knowledge.[59] As he put it, 'civil power is an inflexible thing, and is deaf to all kinds of argument and persuasion; so that truth has no chance where it prevails'.[60] Priestley had been stimulated to consider broader questions concerning civil and political liberty by *Thoughts on Civil Liberty, Licentiousness, and Fashion* (1765) by Dr John Brown (1715–66), a skilful essayist and critic of eighteenth-century culture and society. Brown's recommendation of a uniform Spartan-style state education as the best way of producing virtuous citizens roused Priestley to defend educational choice and diversity, and his reply was eventually incorporated into his *Essay on Government*. The second edition of the essay also incorporated his reply to Dr Thomas Balguy (1716–95), Archdeacon of Winchester, who had defended the authority of the established church in a sermon of 1769.[61] Once again Priestley defended independence from state control. This led him to assert the importance of freedom of the press, of religion independent of the state, and of universal toleration. Candid public debate was the best means of furthering truth and, most importantly, religious truth. Acting on such ideals, he became involved in pamphleteering on various issues relating to toleration, and was often more of a hindrance than a help to the causes he supported, most notably in relation to the repeal of the Test and Corporation Acts. The real substance of his position was, however, already articulated in the first edition of the *Essay on Government*. Here we find him at his best and, arguably, most distinctively radical in developing Locke's theory of toleration, in taking on widely held prejudices and in arguing for a free and open society, in which rival opinions could be expressed in the spirit of candid enquiry.

[58] Ibid. 59.   [59] Priestley, *Essay on Government*, 54–5.

[60] Priestley, *Letter to the Author of Remarks on Several Late Publications*, 16.

[61] Thomas Balguy, *A Sermon Preached at Lambeth Chapel, on the Consecration of the Right Rev. Jonathan Shipley, ... February 12, 1769* (London, 1769).

RELIGIOUS LIBERTY

Priestley was by no means the first to argue for complete freedom of conscience. William Popple in his translation of Locke's *Epistola de Tolerantia* (1689) added a preface without Locke's concurrence, in which he contended for 'absolute liberty, just and true liberty, equal and impartial liberty' on the basis that no single authority had the right to invade the civil rights of individuals 'upon pretence of religion'.[62] The principle, however, had not been applied to religious minorities in England. In particular, many who argued for complete freedom of conscience combined such views with virulent hostility towards the Roman Catholics. Indeed Popple was cited by the anti-Catholic Archdeacon of Cleveland, Francis Blackburne (1705–87) in his *Confessional* (1766).[63] Blackburne had been encouraged to publish the work by his friend Thomas Hollis of Lincoln's Inn (1720–74), who was a vigorous orchestrator of anti-Catholic propaganda in the mid-century. His prejudices were shared by all those encompassed by the Commonwealth tradition, including many dissenters.[64] Priestley was himself deeply opposed to Papal hierarchy and to Roman Catholic theology, but crucially he refused to exclude Roman Catholics from his arguments for toleration. Locke had provided a framework for exclusion by arguing that those who did not recognize the supreme authority of the state and those whose teachings could undermine the moral order should be excluded from toleration. On the latter count he excluded atheists from toleration for he believed

---

[62] John Locke, *Epistola de Tolerantia. A Letter on Toleration* (1689), Latin text and preface, ed. R. Klibansky; English trans. and intro. J. W. Gough (Oxford: Clarendon Press, 1968), 164.

[63] [Francis Blackburne] *The Confessional: Or, A Full and Free Inquiry into the Right, Utility, Edification, and Success, of Establishing Systematical Confessions of Faith and Doctrine in Protestant Churches*, 3rd edn., enlarged (London, 1770), Preface to the 1st edn., pp. liii–liv, lxv, xcvii–c.

[64] On Blackburne see Chapter 5. On the tradition see Caroline Robbins, *The Eighteenth-Century Commonwealthman. Studies on the Transmission, Development and Circumstance of English Liberal Thought from the Restoration of Charles II until the War with the Thirteen Colonies* (1959, 3rd repr. with a new Preface by the author, New York: Atheneum, 1968). See also John Trenchard and Thomas Gordon, *Cato's Letters or Essays on Liberty, Civil and Religious, and Other Important Subjects*, four volumes in two, ed. and annotated Ronald Hamowy (1720–3; Indianapolis: Liberty Fund, 1995), I, Introduction, pp. xxii–xxiii.

that they did not recognize the moral order: 'promises, covenants, and oaths, which are the bonds of human society, can have no hold upon or sanctity for an atheist'. Roman Catholics, although not mentioned by name, clearly came within the criteria for exclusion. Their ultimate allegiance was to the Pope and the Pope had the power to dispense with moral obligations, for Catholics believed that no faith was to be kept with the heretic.[65] Priestley believed that Locke's principles formed the basis for a more comprehensive notion of toleration. They rested upon the separation of church and state. He had, moreover, suggested that 'practical opinions, although not free from error, if they do not aim at domination over others or civil impunity, there can be no reason why the churches in which they are taught should not be tolerated'.[66] Priestley was therefore mortified to discover that John Brown had cited Locke's authority for including extra restrictions on religious liberty in his new Sparta.[67] For Priestley, religious liberty was a branch of civil liberty, and, as with civil liberty, he combined a general predisposition against state interference with arguments drawn from experience. Anti-Catholic propaganda for the continued exclusion of Catholics from citizenship was rich in examples of Catholic persecution and disloyalty.[68] Priestley deplored persecution but drew a very different lesson from history. He argued that, 'Those societies have enjoyed the most happiness, and have been *ceteris paribus*, in the most flourishing state, where the civil magistrates have meddled least with religion.'[69] Priestley did not deny that there was a relationship between belief and action, but he saw no reason to discriminate against any particular beliefs. He believed that all religions were conducive to good behaviour and the 'good order of society'. In a situation of complete toleration they would compete for the distinction of serving best the civil magistrate. No one religion would be privileged by

---

[65] Locke, *Epistola de Tolerantia*, 131–5.   [66] Ibid. 135, § 4.

[67] Priestley, *Essay on Government*, 128–9. See Margaret Canovan, 'Two Concepts of Liberty—Eighteenth-Century Style', *P-PN*, 2 (1978), 27–43.

[68] See Martin Fitzpatrick, 'Joseph Priestley and the Cause of Universal Toleration', *P-PN*, 1 (1977), 3–30.

[69] Priestley, *Essay on Government*, 110–11; this echoed his views on education, 85–7.

the magistrate. The alliance between the Anglican Church and the state, cherished by Balguy and its main apologist William Warburton (1698–1779), Bishop of Gloucester, would be unnecessary. All religions would be independent of the state and exist on the basis of equality. Cutting away the limitations which Locke had placed on complete toleration, Priestley suggested that men should be tried for their deeds, not their words. No religion should be regarded as criminal, and no opinion should be outlawed. He pilloried Brown for allowing individuals to think for themselves at the price, so Priestley argued, of keeping their thoughts to themselves and never publicly expressing them.[70] Brown was fearful of the impact of unconventional opinions on the social order and attacked an assortment of writers from earlier in the century, including the third Earl of Shaftesbury, Viscount Bolingbroke, Bernard Mandeville, John Trenchard, Thomas Gordon, Anthony Collins, and Matthew Tindal.[71] They had undermined religious and civil liberty, and were 'public enemies of their country and mankind'.[72] Brown was convinced that freedom of thought, of which they were exemplars, led to licentiousness and that unassisted human reason was a 'poor and unprofitable...Possession'.[73] Opinions therefore needed to be controlled through uniform education, a national religion and the policing of writers and their publications which offended against public virtue and undermined 'the essential principles of religion'.[74] Priestley's response was that 'unbounded free inquiry...may certainly be attended with some inconvenience, but it cannot be restrained without infinitely greater inconvenience'.[75] He also tended to think that freedom of enquiry was a good in itself for it provided the means of testing established truths, confirming some and rooting out those that were erroneous. From his point of view the writers feared by Brown would have rendered a service by testing received opinion. In his familiar optimistic mode, Priestley asserted that principles subversive of religion and civil society could easily be defeated for 'they must be evidently false and easy to refute'. So for him, there

---

[70] Priestley, *Essay on Government*, 275–6.
[71] John Brown, *Thoughts on Civil Liberty, on Licentiousness, and Faction* (Dublin, 1765), 99–110.
[72] Ibid. 110.   [73] Ibid. 38.   [74] Ibid. 174–84, at 176.
[75] Priestley, *Essay on Government*, 279.

should be no restraint on opinion, no Lockian tests of citizenship. Those who committed criminal acts in the name of religion, even as dire as murder, should be tried for their actions not their opinions.[76] He thought the risks of such a policy small in comparison to the damage that civil interference in religion created. Moreover, he believed that dissenters should not wait for complete freedom of religious expression but should act as if it existed and if necessary take the consequences. The advice he gave them was not sectarian but intended for the good of all:

It would be an infinite advantage to all states if the following maxims were adopted by all their members, viz to think with freedom, to speak and write with boldness, to suffer in a good cause with patience, to begin to act with caution, but to proceed with vigour.[77]

Priestley's belief in the need to separate church and state was fortified by his religious primitivism, for true Christianity had not required the assistance of the state.[78] Although this view was founded on revelation, it was an aspect of his broader concern for '*promoting useful knowledge*'.[79] Religious liberty, although a prime concern for Priestley, was thus incorporated in his ambition for a state which left its citizens free to develop their ideas as they wished, and included not only Christians but non-Christians and atheists. It was in keeping with this position that Priestley exhorted the dissenters, who were at the time seeking a minor repeal of penal laws relating to them alone, to take their stand not as Christians but as men and to 'ask at once for the repeal of all penal laws which respect matters of opinion.... ask for the common rights of humanity'.[80] He aimed to appeal to all men irrespective of creed. He also believed that universal toleration was not only consonant with Christianity, but that persecution offended against the Christian principle, '*to do unto others as we would that they should do to us*'.[81]

---

[76] Ibid. 118, 121–2.
[77] Joseph Priestley, *A Letter of Advice to those Dissenters who Conduct the Application to Parliament for Relief from Certain Penal Laws* (1773), Rutt, XXII, 455.
[78] Priestley, *Essay on Government*, 173.   [79] Ibid. 149.
[80] Priestley, *Letter of Advice*, Rutt, XXII, 442–3.
[81] Joseph Priestley, *A Free Address to Those who have Petitioned for the Repeal of the Late Act of Parliament in Favour of the Roman Catholics* (June, 1780), Rutt, XXII, 514.

PROGRESS, EXPERIMENTATION, AND FREE ENQUIRY

Priestley believed that it was the intention of providence that men and women should discover things for themselves, that 'as far as possible' they should be *'self taught'*.[82] Progress occurred this way and it was almost invariably wrong and unwise for government to interfere in the process.[83] Edmund Burke (1729/30–97) MP, a politician and political philosopher in the conservative Enlightenment mould, was deeply suspicious of what he regarded as the abstract ideas of radicals including Priestley. 'Government,' he argued, 'is a contrivance of human wisdom, to provide for human *wants*. Men have a right that these wants should be provided for by this wisdom.'[84] For him, religion was amongst those wants to be provided for by government through an established church. Priestley's predictable counter argument was that 'in many things besides the article of religion, men have busied themselves *legislating* too much, and when it would have been better if individuals had been left to think and act for themselves'.[85] As Peter Miller has argued, his 'fundamental insight' is that if the 'civil magistracy' acts wisely, and 'take as little upon its hands as possible,' 'the public good does not disappear, but is best served by leaving individuals responsible for what had heretofore been seen as part of the necessary task of government'.[86]

An advocate of minimalist government, Priestley believed that experimentation in government would favour *'unbounded liberty'*.[87] Yet if it were to be discovered through experimentation that government was the most effective agency for improving a particular

---

[82] Priestley, *Essay on Government*, 263.   [83] Ibid. 119–20.

[84] Edmund Burke, *Reflections on the Revolution in France* (1790), in *The Writings and Speeches of Edmund Burke*, gen. ed. Paul Langford, VIII, *The French Revolution, 1790–1794*, ed. L. G. Mitchell (Oxford: Clarendon Press, 1989), 110.

[85] Joseph Priestley, *Letters to The Right Honourable Edmund Burke occasioned by his Reflections on the Revolution in France*, 2nd edn. corrected (Birmingham, 1791), Letter vi, 'Of the Interference of the State in Matters of Religion', 55.

[86] Peter N. Miller, *Defining the Common Good: Empire, Religion and Philosophy in Eighteenth-Century Britain* (Cambridge: CUP, 1994), 345, citing Priestley, *Essay on Government*, 58. Cf *Priestley: Political Writings*, ed. Peter N. Miller (Cambridge: CUP, 1993), pp. xviii–xix. See also James Dybikowski, review of *Priestley: Political Writings*, ed. Miller, *E&D*, 15 (1996), 118–27.

[87] Priestley, *Essay on Government*, 115.

aspect of society, then he would have no ideological objection to the government taking on those powers.[88] Of course, in matters of great consequence the people needed to approve any proposed changes, but in lesser matters he suggested that the government could try things out and take on appropriate powers if the experiment succeeded. With his usual candour, he accepted the role of elite leadership in such matters, and said so even in the process of criticizing the government. In 1787, in his letter to the Prime Minister, William Pitt the Younger (1759–1806), he wrote:

The minds of the higher ranks in any community may well be presumed to be more enlightened than those of the lower. It is therefore their proper business to speculate, to devise plans for the public good, and to make trial of such as promote the best.[89]

It is hardly surprising that Priestley, the scientist, believed that science provided the model for general human progress. His contemporaries recognized his contribution to the theory of progress. The supreme theorist of enlightened progress, the Marquis de Condorcet, singled out Priestley, his friend Richard Price and the French enlightened statesman, Anne-Robert-Jacques Turgot, for developing the idea of the indefinite progress of the species.[90] In Priestley's case, this came about through the progress of knowledge, and although his ultimate vision of progress was religious, his God was truth even at the possible expense of Christian truth. Although he had no doubt that Christianity could 'stand the test of the most rigorous examination', he was prepared to argue that 'we can only wish for the prevalence of Christianity on the supposition of its being *true*; and if it fall before the influence of free inquiry, it can only do so in consequence of its not being true'.[91] In this he followed David Hartley, who argued that in an open society 'errors will combat one another, and leave truth

---

[88] Ibid. 58–9.   [89] Priestley, *Letter to the Right Honourable William Pitt*, 9.

[90] Jean-Antoine-Nicolas Caritat, Marquis de Condorcet, *Esquisse d'un tableau historique des progrès de l'esprit humain* (1795 posth.), ed. O. H. Prior (1933), intro. by Yvon Belaval (Paris: Librairie Philosophique J. Vrin, 1970), 166.

[91] Joseph Priestley, *The Importance and Extent of Free Inquiry in Matters of Religion: A Sermon, Preached before the Congregations of the Old and New Meeting of Protestant Dissenters at Birmingham. November 5, 1785. To Which are Added, Reflections on the Present State of Free Inquiry in this Country* (Birmingham, 1785), 23.

unhurt'.[92] For Priestley, the quest for religious knowledge was endless not only in this world but probably in the next.[93] He hoped that free enquiry would cause the fall of establishments of religion, which he regarded as obstacles to the progress of religious truth. Indeed, he won notoriety by envisaging that free enquiry was metaphorically 'laying gunpowder grain by grain under the old building of error and superstition, which a single spark may hereafter inflame, so as to produce an instantaneous explosion', with such drastic results that the edifice could never again be rebuilt.[94]

Although for Hartley and Priestley the supreme aspiration was for religious progress, their emphasis on the pursuit of knowledge married to a belief in the power of knowledge undoubtedly furthered secular ideas of progress. Yet from a strictly secular point of view there were flaws in Priestley's idea. Both Turgot and Condorcet believed that progress was inevitable but in the past it had not been inevitable in single societies: as one society regressed it passed the baton of progress on to another. Condorcet believed that the development of the Enlightenment in Europe ensured that retrogression would in future be prevented and progress could become a more even process. Knowledge was the key. The continued development of scientific knowledge and the percolation of knowledge through society would lead to real improvements in the standard of life. Priestley's views were not very different, but he differed from Condorcet in believing that progress was ultimately the working out of divine intentions, and that revelation indicated that the end of the process was the inauguration of the millennium.

Belief in progress as a dispensation of providence caused several problems. The first was that Priestley could not explain in historical terms why certain events of epochal significance occurred. Secular progressivists could offer a range of explanations, such as, for disastrous events, ignorance, tyrannical power structures, and

[92] David Hartley, *Observations on Man, his Frame, his Duty, and his Expectations*, 2 vols. (1749; 5th edn. London: J. Johnson, 1791), II, 368.

[93] Priestley, *Importance and Extent of Free Inquiry*, 7.

[94] Ibid. 40–1. The gunpowder metaphor may have been suggested by John Jones, author of *Free and Candid Disquisitions* (1749), see [Blackburne] *The Confessional*, Preface to the 1st edn., xv, n.'f'., citing John White, *Free and Impartial Considerations on the Free and Candid Disquisitions* (1751).

man's limited control over nature. Priestley, of course, deployed such arguments but he shifted easily from historical to providentialist explanations, a strategy unavailable to secular historians who were hidebound by their belief that 'no effect is produced without an adequate cause'.[95] As a result, Priestley argued, even the historian Edward Gibbon (1737–94) could not explain the rapid rise of Christianity. He failed to recognize the crucial significance of divine intervention through miracles for the progress of the new faith.[96] To put the problem another way, historians confined their explanations to secondary causes related to historical facts, a point made by Gibbon,[97] whereas Priestley switched from secondary causes to primary causes whenever explanations based on secondary causes seemed inadequate. The second problem caused by the association of Priestley's progressivism with his providentialism is that the latter was tied to a millennial agenda which he was confident would be fulfilled however change occurred. Millenialism came in different forms—one gradualist, which could easily be harmonized with secular gradualism, and which accorded with Priestley's Hartleian associationism and materialism by which the development of the understanding and the advancement of happiness occurred by degrees;[98] the other catastrophic, which, if reconcilable in some senses with ideas of progress, was also likely to bring in its train misery and hardship. These alternatives meant that Priestley could hedge his bets. The progress of knowledge could be gradual as would be the development of human happiness, or it could have an explosive effect by sweeping away barriers to progress.[99]

The chameleon-like nature of Priestley's millenialism led him to view dreadful contemporary events as part of the purposive plan of providence and somehow to believe that this did not impair his belief in progress. It is here that one can agree with Geoffrey Cantor that he 'could (despite his proclaimed rationalism) erect balsawood

[95] Joseph Priestley, *An History of the Corruptions of Christianity*, 2 vols (Birmingham, 1782), II, 443.

[96] Priestley, *History of the Corruptions of Christianity*, II, 444, 455–6.

[97] Edward Gibbon, *The History of the Decline and Fall of the Roman Empire. By Edward Gibbon, Esq; Volume the first* (London, 1776), 450.

[98] Priestley, *History and General Policy*, II, Lecture lxiv, 269.

[99] See Martin Fitzpatrick, 'Joseph Priestley and the Millennium', in Anderson & Lawrence, 29–38, esp. 34–5.

bridges across the deepest intellectual chasm'.[100] From the outset of the revolution in France, and especially after he himself suffered in the Birmingham riots, his judgement of contemporary events was often inconsistent. It may have been brave of him to declare after the riots that 'violence is temporary, but truth is eternal', but he escaped the physical effects of violence, whereas many in France did not.[101] His extraordinarily optimistic outlook can be attributed to his underlying belief that all things, evil as well as good, were necessitated by the will of God. It alarmed contemporaries such as Richard Price, but was central to his understanding of the way change occurred.[102] If it led to gaps in his explanatory theory, his sense that knowledge could sometimes cause dramatic change was correct even if it weakened the development of a coherent gradualist theory of progress.

The inspiration for so many eighteenth-century theorists of progress was the statesman and natural philosopher, Francis Bacon (1561–1626). He was amongst the first to argue that knowledge should become the handmaiden of human well-being. He also believed that such a view was authenticated by revelation. The fruits of the tree of knowledge could emancipate humans from the fall from grace caused by their initial selfish desire for knowledge.[103] If there is a bridge between the polarities of Priestley's views of progress, it lies in his belief that knowledge was growing exponentially and that progress would be ever accelerating.[104] This he stated clearly at the outset of his *Essay on Government*. As knowledge grows so would it be subdivided and become more specialized, producing greater efficiency in the pursuit of understanding and increasing mutual dependence in the process:

---

[100] Geoffrey Cantor, review of Anderson & Lawrence, *E&D*, 8 (1989), 125–9 at 128.

[101] Rutt, II ii, 145–56, Priestley to the Chairman of the Committee of the Revolution Society, 22 Aug. 1791. For Priestley's attitude to truth and that of fellow rational dissenters see Martin Fitzpatrick, 'Toleration and Truth', *E&D*, 1 (1982), 3–31.

[102] See Martin Fitzpatrick, ' "Through the glass of history"; Some Reflections on Historical Knowledge in the Thought of Joseph Priestley', *E&D*, 17 (1998), 172–209.

[103] See John Hedley Brooke, *Science and Religion: Some Historical Perspectives* (Cambridge: CUP, 1991), 22.

[104] Joseph Priestley, *Disquisitions relating to Matter and Spirit*, 2 vols., (1777; 2nd edn. improved and enlarged, Birmingham, 1782), II, 151. Cf. *A Letter of Advice*, Rutt, XXII, 455.

knowledge, as Lord *Bacon* observes, being *power*, the human powers will, in fact be enlarged; nature, including both its materials, and its laws, will be more at our command; men will make their situation in this world abundantly more easy and comfortable; they will probably prolong their existence in it, and will grow daily more happy, each in himself, and more able (and, I believe, more disposed) to communicate happiness to others.[105]

This was the point at which he envisaged the end of the world being 'glorious and paradisaical', which brings us back to his belief that government would be instrumental in this process by interfering as little as possible in the lives of its subjects. For all the flaws in his notion of progress, he can be placed amongst those, as Robert Nisbet has noted, who contributed to the idea of progress as freedom.[106] As Priestley himself put it towards the close of his *Essay on Government*, 'it is an universal maxim, that the more liberty is given to every thing which is in a state of growth, the more perfect it will become'.[107]

Priestley's belief in providential progress was central to his political philosophy but it also tended to blunt its analytical edge. Once one accepts his assumption, it is easy enough to see how he might think that development of independence would further the development of the community, that individual happiness would contribute to the overall general well-being, that people, freed from the constraints of the corrupt old world, would realize their true potential and not require disciplining, that the pursuit of one's economic interests would not conflict with Christian compassion for others, nor would there be any conflict between *laissez faire* and government acting for the general good. This can be seen in his more euphoric utterances. In the last of his *Letters to Burke*, he sees events in America and in France as presaging a transformed state of mankind. He outlines this state as one in which European powers would give up their empires. In future their contact with other parts of the world would only be for 'mutual advantage'.[108] The causes of foreign and civil wars would be eliminated. There would be no need for standing armies. Government would be cheaper and more efficient, and taxes lower

---

[105] Priestley, *Essay on Government*, 4–5.
[106] Robert Nisbet, *History of the Idea of Progress* (London: Heinemann, 1980), 200–1.
[107] Priestley, *Essay on Government*, 258–9.
[108] Priestley, *Letters to Burke*, Letter xiv, 143–55, at 147.

(as Paine envisaged later in part two of *Rights of Man*). If there was any superfluity of funds it would be employed for public works 'of public utility, which are always wanted',[109] such as canals, bridges, roads, public libraries, and public laboratories. He reminded Burke that this was the 'happy state of things' foretold in ancient prophecy and added prosaically, 'this is a state of things which good sense, and the prevailing spirit of commerce, aided by Christianity and true philosophy, cannot fail to effect in time'.[110] In this vision, individual liberty, public utility, Christian virtue, and economic progress could all happily co-exist.

PRIESTLEY THE RADICAL

Priestley's reputation as a subversive radical was derived far more from his attitude to contemporary events, informed as it was by his providential optimism, than from an appreciation of his philosophical arguments for civil liberty. There was a long tradition of hostility towards religious dissent exemplified by the statement of Priestley's formidable Anglican critic, the Revd Samuel Horsley (1733–1806), that 'the principles of a Non-conformist in religion and a Republican in politics, are inseparably united'.[111] In his eyes the most dangerous dissenters were heterodox like Priestley. Those who sought a second religious reformation he described as 'those concealed instruments of vengeance on their devoted country'.[112]

Priestley replied to accusations of republicanism by claiming that he was '*a trinitarian in politics* though an *unitarian in religion*'.[113] Priestley in denying that he was a republican used the term in the popular sense of favouring a non-monarchical state, but there are elements in his thought which may be regarded as republican in the broader classical republican tradition. He favoured mixed

---

[109] Priestley, *Letters to Burke*, 148.   [110] Ibid. 150.

[111] Samuel Horsley, *A Review of The Case of the Protestant Dissenters; with Reference to the Corporation and Test Acts* ... (London, 1790), 29.

[112] Samuel Horsley, *Remarks Upon Dr Priestley's Second Letters to the Archdeacon of St. Albans* (London, 1766), 80.

[113] Priestley, *Familiar Letters*, 89.

government not only in the sense of a balance of powers, but he also believed, following the eminent French *philosophe* Montesquieu (1689–1755), in the separation of powers, although the supreme authority should lie in the legislature.[114] However, as his central concern was with civil liberty he did not share the classical republican concern with political participation as the hallmark of civic virtue. This does not mean that Priestley was uninterested in political reform, but he did not think it essential that everyone should participate in the political process, nor that participation was a key constituent of liberty, as it was for Price. His emphasis on the priority of civil liberty, on individual independence over collective harmony, distances him from classical republicanism. We have seen that he allowed a very limited role for government in securing the public good. His emphasis on civil liberty led him to prefer the 'arbitrary will' of the individual not just to the will of the majority but to the 'united reason of the whole community'.[115] Indeed, he thought that mixed government required 'every man's educating his children in his own way'.[116] However, he was not preoccupied, as classical republicans were, with creating a constitution in which the forces of monarchy, aristocracy, and democracy were balanced. Priestley had a limited interest in the different forms of government. The form of government was much less important than the power which it exercised.[117] He was anxious that a fixed model of government, advanced as it might be for its time, would impede future progress, and he favoured experimentation in government.[118] This attitude may partly account for his willingness to change his mind during contemporary debate about the best form(s) of government and to contemplate republicanism in its anti-monarchical form. There is no doubt that when he settled in America he was comfortable with republican government. The question is whether he had been a covert republican for many years before that.

---

[114] Priestley, *History and General Policy*, II, Lecture xxxix, 67–8.

[115] Priestley, *Essay on Government*, 52.

[116] Joseph Priestley, *An Essay on a Course of Liberal Education for Civil and Active Life* (London, 1765), 207. This was incorporated in his *Essay on Government*, 106–8.

[117] Priestley, *Essay on Government*, 48–9, 51–2.

[118] Priestley, *History and General Policy*, II, Lecture xxxviii, 52.

When he described himself as a 'trinitarian in politics' Priestley also claimed that the dissenters 'are friends to *limited monarchy*, in which a king may do much good, and can do but little harm'.[119] In the summer of the following year, 1791, an anonymous tract, *A Political Dialogue on the General Principles of Government*, was published. This was presented as a sequel to *The Present State of Liberty in Great Britain and her Colonies* of 1769, also published anonymously. There is no direct authentication for the dialogue, although traditionally it has been attributed to him. Priestley experts differ as to its value. Whereas Jenny Graham believes it provides a key insight into Priestley's political ideas, Robert Schofield, author of the recent two-volume study of Priestley, doubts whether he wrote it.[120] But if the jury is still out, we may ask how far the ideas in the tract differ from Priestley's political philosophy up to that date. The differences may be listed as follows: it is an anti-monarchical tract, it emphasizes the importance of a single will in politics, and favours the French revolutionary preference for unicameral government, although it does not rule out a mixed system of government so long as the checks and balances in such a government are extremely limited. In other respects it does not depart significantly from Priestley's political philosophy to date. It is not a levelling democratic tract. It attacks titles and privileges but not hereditary wealth, and in its proposals for rearranging the representative system it argues that the representatives chosen would be 'the most respectable members of the society'.[121] However, the closest parallel with Priestley's ideas can be found in its predictions for change. Progress occurs through the power of enlightenment, for 'it is *opinion* that governs the world'. Genuine progress only takes place when opinion is ready for it: 'till the general opinion in any country concerning the foundation, the nature, and the uses of government, be changed, all useful revolutions will be impossible, or not permanent.'[122] This leads to a reassuring

---

[119] Priestley, *Familiar Letters*, 10–14. Cf. Voltaire, *Letters concerning the English Nation* (London, 1733), 53.

[120] Schofield, II, 1282 n.43; cf. Jenny Graham, 'Revolutionary Philosopher', part one, 58–9; 'Revolutionary Philosopher', part two, 23–7.

[121] *A Political Dialogue on the General Principles of Government*, Rutt, XXV, 88.

[122] *Political Dialogue*, 104; on opinion, cf. *History and General Policy*, II, Lecture, xliii, 116–19. The idea that opinion governs the world was not exclusively radical; see Gunn, *Beyond Liberty and Property*, 264–6.

concluding passage which portrays change in terms of non-violent reformation rather than revolution and stresses its gradual nature, for the people generally are 'averse to innovations.'[123] But not all the observations in the pamphlet were so reassuring. Enlightenment had led to revolution in France. In Britain, hostility to enlightened ideas would be counterproductive. With sublime confidence it pronounces that 'whatever is *true* and *right* will finally prevail, and the more violent the opposition, the more firmly will it be established in the end; because opposition excites attention, and this is all that is necessary to the perception of any truth'. Attacking enlightenment ideas is clearly a perilous enterprise. Those in power would be well advised to 'listen to proposals of reform, rather than run the risk of such convulsions as may be the consequence of an obstinate refusal to reform any thing'.[124] This sounds like Priestley the providential optimist—enlightened change would take place one way or another. It could not be permanently resisted.

Even if we accept that Priestley was the author of *A Political Dialogue*, the shift into republicanism does not constitute a marked departure from his primary concern with civil liberty. Politics was always important to him, but political life was always subordinate to civil life. Even in the dialogue the indications are that the role of the state is to be limited. The tract proposes that, in a reformed state, officeholders would be appointed only for a short term and paid minimal salaries.[125] Such a system would dispense with the services of those who had gained valuable experience in office. Apparently that would not cause problems for 'the business of states is not so difficult'.[126]

CONCLUSION

What might we conclude? It has been argued that the most important dimensions of Priestley's political philosophy are his delineation of a specific sphere for civil liberty, his arguments for freedom of inquiry,

---

[123] *Political Dialogue*, 108.   [124] Ibid. 106.
[125] Ibid. 88–9.   [126] Ibid. 91.

and his belief that political activity should aim at creating the optimal conditions for preserving civil liberty and for a free and open society in which truth would progress. Both in his insistent arguments for liberty of thought and in his radicalization of Locke on sovereignty and toleration he conformed and contributed to major trends within the Enlightenment.[127]

This is not to suggest that there is broad agreement in interpreting Priestley's political philosophy. Priestley was a prolific writer, and there is a considerable range of sources for his political ideas, varying from correspondence, sermons, pamphlets, and tracts to carefully composed treatises. He was very aware of the different audiences he was addressing and deliberately varied his tone. He was also given to writing in haste and in an injudicious way. In interpreting his ideas, I have generally taken the view that the more considered works, which he himself regarded as authoritative, provide a better insight into his political philosophy than those written for specific occasions. One may take a different view, namely that greater insight into his ideas and feelings may be found in more ephemeral works in which, it could be suggested, he lets his guard down. It is also important to bear in mind that Priestley lived through a turbulent period and that is reflected in the ideological richness as well as confusion of the period.[128] It is unsurprising therefore that there is a great variety of interpretations of his ideas; the Selected Bibliography acts as a basic guide to them.

I began this chapter by suggesting that it is important for a true appreciation of Priestley's political ideas that his radical reputation should be understood. But it is also true that his radical reputation was fairly quickly forgotten—if caricature is anything to go by—soon after his departure to America.[129] Over the ages it is Priestley the scientist who has been remembered. His legacy was, however, more rounded than that. His greatest influence naturally was on

[127] See Stephen Eric Bronner, *Reclaiming the Enlightenment: Towards a Politics of Radical Engagement* (New York, Chichester, West Sussex: Columbia University Press, 2004), esp. 41–60, 'Inventing Liberalism'.

[128] See Mark Philp, 'The Fragmented Ideology of Reform', in Mark Philp (ed.), *The French Revolution and British Popular Politics* (Cambridge: CUP, 1991), 50–77, at 54–5.

[129] Fitzpatrick, 'Priestley Caricatured', 206.

the community which he served, the rational dissenters, and their Unitarian successors. They were won over by his arguments for universal toleration, and, almost exclusively amongst Protestant dissenters, consistently advocated toleration for Roman Catholics. More importantly Priestley's advocacy of the pursuit of knowledge in all its aspects and the application of that knowledge to the improvement of society was inspirational for the civic mindedness which was already emerging in Priestley's time,[130] notably in the new industrial cities, and which became a central feature of nineteenth-century Britain. Priestley's belief that civil liberty was not a sanction for individual selfishness but was essential for the development of civic virtue was in a sense confirmed by the emergence of a vibrant Victorian urban culture in which Unitarians played a hugely influential role. Only towards the end of the nineteenth century did the limitations of that culture become evident, and the state began to take over many of the functions performed by philanthropists, charities, and city authorities. Priestley's ideas have had their heyday, but have they completely had their day? One might suggest that in the new twenty-first century in which problems of religious co-existence have become acute and the state over-governs our lives, his arguments for a tolerant, free, and open society, dedicated to the pursuit of knowledge in all its forms and always willing to re-educate itself, are well worth revisiting.

[130] For an exposition and critique of such trends see Isaac Kramnick, 'Eighteenth-Century Science and Radical Social Theory: The Case of Joseph Priestley's Scientific Liberalism', in Schwartz & McEvoy, 57–92, esp. 80–6.

5

Joseph Priestley and the Complexities of Latitudinarianism in the 1770s*

G. M. Ditchfield

> Many blame him, and he may be perhaps, sometimes to be
> blamed, for publishing in too hasty a way. But perhaps it is
> owing to this very temper that he publishes at all, and therefore
> great allowances should be made, where needed, of this sort.
>
> (Theophilus Lindsey, writing of Priestley, 10 January 1773)[1]

INTRODUCTION

Few Protestant dissenters, or indeed religious writers of any kind,
achieved so high a public profile in the eighteenth century as did
Joseph Priestley. With the possible exceptions of Benjamin Hoadly
(1676–1761) and Richard Price, none stimulated such widespread

* I am grateful to those who took part in the discussion at the Priestley conference
on 5 March 2005 for their valuable contributions to the discussion which followed the
papers. In particular I have benefited from the comments of Martin Fitzpatrick, Isabel
Rivers, and David Wykes. I wish to thank my fellow trustees of Dr Williams's Library,
and the Literary and Philosophical Society of Newcastle upon Tyne for permission to
quote from manuscripts in their possession. Quotations from the letters of Theophilus
Lindsey to William Tayleur are reproduced by courtesy of the University Librarian and
Director, JRUL. Part of the research for this chapter was financed by a grant from the
British Academy, which I acknowledge with gratitude.

[1] Rutt, I i, 223, n. §§.

and prolonged controversy. To some extent, the high level of dis-putation may be attributed to the breadth of Priestley's intellectual interests, which, as the present volume amply demonstrates, ranged from electricity to biblical criticism, from natural philosophy to the writing of history. In no areas of his activity, however, did he arouse more passionate conflict than in those of theological doctrine, church government, and politics. He was well aware of the way in which his theological opinions made him a target not only of criticism, but also, he believed, of personal abuse. His reply in 1784 to the strictures of the *Monthly Review* upon his *Letters* to Samuel Horsley was plaintive in tone. He wrote

My friend, Mr Lindsey has, in several publications, largely insisted upon *the unitarianism of the primitive christian church* (the very same thing that has roused all the rage of the present Reviewer) without the least note of disapprobation from his predecessors.[2]

He believed that the *Monthly Review* had become more hostile to his theology over the previous few years; and consequently, opinions expressed by others could be treated in a measured if not uncritical way, but when articulated by him the same opinions provoked furious resentment.[3]

The extent of the opprobrium incurred by Priestley over the course of his career is examined by David Wykes in the opening chapter of this volume. How, it might be asked, had Priestley become by 1784 so controversial a public figure? In some ways, of course, the explanation may be found in the frankness of his style. Theophilus Lindsey came to this conclusion in December 1778 when comparing Priestley with Leibniz. While the latter did not differ '*au fond* as the french say from Dr Priestley', wrote Lindsey, 'he takes care not to stagger his readers by the harshness of his expressions, whereas my friend with a fearless conviction of the truth never uses any softening'.[4] This

---

[2] Joseph Priestley, *Remarks on the Monthly Review of the Letters to Dr Horsley* (Birmingham, 1784), 24–5. The 'present Reviewer' was Samuel Badcock; his 'prede-cessors' were the authors of the *Monthly Review*'s articles on Lindsey's *Apology... on Resigning the Vicarage of Catterick* (London, 1774) and his *Historical View of the State of the Unitarian Doctrine and Worship* (London, 1783).

[3] This was a view shared by Lindsey, all the more strongly in the light of the dissenting connections of the *Monthly Review*.

[4] JRUL, Lindsey Letters, vol. I, nos. 22–3: Lindsey to William Tayleur, 3 Dec. 1778.

chapter proposes to investigate one of the most significant ways in which, through his published work and unpublished correspondence, Priestley had constructed for himself, not altogether intentionally, a reputation as a forceful and at times acerbic author. Its chosen method of so doing involves a particular illumination of one of the best known religious and political phenomena of the eighteenth century. That phenomenon was the affinity—sometimes uneasy but generally resilient—between Anglican latitudinarianism and Protestant dissent, an affinity developed in response to the perception of a common threat from high churchmen of the generation of Francis Atterbury (1663–1732) and Henry Sacheverell (1674?–1724). Even with the mid-century decline of party strife at the national level, many local constituency conflicts were still fuelled by a clash of interests between those of a high church persuasion, and an alliance of low churchmen and dissenters. However, this chapter will suggest that during the 1770s that alliance was placed under considerable pressure and that the complexities which it involved can be illustrated by a focus upon the controversy between Priestley and Benjamin Dawson (1729–1814), at that time the rector of Burgh in Suffolk.

ANGLICAN LATITUDINARIANISM AND PROTESTANT DISSENT

In an important article published in 1988, John Spurr suggested that the term 'latitudinarian' originated in the mid-seventeenth century as a somewhat pejorative expression, applied to those nominally Puritan clergy who retreated from the rigours of Calvinism and conformed to the re-established Church of England after 1660.[5] Spurr identified a set of opinions widely attributed to latitudinarians of Charles II's reign. They included a moderate Arminianism, an emphasis on the ethical dimensions of religion and on the preaching of morality, the elevation of reason, an attraction towards the 'scientific' methods of

[5] See John Spurr, ' "Latitudinarianism" and the Restoration Church', *Hist. Jnl.*, 31 (1988), 61–82.

intellectual inquiry promoted by the newly formed Royal Society, and a tolerant attitude towards dissenters. But Spurr showed that attitudes of this sort were in fact widely shared among Restoration clergymen as a whole and questioned the existence of an organized latitudinarian 'party' in the Restoration Church.

But gradually, and especially after 1688–9, a more distinctive latitudinarian mentality emerged, graced by post-1689 bishops such as Gilbert Burnet (1643–1715) and enhanced by the Whig ethos of Cambridge University, where the 'new' science inspired by Isaac Newton accorded well with theological speculation.[6] Latitudinarian clergymen contributed substantially to the intellectual climate which some historians have come to regard as a clerical enlightenment.[7] Hence by the early, and even more by the middle years of the eighteenth century, latitudinarianism had achieved a far greater level of respectability. As Martin Fitzpatrick has shown, eighteenth-century latitudinarians, like their Restoration predecessors, were distinguished by a distaste for sacerdotalism, an acceptance of rationality as entirely consistent with revelation, and a Protestant optimism about the ability of the human mind to read and interpret the Scriptures independently, according to conscience. As Fitzpatrick neatly puts it,

[Latitudinarians] were tolerant of differences, stressed the common core of Christianity and placed the creeds and dogma at the margins of their concerns. They were not prepared to allow philosophical differences to outweigh their commitment to moderation and, in their different contexts, to the *via media*. Many still hoped for a comprehensive establishment.[8]

A continuing hostility towards Catholicism made Protestant unity, in the form of comprehension of dissent within a reformed Church, a priority. On terms such as these, latitudinarians and dissenters could,

---

[6] See, especially, John Gascoigne, *Cambridge in the Age of the Enlightenment: Science, Religion and Politics from the Restoration to the French Revolution* (Cambridge: CUP, 1989), chs. 2–3.

[7] See, in particular, B. W. Young, *Religion and Enlightenment in Eighteenth-Century England: Theological Debate from Locke to Burke* (Oxford: OUP, 1998).

[8] Martin Fitzpatrick, 'Latitudinarianism at the Parting of the Ways: A Suggestion', in John Walsh, Colin Haydon, and Stephen Taylor (eds), *The Church of England c.1689–c.1833: From Toleration to Tractarianism* (Cambridge: CUP, 1993), 209–27, at 209.

148 *Joseph Priestley*

to quote Fitzpatrick, 'co-exist for the most part in mutual admiration'.[9]

Hence Benjamin Hoadly, in *The Reasonableness of Conformity to the Church of England Represented to the Dissenting Ministers*, published in 1703, had urged dissenters to rejoin the Church of England, arguing that they had no good cause to remain outside it. With a characteristic latitudinarian plea for sincerity, he criticized the practice of occasional conformity as a denial of individual authenticity as well as a profanation of the sacrament.[10] Mindful of the threat, as he saw it, from nonjurors and from Catholicism, and with the prospect of a Jacobite restoration in the background, Hoadly appealed to dissenters to end the disunity among English Protestants:

It grieves me to see a Church torn to pieces, it's members divided from one another, Discord triumphing upon the ruins of Unity, and Uncharitableness reigning without controul; and all this brought about by men of seriousness and consideration, men that profess they desire nothing more than the edification, and perfection of this very Church. Had You asked the Enemies of this Church and Nation; (those whom it hath so gloriously and successfully opposed;) which way You should take to ruine both Church and Nation; they would have thought of no other, but the encouraging such a *separation*: and they may well be pleased that You think *separation* your duty in order to *a farther reformation.*[11]

Hoadly hoped to persuade the Church of England to relax the barriers—notably the sacramental and Thirty-Nine Articles tests—which stood between conscientious dissenters and the possibility of a re-united Protestantism. It was a plausible aspiration, especially as the sense of a threat to the Church posed by dissenters faded considerably in the middle years of the eighteenth century. The public image of dissent was represented by the eirenical ethos of ministers such as Isaac Watts and Philip Doddridge, and local relationships between clergymen and their dissenting fellow citizens were frequently quite

[9] Fitzpatrick, 'Latitudinarianism', 210.
[10] See William Gibson, *Enlightenment Prelate: Benjamin Hoadly, 1676–1761* (Cambridge: James Clarke, 2004), 67ff.
[11] Benjamin Hoadly, *The Reasonableness of Conformity to the Church of England, Represented to the Dissenting Ministers. In Answer to the Tenth Chapter of Mr. Calamy's Abridgement of Mr. Baxter's History of his Life and Times, Part II*, 2nd edn (London, 1703), 114.

harmonious and could involve cooperation in philanthropic endeavour.[12]

W. M. Spellman insisted on the doctrinal orthodoxy—especially the Trinitarian orthodoxy—of the leading latitudinarian churchmen of the late seventeenth century.[13] But by the middle and later years of the eighteenth century, if not earlier, one notable—and interesting—characteristic of the latitudinarian ethos was a willingness to engage with heterodoxy over the doctrine of the Trinity—in its Arian and even its Socinian forms—on the assumption of a shared basis of Christianity, rather than regarding heterodoxy as beyond the pale of Christianity and therefore untouchable. Hence the rational dissent of Priestley's generation, as well as orthodox dissent, could participate in the affinity with latitudinarianism. For this and other reasons, there is no necessary inconsistency between Jonathan Clark's location of the springs of radical ideology among Socinians and John Gascoigne's detection of that ideology within Anglican latitudinarianism.[14] As the brief entry in the third edition of the *Oxford Dictionary of the Christian Church* perceptively notes, latitudinarianism 'could encourage a prosaic, commonsense piety which occasionally harboured heterodoxy concerning the Trinity'.[15] A measure of (often carefully coded) theological radicalism could exist within the Church as well as among rational dissenters.

One feature of the alliance was an alignment in politics between latitudinarians and dissenters in electoral support for the Whig party. Indeed, as James Bradley puts it, 'the alliance between Dissenters and Low-Church Anglicans at the local level...was the very basis for the definition of local Whig parties'.[16] An example of its practical

---

[12] For an example of such cooperation at local level, involving Whig and Tory interests, see Adrian Wilson, 'Conflict, Consensus and Charity: Politics and the Provincial Voluntary Hospitals in the Eighteenth Century', *EHR*, 111 (1996), 599–619.

[13] W. M. Spellman, *The Latitudinarians and the Church of England, 1660–1700* (Athens, GA: University of Georgia Press, 1993).

[14] J. C. D. Clark, *English Society, 1660–1832: Religion, Ideology and Politics during the Ancien Regime* (Cambridge: CUP, 2000), ch. 4; John Gascoigne, 'Anglican Latitudinarianism and Political Radicalism in the late Eighteenth Century', *History*, 71 (1986).

[15] F. L. Cross (ed.), E. A. Livingstone (rev.), *The Oxford Dictionary of the Christian Church*, 3rd edn., rev. (Oxford: OUP, 1997), 956. It is a matter for surprise that the entry for 'Latitudinarianism' in this important volume consists of only 79 words.

[16] Bradley, 113.

operation may be found in the mid-1770s. As the dispute between
Britain and its North American colonies deteriorated to the point
of war in 1775–6, high churchmen tended to support the ministry of Lord North (who, after all, from 1772 was Chancellor of
Oxford University) and to identify with the Episcopal Church in
the colonies. Significantly, the cult of Charles I, and the excoriations
of the sinfulness of rebellion preached in the annual 30 January
sermons commemorating his execution, underwent something of a
resurgence in the 1770s.[17] By contrast, as James Bradley's analysis
has demonstrated, dissenters and low church Anglicans combined in
quite substantial numbers in the promotion of petitions to king and
Parliament in favour of conciliatory rather than coercive measures
towards the British North American colonies.[18] However, a slightly
earlier opportunity for cooperation along these lines had arisen in
1772–4 with the issue of subscription to the Thirty-Nine Articles of
the Church of England. There was in principle a shared opposition
to the authority of the magistrate in spiritual matters and to the
imposition of human formularies as tests of fitness for ecclesiastical
or civil office. The two campaigns, in Parliament, in the country,
and in pamphlet controversy—the Feathers Tavern petition, and the
dissenters' campaign recorded in the Minutes of the General Body
of Dissenting Ministers, held at Dr Williams's Library—had much in
common. Potentially, each stood to benefit from the success of the
other.

PRIESTLEY'S CONTROVERSY WITH
BENJAMIN DAWSON

There were, of course, many shared perceptions between Anglican
latitudinarianism and rational dissent over the topical issues of the
1770s. They included lingering suspicions of the supposedly authoritarian intentions of George III; concern over threats to domestic

[17] See Andrew Lacey, *The Cult of King Charles the Martyr* (Woodbridge: Boydell
Press, 2003).
[18] Bradley, ch. 10.

liberties, particularly after the exclusion of John Wilkes from the House of Commons after his election for Middlesex (1768–9); opposition to the use of force in America, and unease about the concessions to Catholicism in Canada which were built into the Quebec Act of 1774. But there were also fundamental differences. No individual assumed a more visible and important role in the exposure of those differences than Priestley. That role is well illustrated by his brief but very bitter controversy with Benjamin Dawson, which forms the central theme of this chapter.

It was a controversy all the more piquant because Benjamin Dawson had been a dissenting minister before conforming to the Church of England. In fact, he was everything that an eighteenth-century dissenting minister should have been. He was a pupil of Caleb Rotheram's dissenting academy at Kendal and a graduate of Glasgow University, where he was a scholar on Dr Williams's foundation, and was awarded the degree of LLD. He served as a minister to a succession of small dissenting congregations in Staffordshire and in Cheshire and then at St Thomas's Presbyterian church, Southwark. Even after he followed the example of two of his brothers in conforming to the Church of England, which he did in 1758, he remained a sympathizer with dissent. In the later 1760s he resided at Warrington as the private tutor to Sir Benjamin Ibbetson of Leeds, who was a pupil at Warrington Academy where at the same time Priestley was tutor in languages and belles lettres (from 1761 to 1767), and he associated with the literary circle of John Aikin.[19] Moreover Benjamin Dawson's brother Obadiah remained a dissenter and was a member of Priestley's congregation at Mill Hill chapel, Leeds. Even after conforming, Dawson himself maintained good personal relations with some individual dissenters.

In 1771 Dawson edited for publication the *Free Thoughts on the Subject of a Farther Reformation of the Church of England*, written by the Anglican clergyman John Jones, vicar of Alconbury (1700–70). Jones by this time was best known as the author of the *Free and Candid Disquisitions relating to the Church of England*, published anonymously (in 1749), and an effective plea for large-scale church

---

[19] For Dawson's career, see Brian Young's entry in the *Oxford DNB*. Dawson was rector of Burgh from 1760 until his death in 1814.

reform including a much reduced form of clerical subscription. In the commentary which he provided to this work, Dawson identified himself fully with Jones's conclusions and the means by which he had reached them. Indeed he claimed that Jones had requested him to undertake the publication.[20] In the preface (unpaginated), Dawson stated:

The end of the controversy, it should be remembered, is the improvement of our ecclesiastical establishment, more particularly in the removal of those restraints upon religious freedom, which were unhappily admitted into it at the first, and are suffered to continue in it, though evidently to its discredit and disadvantage, if not immediate danger.

Dawson stressed the desirability of the exertion of 'all the friends of religious truth and freedom to excite attention to the original principles of protestantism' in order to bring about the desired reformation. He demonstrated his own commitment to the latitudinarian ideal by writing a series of effective defences of *The Confessional*, the learned critique of subscription to human formularies published by Francis Blackburne, Archdeacon of Cleveland, in 1766.[21] He was recognized publicly by Blackburne as his chief ally in the subsequent controversy. In the third edition of the *Confessional* (1770), Blackburne described him as 'an incomparable writer, one whose superiority in this disputation will be acknowledged and admired in distant times'.[22] As if to justify Blackburne's encomium, Dawson served as secretary to the Feathers Tavern Association, formed in the summer of 1770. He was one of the signatories to the petition which it circulated in 1771–2 for the abolition of the system of subscription to the Thirty-Nine Articles for Anglican clergymen and English undergraduates.[23]

[20] *Free Thoughts on the Subject of a Farther Reformation of the Church of England; In Six Numbers: to which are Added, the Remarks of the Editor. By the Author of a Short and Safe Expedient for Terminating the Present Debates about Subscription.* Published by Benjamin Dawson, LLD (London, 1771).

[21] Dawson published a series of pamphlets in support of Blackburne, of which the most notable was *An Answer to Letters concerning Established Confessions of Faith; Being a Vindication of the Confessional* (London, 1769).

[22] [Francis Blackburne] *The Confessional: Or, a Full and Free Inquiry into the Right, Utility, Edification and Success, of Establishing Confessions of Faith and Doctrine in Protestant Churches*, 3rd edn., enlarged (London, 1770), p. vi.

[23] See the (incomplete) list of signatories to the Feathers Tavern petition in the *Monthly Repository*, 13 (1818), 15–18, with Dawson's name under the county of

However, it was clear in all Dawson's work that he was writing from within the frontiers of the Church itself. In his own 'Remarks', appended to his edition of John Jones's work, he seized upon a passage from Priestley's *Considerations on Church Authority* of 1769 in which the latter had asked the rhetorical question 'Who among the clergy, that read and think at all, are supposed to believe one third of the thirty-nine articles of the Church of *England*?' Priestley's purpose had been to protest against the attacks upon ecclesiastical reformers levelled in Archdeacon Thomas Balguy's Lambeth Chapel sermon 'On Church authority', preached at the consecration of Jonathan Shipley in 1769. In that sermon, Balguy had criticized those who 'propose a reformation in the church, while they continue in it', while remaining silent about those who came into the church while disbelieving all or some of its articles. Ominously, Priestley had concluded, 'Men who have come *this way* into the church, have always proved its firmest friends. Having made no bones of their own scruples, they pay no regard to the scruples of others'.[24]

Dawson's response to this allegation of widespread clerical hypocrisy was sharp:

To charge us (at least to insinuate such a charge) with *not believing*, if we read and think *at all, one third* of what we have solemnly subscribed, is more than uncandid and indecent; it is to *detract* from our good name...We are moreover, from the very nature of such a charge, precluded from pleading to it, though we may be perfectly innocent. Conscience may acquit us of insincerity to *ourselves*, but it cannot be *produced* in evidence of our sincerity.[25]

Dawson accused Priestley of claiming in a misleading way that he spoke for 'the generality of dissenters' in expressing so 'uncharitable' an opinion of the Anglican clergy. In an effort to rebut such a claim, he deliberately provoked Priestley by quoting the responses at their respective ordinations of two of Priestley's former Warrington

Suffolk, 17. See G. M. Ditchfield, 'Feathers Tavern petitioners (act. 1771–1774)', *Oxford DNB*.

[24] Joseph Priestley, *Considerations on Church-Authority; occasioned by Dr Balguy's Sermon on that Subject* (London, 1769), 85.

[25] Dawson's edition of *Free Thoughts*, 149.

pupils, Philip Taylor at Liverpool and Robert Gore at Manchester, respectively, in June and August 1770. In each case, the ordinand, when asked his reasons for taking up the dissenting ministry, replied with irenical and even complimentary remarks about the Church of England. As Philip Taylor had put it:

Whilst I enjoy the advantages of a toleration; whilst I am permitted without molestation to worship God in the manner I most approve; I shall think myself bound by the laws of candour, of moderation, and even of gratitude, to refrain from saying, or doing any thing which may give *unnecessary* offence to the professors of that system of religion, which the laws of this kingdom have countenanced and established.[26]

Priestley made his initial riposte in *A Letter of Advice to those Dissenters who Conduct the Application to Parliament for Relief from Certain Penal Laws, with Various Observations Relating to Similar Subjects* (1773), in which he devoted a separate section to Dawson's strictures. He accused Dawson of defending Socinianism in his Sermons preached at Lady Moyer's Lectures and thus contradicting himself by subscribing to Trinitarian articles, not 'in the days of youth and ignorance', but at the age of 29, 'after a most liberal education among the Dissenters, with whom this subject never fails to be fully considered, and well understood'.[27] To Priestley, Dawson's apostasy from dissent was a prime target. He described Dawson's conformity as a 'dark transaction', adding, 'We lament the loss of the men to the dissenting interest, and more lament the wounds which, by their conduct, have been given to the more important interests of truth and probity.'[28]

Priestley proceeded to complain that not only had Dawson conformed, he had then, having benefited from the privileges of establishment and sought preferment therein, had the temerity to assume the character of advocate for religious liberty. His charge was that Dawson, to quote Priestley,

---

[26] Philip Taylor, quoted in Dawson's edition of *Free Thoughts*, 151. Taylor (1747–1831) was assistant minister, then minister, at Kaye Street chapel, Liverpool, 1767–77 and minister at Eustace Street, Dublin, 1777–1831. His fellow pupil Robert Gore (1748?–79) was minister at Cross Street chapel, Manchester, 1770–9.

[27] Priestley, 'Letter of Advice', Rutt, XXII, 466.   [28] Rutt, XXII, 467.

had purposely carried his dissenting principles into the church, because they were more wanted there; though every thing he knew of that church might have made him sensible, that instead of being able to effect her freedom, he must himself continue a slave with her, and to her.[29]

Then he made the decisive point which above all epitomised the difference between him and his antagonist:

The Doctor has...so far renounced the favourite sentiments of the Dissenters, as even to boast of the protection of the civil magistrate, as the crown and ornament of the church of which he is now a member; whereas we think it a disgrace to Christianity, and inconsistent with the true spirit of it, to acknowledge any such obligation to the civil power; and rather boast that our religion stands unconnected with it, and independent of it.[30]

He accused Dawson of hypocrisy, caricaturing him as someone willing to subscribe repeatedly to the Thirty-Nine Articles in return for ecclesiastical advancement. In so doing, Priestley drew a vivid contrast between Dawson's conduct and that of William Chambers, rector of Achurch in Northamptonshire (who, like Francis Blackburne, declined offers of preferment rather than subscribe again), and that of William Robertson of Rathvilly (who had resigned from the Church in 1764). He concluded by repudiating the remarks about the Church made at their ordinations by Philip Taylor and Robert Gore.

There was a particular irony in this confrontation, since both Priestley and Dawson had as their original target Thomas Balguy, Archdeacon of Winchester and one of the severest critics of the Feathers Tavern petitioners. The irony was compounded by the fact that Balguy had been educated in latitudinarian circles and that his father John Balguy (1686–1748), a prebendary of Salisbury, had been a protégé of Benjamin Hoadly. In January 1773 Dawson published *A Letter to the Clergy of the Archdeaconry of Winchester*, which was an attempt to refute Balguy's allegations that the clerical petition against subscription, if granted, would allow heretics and sectaries into the church and threaten the civil as well as the religious establishment. In this work he could not resist a further blow at Priestley when he invited Balguy to decline Priestley's backhanded compliment to him

[29] Rutt, XXII, 467.   [30] Rutt, XXII, 467–8.

to the effect that he had given priority to his good sense over his sincerity when subscribing the Thirty-Nine Articles.

Dawson, however, faced a serious intellectual problem in seeking to counter Balguy's anxieties. While advocating the Feathers Tavern petition and other moves for liturgical reform, he and other latitudinarian clergy had to defend themselves against the accusation—levelled by Balguy and many others—that they were trying to destroy the Church from within. It was an accusation all the more difficult to ignore at a time when disaffection in America, Wilkite agitation (sometimes blasphemous) in Britain, and anti-clerical moves in the House of Commons had revived Anglican fears of internal and external danger. Hence latitudinarians were obliged to emphasize their loyalty, both doctrinally and institutionally, to the state Church. But in so doing, of course, they could not but distance themselves from the essentially voluntarist dissenting ethos so clearly articulated by Priestley. For Dawson was in effect expounding a variant on the Anglican *via media* when he claimed that

The Magistrate in this free land knows a much more effectual method than this [i.e. subscription] of supporting his *Civil authority* against every invasion of it, (happily for all sides) whether from the folly and madness of a *Sectary*, or from the ambition and insolence of a Churchman.[31]

The abolition of subscription to the articles would enhance, not undermine, the authority of the magistrate, which would be all the more respected if it were 'uniformly exerted in protecting his subjects, as well in their *religious*, as in their *civil* rights'.[32] Dawson summarized his response to Balguy's allegations by insisting:

It is therefore most evidently the *improvement*, not the *destruction*, the *reformation*, not the *abolishment* of our present establishment, which is aimed at by the Petitioners. And proposals of this nature have ever been considered by men not more distinguished by their stations in the church, than by their learning, moderation, and withal their attachment to our constitution both in Church and state, not only as harmless, but as worthy of encouragement.[33]

[31] Benjamin Dawson, *Letter to the Clergy of the Archdeaconry of Winchester* (London, 1773), 37.
[32] Dawson, *Letter to the Clergy*, 37.   [33] Ibid. 10.

Dawson upheld the consistency of reason and Scripture and suggested that a general declaration of belief in the Scriptures (as
embodied in the Dissenters' Relief Act of 1779 and reluctantly
accepted by them) would be far preferable to subscription to human
formularies. But in so doing, he went a considerable distance towards
a positive embrace, rather than a tacit acceptance, of the authority of
the state in matters of religion:

We may hope to appear, in future, to have acted with peculiar propriety
and consistency, when we submitted our cause to Parliament, and be considered in that application, not as dissatisfied with the authority claimed
by the Magistrate, but, on the contrary, as fully satisfied therewith, and
therefore suing to the legislative body for an interposition of that authority
to redress a religious grievance, which continues not without a manifest
inconsistence with *his own* establishment, and derogation from *his own*
judgment.[34]

Herein lay the real heart of the controversy. Dawson might criti-
cize the manner in which magisterial authority was currently used,
but he accepted its existence in principle. Priestley on the other
hand denied its very legitimacy. Dawson's arguments accorded a
higher priority to the promotion of unity within the Church as
currently constituted than to a revived scheme of comprehension.
While Priestley's initial target in his *Letter of Advice* had been those
dissenting ministers who conformed to the established Church, his
fiercest fire was reserved for the principle of a state church and
the state imposition of doctrinal formularies. Such indeed were his
suspicion of parliamentary authority in the religious sphere and his
reluctance to confer indirect legitimacy upon it by seeking favours
from it that he was not one of the earliest campaigners on behalf
of the dissenters when they followed the example of the Feathers
Taverners and launched their own petition for reform of the subscription laws.[35] Between Priestley and Dawson there was undoubtedly an element of personal dislike. But their controversy had far
deeper roots and involved very much more than a clash of persona-
lities.

---

[34] Dawson, *Letter to the Clergy*, 48.
[35] Priestley, *Letter of Advice*, Rutt, XXII, 441, where Priestley described himself as
'a silent but not an uninterested spectator'.

THE IMPORTANCE OF THE SUBSCRIPTION
ISSUE, 1772–4

The problems inherent in the relations between latitudinarianism and dissent may be detected in a private but very sharp disagreement between Priestley and Theophilus Lindsey, which arose at the very beginning of the subscription campaign early in 1772 and smouldered for two further years. Although when writing to Lindsey in March 1772 Priestley expressed support for the aims of the clerical petitioners, he added that it was absurd and futile for Anglican clergymen to appeal to Parliament:

You must permit us Dissenters... however, who are not used to the idea even of *spiritual superiors*, to smile at your scheme as an application to the *powers of this world* for a reformation in the business of religion. As the disciple of a master whose kingdom is not of this world, I should be ashamed to ask any thing of temporal powers, except more peace and quietness, which being temporal blessings, they may bestow; but I should be sorry to make any application to them, which should imply an acknowledgement of their having *other* kind of power. The more I think of an application to such a house of Commons, or such a parliament as ours, on the subject of religion, the more does the absurdity of it strike me. But I shall say no more on this subject, lest I should offend you. I really did not mean to say so much.[36]

At that point, in the spring of 1772, it was far from certain that Lindsey, John Jebb, the Cambridge don and strong critic of the system of clerical subscription, or, indeed, anyone else would actually resign from the Church over this question. It was not until two years later, and only when Lindsey's resignation of the vicarage of Catterick was an accomplished fact, that Priestley published his *Letter to a Layman, on the Subject of the Rev. Mr Lindsey's Proposal for a Reformed English Church upon the Plan of the Late Dr Samuel Clarke*. In this work he praised Lindsey's aspirations for a broader liturgical basis for the Church, and also commended Lindsey's *Apology*. But he had a powerful polemical motive for doing so; he could then cite Lindsey's failure to achieve an internal reformation of the Church of England

---

[36] Priestley to Lindsey, 2 Mar. 1772; Rutt, I i, 160.

as firm evidence of its incorrigible corruption, and as a further reason to oppose any form of state establishment in religion. When Lindsey wrote to the dissenting minister William Turner (1714–94) of Wakefield, 'D^r. Priestley is indeed a warm and true friend to me, and to the cause of God's truth which he has most earnestly at heart. He has signified to me his kind efforts in my behalf and their success', he referred not to the Feathers Tavern petition but to his decision to set up an independent Unitarian chapel at Essex Street in London.[37]

Behind these exchanges lay three distinct sources of strain in the affinity between latitudinarianism and dissent. In the first place, Priestley detected in the conformity of Benjamin Dawson the dangerously seductive attractions of the Church of England, attractions gilded by the prospects of upward social mobility, favourable marriage alliances, and career advancement. There was nothing new, of course, in dissenting anxiety about the decay of their interest, a cause of concern to the generation of Philip Doddridge as well as to that of Priestley.[38] In the 1770s, however, it was exacerbated by the realization not only of the fall in dissenting numbers in the middle years of the eighteenth century, but by the divisive effects of evangelical Calvinism. One result of this development was a serious split among the General Baptist body in 1770, with the secession from it of a substantial number of adherents under the leadership of the former Wesleyan preacher Dan Taylor.[39] Priestley himself on several occasions expressed pessimism over the state of rational dissent, while Richard Price was to complain in 1778, 'The truth is . . . that the Dissenting interest, particularly in and about London, is declining very fast.'[40] The more closely that latitudinarianism compromised with, and accommodated itself to, the establishment, the more isolated would rational dissent become. It would be dangerously positioned between a more comprehensive and authoritarian Church on the one

[37] DWL MS 12.44, (11), Lindsey to William Turner of Wakefield, 5 Jan. 1774.
[38] See in particular Doddridge's *Free Thoughts on the Most Probable Means of Reviving the Dissenting Interest* (London, 1730).
[39] See Raymond Brown, *The English Baptists of the Eighteenth Century* (Didcot: Baptist Historical Society, 1986), pp. 67–70.
[40] *The Correspondence of Richard Price*, ed. D. O. Thomas and Bernard Peach, 3 vols (Durham, NC: Duke University Press and Cardiff: University of Wales Press, 1983–94), II, 33.

hand, and an evangelically revived orthodox dissent with an increasingly conservative theological agenda, on the other.[41]

Secondly, latitudinarians and dissenters shared, to some extent, the anxiety that the early years of George III's reign had been accompanied by a more 'authoritarian' tone in secular and spiritual affairs—the familiar Whig myth. Immediately before the re-emergence of the subscription issue, Priestley and the Independent minister Philip Furneaux (1726–83) of Clapham had been involved in a dispute with William Blackstone. They had felt it necessary to devote considerable energy to resisting the great jurist's efforts to limit the libertarian implications for dissent of Lord Mansfield's celebrated judgement—that nonconformity was not a crime at law—in the Evans case of 1767.[42] Yet it seemed that many clergymen from Cambridge Whig or from latitudinarian backgrounds either rallied to the Court—Thomas Balguy, Archdeacon of Winchester, and Richard Hurd (1720–1808), Archdeacon of Gloucester, and from 1775 Bishop of Coventry and Lichfield, being obvious examples—or confined their expressions of unease to carefully coded forms, as exemplified by Jonathan Shipley's 1770 sermon before the House of Lords.[43] To many dissenters, the final proof was provided by the very limited clerical support for the Feathers Tavern petition. Lindsey's letters repeatedly record his discouragement when canvassing for signatures. His scorn for the reluctance of Peter Peckard, of Madgalene College, Cambridge, to sign, encapsulates this attitude: 'I fear Peckard does not speak home, because he seeks Preferment and would not petition with us.'[44]

---

[41]   This was something which Lindsey recognized; 'For these rational Dissenters as they are called are manifestly crumbling away every day, and they and their families sliding back into the Trinitarian worship of the Ch. of E'; JRUL: Lindsey Letters, vol. I, no. 34: Lindsey to William Tayleur, 29 Nov. 1780.

[42]   For the background to this controversy, see Richard Burgess Barlow, *Citizenship and Conscience: A Study in the Theory and Practice of Religious Toleration in England During the Eighteenth Century* (Philadelphia: University of Pennsylvania Press, 1962), 160–70.

[43]   Jonathan Shipley, *A Sermon [on Isaiah xxxiii. 6] preached before the House of Lords...January 30, 1770* (London, 1770).

[44]   DWL MS 12.44 (6), Lindsey to Turner, 2 June 1772. On 23 June 1772 Lindsey added 'I have not seen Peckard's sermon; but I am told it is but a trimming one' (DWL, MS 12.44 (7)). See John Walsh, 'Peter Peckard: Liberal Churchman', in John Walsh and Ronald Hyam, *Peter Peckard: Liberal Churchman and Anti-Slave Campaigner*,

Thirdly, as Martin Fitzpatrick has demonstrated, Priestley was already well on the way towards the development of his theory of 'universal toleration'.[45] By contrast, there remained within the mentality of many latitudinarians a deep suspicion of Catholicism. Archdeacon Francis Blackburne in particular, abetted by the wealthy dissenting bibliophile and propagandist Thomas Hollis, believed that Catholic numbers were increasing and that they posed an internal and external threat. In 1767 the bishops even commissioned a survey into the extent of those numbers.[46] A key reason for Blackburne's bitter opposition to Lindsey's secession from the Church was his conviction that Protestant unity was all the more necessary at such a time. In his will he bequeathed just £10 to Lindsey's wife, his own stepdaughter (although later, in a codicil, he increased the bequest to £20).[47] To Blackburne and others, the Catholic Church was incapable of change and would always be inseparably linked to persecution. Even the suppression of the Jesuit order by Clement XIV in 1773 did nothing to lessen this sentiment; the death of that Pope in 1774 was widely interpreted as the result of poisoning by the Jesuits. To Priestley, Protestant unity on the basis of such a level of intolerance was a contradiction in terms. As he wrote to Lindsey on 18 December 1769: 'You smile at my *nostrum*, as you call my sentiments concerning the poor papists, and I smile at your panic concerning them. I hope that we shall continue to think for ourselves, to smile at and bear with one another. We see things in very different lights.'[48] Lindsey, indeed, was relatively slow to follow Priestley in the direction of 'universal toleration'. In his *Farewell Address* on resigning the vicarage of Catterick in 1773, he had admonished his parishioners about papists, *'against whose seducing arts I beg you to be continually upon your guard'*, and of whom a considerable number are recorded as resident in

---

Magdalene College Occasional Paper, no. 16 (Magdalene College, Cambridge, 1998), 1–14. See also Young, *Religion and Enlightenment*, 59–62.

[45] Martin Fitzpatrick, 'Joseph Priestley and Universal Toleration,' *P-PN*, 1 (1977).

[46] See Colin Haydon, *Anti-Catholicism in Eighteenth-Century England c. 1714–80: A Political and Social Study* (Manchester: Manchester University Press, 1993), 191ff.

[47] G. M. Ditchfield, 'Testaments of Faith: A Comment on some Unitarian Wills in the Age of Theophilus Lindsey', *TUHS*, 22, no. 2 (2000), 133.

[48] Priestley to Lindsey, 18 Dec. 1769; Rutt, I i, 104–5.

the region of Catterick.[49] Not until the Gordon Riots of June 1780 helped to convince him that English Unitarians and Catholics shared a common victimhood did Lindsey come to share Priestley's view.[50] Benjamin Dawson, too, evinced a Blackburne-like degree of paranoia over Catholicism. His *Letter to the Clergy of the Archdeaconry of Winchester* complained that 'the maxims of the *Romish* church begin to be disseminated *openly* among his Majesty's subjects' and that 'Popery', and not the petitioning clergy, was the Church of England's real enemy. He arraigned Balguy for espousing 'Popish' principles of authoritarianism and insisted that 'the argument cannot conclude in favour of a requisition to subscribe the 39 Articles, or any other *unscriptural* formulary of religion, without bringing us ... *directly to Popery*'.[51] Latitudinarian anxieties were heightened by the Quebec Act of 1774, hastily passed into law at the very end of the parliamentary session. Many of those who took a particularly rigorously 'Protestant' view of the Church of England, such as Shute Barrington—one of the few bishops nominated during the ministry of the latitudinarian (and subsequently Unitarian) Duke of Grafton—persisted with that attitude and applauded the fall of the Papacy in 1799. There were, of course, dissenters as well as latitudinarians who detected the spirit of 'Popery' within the Church of England. But to Priestley and his fellow rational dissenters such an attitude was at variance with Enlightenment notions of the free circulation of opinions and the belief in the ultimate triumph of truth in a free market of intellectual enquiry.

These considerations of principle help to explain why there were significant differences between the Feathers Tavern petitioners and the campaign of the General Body of Dissenting Ministers. Partly for tactical reasons the dissenters emphasized the differences between their petition and that of the clerical reformers. Dissenters, they and their parliamentary advocates argued, were not part of a state church and did not enjoy its emoluments; hence they could

[49] Theophilus Lindsey, *A Farewel Address to the Parishioners of Catterick* (London, 1773), 5.

[50] G. M. Ditchfield, ' "Incompatible with the very name of Christian": English Catholics and Unitarians in the Age of John Milner', *Recusant History*, 25 (2000), 52–73.

[51] Dawson, *Letter to Clergy of the Archdeaconry of Winchester*, 4–5, 43.

not and should not be subjected to its doctrinal articles. Dissenting denominations were free to impose or not to impose their own doctrinal tests if they saw fit. The Church of England was a state Church, with all the privileges and advantages that established status conferred; a measure of parliamentary superintendence could thus logically be justified. Hence the dissenters' petitions repeatedly won majorities in the House of Commons, while the Feathers Tavern petition was twice defeated there, on the second occasion (in May 1774) without even a division.

To Lindsey, this implicit endorsement of so erastian a view of church–state relations was a cause of dismay. On 12 April 1772 he wrote to complain to the dissenter William Turner of Westgate chapel, Wakefield that a widening of the difference between the objectives of the two campaigns could only harm them both:

I do not know whether you have seen the *printed Case* of the Dissenters, as given to the Members on this occasion. A friend sent it to me, and remarked that Reason xii seemd rather to[o] *invidiously* he says, I woud say, *heedlessly* given on this occasion. It is this—'Because the reasons for which Subscription is deemed necessary under an establishment [*sic*], do not extend to the case of a Toleration'.

[It seems] *your* Advocates in the house, almost all [en]larged upon the difference between the two [petitions, yours] and our's. But this coud be only owing to their ignorance, and political notions of religion. If they believe the SS. [i.e. the Scriptures] to be of divine authority, and pay any regard to the natural rights of conscience, they must relieve all Subjects equally from such a yoke.[52]

The implication was that dissenters were prepared to accept, tacitly, the principle of subscription for the Anglican clergy. Priestley, indeed, told Lindsey privately that he thought this twelfth reason of the dissenters' case to be 'very proper'.[53] What else, he might have asked, could one expect of a state Church? To him, it was a delusion, a contradiction in terms, to expect serious liberalization from within the established Church, especially one dominated by what he famously derided as 'the old building of error and superstition', beneath which

[52] DWL MS 12.44 (5), Lindsey to Turner, 12 April 1772.
[53] Priestley to Lindsey, April 1772; Rutt, I i, 169.

he claimed, in a metaphorical sense, to be 'laying gunpowder, grain by grain'.[54]

This greatly increased Lindsey's concern about Priestley's attacks upon Dawson. He thought that Priestley was unjust to the Feathers Tavern petitioners and that his contribution was unhelpful. Instead, he yearned for the prolongation of the alliance between latitudinarianism and dissent:

I have mentiond to him [Priestley] ... a report that had given me much concern, vizt. that he was going to attack D^r. B. Dawson in form, and thro' him our Petition and the Petitioners. I could not be easy, however, so confidently was it asserted, with^t. making him acquainted with it. We have surely one comon cause. We are brethren, and sh^d. not quarrel by the way. And tho' others are irritable, and cannot stifle resentment, I think D^r. Priestley has too much christian spirit and benevolence to enter into a personal controversy at any time, much less into such a controversy at this time.[55]

In reply to a (regrettably lost) letter of protest from Lindsey, Priestley replied:

I am truly sorry that I made the observation in my last on your application to parliament, in which I am really much interested, and in the success of which I shall most sincerely rejoice. I cannot help thinking, however, that an application to temporal powers to remove religious grievances is a very different thing in those who continue in a state of voluntary subjection to them, and in those who never owned their authority. In the former case a request to make any alteration seems to be a recognition of a power either to make it or not to make it; whereas in the latter case, it is only desiring a person to recede from a claim, which never has been, and never will be acknowledged. It is possible, however, that you and I may differ in several of our ideas on this subject ... I should be very sorry if this inadvertence should have displeased you.

But he was nonetheless unrepentant:

I cannot help smiling at the anxiety you express about my apprehended controversy with Dr Dawson, not being able to imagine how it could be of any disservice to you as petitioning clergy ... this is the man, though living in contradiction to every principle of the Confessional, is considered by the

---

[54] Joseph Priestley, *The Importance and Extent of Free Enquiry in Matters of Religion* (Birmingham, 1785), 40–1.

[55] LPN, MS 59 (c), Lindsey to William Turner, 24 Apr. 1772.

author of it as his best supporter in the controversy. Were I the author of that work, I should think myself under a necessity of disclaiming all connection with him. It was certainly petulant and foolish in him to attack me as he has done. His brother Obadiah, who is one of my hearers, said to me upon the occasion, 'I do not know what my brother meant by attacking you, but I know he hates the Dissenters'. I am afraid his case is that of one who hates the light because his deeds are evil.[56]

Lindsey was far from mollified. Although he confided that 'Dr Priestley is incapable of writing any thing to disparage us or our cause',[57] he awaited with anxiety the publication of his friend's *Letter of Advice to those Dissenters who Conduct the Application to Parliament for Relief from Certain Penal Laws.* In August 1773 he wrote to William Turner in Wakefield:

These are matters I have heard bandied about in my late travels; and greater will be the outcries of some people when D^r P's intended work[58] appears— in which he proposes to makes [*sic*] reprisals on one *of us* who had indeed wantonly attacked him. I prevented this retaliation being earlier made and thought the thing w^d have been put up with: But the Doctor must judge what is properest for himself to do. I rec^d. a few lines from him at the time you did, with some intimations of the same kind.[59]

Two months later, he added:

He [Priestley] has sent me his pamphlet already printed, but which he thinks to alter, and desired my free sentiments upon it. And I have told him, what indeed appears to me, that *the Letter of advice* will certainly disserve the Dissenting clergy in the object of their present application to Parliament by alarming men's minds.[60]

He referred several times to Priestley's disputation with Dawson, complaining to John Jebb in March 1773 that 'Such little petulancies may as well be spared'.[61] He claimed, indeed, to have acted as

---

[56] Priestley to Lindsey, 'about April 1772'; Rutt, I i, 167–8.
[57] Lindsey to John Jebb, 2 Mar. 1773; Rutt, I i, 235, n. †.
[58] This work was Priestley's *Letter of Advice to those Dissenters who Conduct the Application to Parliament for Relief from Certain Penal Laws, with Various Observations Relating to Similar Subjects* (London, 1773).
[59] LPN MS 59 (g), Lindsey to Turner, 10 Aug. 1773.
[60] DWL MS 12.44 (9), Lindsey to Turner, Oct. 1773.
[61] Lindsey to Jebb, 2 Mar. 1773; Rutt, I i, 235, n. †.

a restraining influence upon his friend. But what was to become a close intellectual collegiality between them was greatly facilitated by Lindsey's departure from the Church and his formal and open, as distinct from unofficial, assumption of the mantle of rational dissent. As I have suggested elsewhere, it was Priestley, more than any other individual, who eased Lindsey's own journey into dissent.[62] Dawson, by contrast, was accused in a pseudonymous letter to the press of excluding dissenters from open endorsement of the Feathers Tavern petition; 'That gentleman will not permit a Dissenter's name to appear in his list: he fears to alarm the King and his friends'.[63]

CONCLUSION: LATITUDINARIANISM AND DISSENT AT THE END OF THE 1770s

Where, then, did the outcome of the subscription controversy leave the affinity between latitudinarianism and dissent? In 1779, dissenting ministers and schoolmasters did obtain a measure of relief, but for latitudinarian clergymen there was only one escape from the stark choice between subscription or secession. That was the route taken by Francis Blackburne and others of the older generation, who declined further subscription to the Thirty-Nine Articles. This, as Martin Fitzpatrick has shown,[64] was a position that was wide open to the charge of intellectual dishonesty, at a time when Enlightenment values and incipient Romanticism in unlikely combination were serving to discredit such prevarication and to elevate the discovery and expression of the authentic self. We know that in the event very few clergymen seceded from the Church in response to this dilemma—far fewer, for instance, than the number of evangelical clergymen who departed from the Church of England in the first half of the nineteenth century. Those few who did secede did so in peculiar individual circumstances, often as a last resort, and generalization from such cases is difficult

---

[62] See G. M. Ditchfield, 'The Preceptor of Nations: Joseph Priestley and Theophilus Lindsey', *TUHS*, 23, no. 2 (2004), 495–512.

[63] Letter of 'A.B.', dated 'Chelmsford, Oct. 5', *General Evening Post*, 17–19 Oct. 1771.

[64] Fitzpatrick, 'Latitudinarianism', 223–7.

and of little value. The dreaded labels of 'schism' and 'schismatic' still carried much odium.

Critics of Trinitarian orthodoxy who remained within the Church—such as Peter Peckard, who in 1794 became Dean of Peterborough, John Conant, rector of Hastingleigh in Kent, John Hey, Norrisian Professor of Divinity at Cambridge, or even Bishop Richard Watson—were unmolested, if rarely preferred. But there was a deep and widening gulf between those bred as churchmen who above all feared being cut adrift, and dissenters, who could pursue popular, often unlettered evangelical Calvinism at one extreme, and—in Priestley's case—intellectual speculation embracing Socinianism at the other. Blackburne's letters to Lindsey from the 1750s and early 1760s, more than 100 of which are preserved in Dr Williams's Library, help to explain why so few clergymen of his inclination resigned. One of the few was another of Blackburne's sons-in-law, John Disney, who joined Lindsey as co-minister of Essex Street chapel in 1782. Lindsey sadly noted that Blackburne thought 'that the original sin lies with me in drawing his son-in-law out of the church'.[65] Blackburne's reasons for holding so implacable a view were twofold. Outside the Church he detected only religious anarchy:

I have seen so much to dislike in all our religious Associations, that I own I never could think of joyning with any of them. There is such a cursed tendency in them all to the vortex of an Establishment that I think it better rather to be actually *in* a bad one, than in that intermediate state which has most of the Evils of the worst and none of the Advantages of any.[66]

Some latitudinarians, indeed, such as Edmund Law and William Paley, would not even sign the Feathers Tavern petition. But the fear of being cut adrift was doctrinal as well as institutional. Socinianism, quite apart from its uncertain legal status, was widely perceived to be subversive of the moral as well as the ecclesiastical order. Blackburne became convinced that fully fledged Socinianism was a theological step too far; its open profession gave dangerous ammunition to enemies of the Church. During his last years he penned the vehement tract *An Answer to the Question, Why are You not a Socinian?* It was

---

[65] Lindsey to Joshua Toulmin, 28 Nov. 1782; Thomas Belsham, *Memoirs of the Late Reverend Theophilus Lindsey* (London: Centenary edn., 1873), 100.

[66] DWL MS 12.52 (32), Blackburne to Lindsey, 14 Feb. 1757.

not published in his lifetime and only appeared in the edition of his collected works in 1804.[67] Nor was Blackburne the only supporter of the Feathers Tavern petition who strongly disapproved of Lindsey's secession; others, too, held that his departure weakened the latitudinarian cause.[68] In doing so, Lindsey probably also played some part in weakening the Church's fundamental Protestant credentials, thus making a reunion with dissent even more unlikely in the longer term.

Priestley's central objections to a state church made him particularly critical of those who questioned its articles, but remained within it—especially after Lindsey's resignation. He believed that there were many of them: he noted in 1782 'Were all the speculative Unitarians in the church of England to become serious christians, and consequently think it their duty to leave it, the desertion would be very conspicuous and alarming'.[69] To him an established Church could never be anything but an established Church—it would remain objectionable in principle, incapable of fundamental reform without destroying itself and always prone to the abuse of authority. He contrasted the close association between dissenting ministers and their congregations, which, in an ideal world, would freely have chosen them, with the undemocratic nominations to church livings of the established clergy. 'The people belonging to the established church', he wrote, 'are like the *vassals* of the Polish nobility, or the mere *live stock* of a farm, delivered over, as *parcel of the estate*, to every successive incumbent'.[70]

Priestley never forgot that he was the heir to the dissenting tradition and to the voluntary principle and opposition to a state religion which were fundamental to its teaching. A particularly effective expression, though one that remains rather underestimated, of that tradition in the mid-eighteenth century was Micajah Towgood's *A Dissent from the Church of England Fully Justified*, which was first published in 1753 as the distillation of his earlier thoughts and which

---

[67] See *The Works, Theological and Miscellaneous...of Francis Blackburne* (7 vols, Cambridge, 1804), I, pp. cxx–cxxvi.

[68] A point made by Rivers, II, 350.

[69] Joseph Priestley, *The Proper Constitution of a Christian Church, Considered in a Sermon Preached at the New Meeting in Birmingham, November 3, 1782* (Birmingham, 1782), p. ix.

[70] Priestley, *Considerations on Church-Authority*, 61.

reached an eleventh edition in 1809.[71] Of those dissenters who followed Towgood's line of argument, one of the most persuasive was Thomas Mole, a predecessor of Richard Price as minister to the Gravel Pit Meeting, Hackney. In *The Case of a Dissent and Separation from a Civil Establishment of the Christian Religion Fairly Stated* he asserted:

A Dissenter is a character in perfect consistence with the divine establishment of the Christian religion, to which we are sincere and intire conformists, and stands in opposition to that of *assenters* and *consenters* in a civil establishment, who are *nonconformists* to the word of God.[72]

Priestley regarded apostasy from that tradition, such as that committed by Benjamin Dawson, with the same intense disapproval as that which Blackburne reserved for seceders from the established Church. This was one reason why his controversy with Samuel Badcock (1747–88) during the 1780s was tinged with a particular measure of acidity: Badcock was not only a dissenting minister who conformed to the Church but, in his earlier capacity, had contributed to Priestley's *Theological Repository*. He lamented in 1784,

At one time no man was more attached to me than Mr. Badcock. He took a journey of 100 miles to see me. But finding it necessary, (in order to make his peace with his orthodox friends,) he renounced all correspondence with me and other heretics.[73]

It was not Priestley nor Dawson, but Lindsey, together with his fellow seceders from the Church of England such as John Disney, Edward Harries, John Hammond, William Frend, and (a little later) Francis Stone, who straddled the divide between latitudinarianism and dissent.[74] Even in 1780, after six years as a Unitarian minister in London, Lindsey could admit that he still had, as he put it, something

---

[71] Moreover Towgood was one of the first authors to use the term 'Rational Dissenters' in a manner that would have been recognizable to Priestley; see his *A Dissent from the Church of England Fully Justified* (London, 1753), 294. Towgood (1700–92) was minister of James's meeting (from 1760 George's meeting), Exeter, from 1750–82.

[72] Thomas Mole, *The Case of a Dissent and Separation from a Civil Establishment of the Christian Religion fairly stated* (London, 1772), 158.

[73] Priestley to Caleb Rotheram, 28 February 1784; Rutt, I i, 374. See also *Gentleman's Magazine*, LVIII, ii (1788), 868–70 and 781–3. Badcock had served as a dissenting minister at Barnstaple but was best known as a contributor to the *Monthly Review*.

[74] See G. M. Ditchfield, 'Feathers Tavern petitioners'.

of 'the habits of a Churchman upon me'.[75] He retained a lifelong commitment to liturgical worship (with a reformed liturgy, drawn of course from the impeccably latitudinarian Samuel Clarke)[76] and never adopted the extempore approach preferred by dissenters. He continued to retain close links with non-resigning Anglican clergy such as Edmund Law, Christopher Wyvill, William Frend (until his deprivation from his college fellowship), and Robert Edward Garnham in Cambridge. Perhaps there was even a hint of affectation when in October 1774 he wrote of himself and William Turner of Wakefield as 'us dissenters'.[77]

But it was Priestley, not Lindsey, who most clearly—even brutally—revealed the complexity of the affinity between latitudinarianism and dissent and its ultimate fracture. As a controversialist, Priestley's primary commitment was to candour, courteously conducted, but unyielding in principle. He would never be, in Thomas Mole's words, 'a nonconformist to the word of God'. Integrity was more important than the 'politeness' which sections of the English elite made into something of a cult in the eighteenth century. Towards the end of Priestley's life, latitudinarianism was frightened by the French Revolution to the extent of receding from its previous radicalism. There were few episcopal successors to latitudinarian bishops such as Jonathan Shipley, Edmund Law, John Hinchliffe, and Richard Watson. Henry Bathurst of Norwich is a distinctly rare exception (and even he secured no further translation). The ramifications of Priestley's controversy with Benjamin Dawson lend more support to Martin Fitzpatrick's somewhat pessimistic diagnosis of the dilemmas of latitudinarianism than to John Gascoigne's rather more cheerful assessment of its condition in the later eighteenth century.

There remained areas of intellectual common ground between nineteenth-century Broad Churchmen and English Unitarians. Their affinities were evident, for example, in the spheres of higher criticism,

[75] JRUL, Lindsey Letters, vol. I, no. 34, Lindsey to William Tayleur, 29 Nov. 1780.
[76] [Theophilus Lindsey] *The Book of Common Prayer Reformed, According to the Plan of the Late Dr Samuel Clarke* (London, 1774, with further editions in 1774 and 1785). Samuel Clarke's copy of the *Book of Common Prayer*, interleaved with and Clarke's additions and alterations, may be found in the British Library, C.24.b.21. It was originally presented to the British Museum in 1768; see J. P. Ferguson, *Dr Samuel Clarke. An Eighteenth-Century Heretic* (Kineton: The Roundwood Press, 1976), 224.
[77] DWL MS 12.44 (20).

biblical inspiration and miracles, and liturgical practice.[78] Similarly, there were theological sympathies between the Whiggishly inclined Noetics of Oriel College and the leading lights of liberal dissent. But the furore surrounding the decision in 1838 of Edward Maltby (1770–1859), Bishop of Durham, to subscribe to a book of sermons published by the Unitarian William Turner (1761–1859) of Newcastle upon Tyne emphasized the gulf which existed between that period and the mid-eighteenth century. Nine years later criticisms of the appointment of R. D. Hampden (1793–1868) as Bishop of Hereford were similarly revealing. The expansion of evangelical dissent, much of it determinedly Calvinist, together with the renewed perception of nonconformity as a threat in the post-1789 world, ended the older and more comfortable types of connection between Church and dissent. Priestley's role in this development was a central one, and an exposure of the difficulties and complexities in the relationship between latitudinarianism and dissent may be regarded as one of his legacies.

Even at the height of their disagreement in 1772, Lindsey could write of Priestley, 'Whatever others do, our Friend does not put his candle under a bushel, but boldly and honestly holds it up, *in his own hand*, to give light to others as well as himself'.[79] The light of Priestley's illumination was sometimes harsh. But one crucial feature of the ecclesiastical landscape upon which it fell has been the theme of this chapter.

---

[78] See Dennis G. Wigmore-Beddoes, *Yesterday's Radicals. A Study in the Affinity Between Unitarianism and Broad Church Anglicanism in the Nineteenth Century* (Cambridge and London: J. Clarke, 1971).

[79] LPN MS 59 (c), Lindsey to Turner, 24 Apr. 1772.

6

Historical Perspectives in the Mind
of Joseph Priestley

Alison Kennedy

INTRODUCTION

Joseph Priestley's insight as a historian of the secular world was keen, practical and incisive, and it produced some interesting perspectives on the understanding and interpretation of the past. It was his theology, however, and his desire to prove historically the tenets of his own Unitarian beliefs that were of prime importance in his intellectual life. Essentially, then, there were two very different historians working in that area of Priestley's mind which was concerned with the investigation of the events and circumstances of past ages. Priestley the historian operated from several important perspectives related to his method which were of great interest, but which marked him essentially as a thinker of the Enlightenment. However, the question of perspective also came into play at a much more fundamental level in his historical approach to theological issues. In this he took on the mantle of the theologian as historian and became a writer absorbed in the historical Biblical criticism he employed to support his radical theological opinions. It is from his role as a historian of the Scriptures that he left behind a scholarly legacy which identifies him as an important link between the radical Enlightenment of rational dissent and the more 'Romantic' historical consciousness of the nineteenth century.

It ought to be remembered, however, that any discussion of the terms 'Enlightenment' and 'Romantic' in relation to the characteristics of any concept is problematic. The relationship between the English Enlightenment and the Romantic period was not easily delineated and the two sets of ideas were often in a state of transition which has never been resolved effectively. Despite this, however, it was usually imagined that the two philosophical periods represented two different frames of mind. The Enlightenment in England tended to be mechanistic, empiricist, and atomistic. It glorified reason and the universality of human nature. Contrastingly, Romantics believed in the reality and diversity of human experience rather than the uniformity of universal abstractions, and in the spirituality of nature and the feelings of the heart rather than dry rationalism. In addition, the essence of the Romantic perspective on human historical forms was organic rather than mechanistic.

These ideas filtered into different approaches to history, which in the Enlightenment mind emphasized the common factors in human experience. Contrastingly, Romantic thinkers appreciated the concrete rather than the abstract and the idea that the diversity of cultures was moulded by history alone. Whatever arose in history was *per se* valuable.[1]

Early works gave little thought to the idea that neither philosophical movement was completely homogeneous. As John B. Halsted pointed out, ideas seldom move as systems.[2] Halsted wrote that in the relationship between Enlightenment and Romantic thought there was a transference and use of old doctrines in new contexts, and that this realization should 'force us to keep in mind how slow and incomplete are revolutions in thought and how strongly the past persists'.[3]

---

[1] Georg C. Iggers, *The German Conception of History* (Middletown, CT: Wesleyan University Press, 1968), 5, 8. Iggers provides the definitive analysis of the historicist idea. For a view of Enlightenment writing, see the introduction by Duncan Forbes to David Hume, *The History of Great Britain* (Harmondsworth: Penguin, 1970), 14–18.

[2] John B. Halsted (ed.), *Romanticism* (London: Macmillan, 1969), 6–7.

[3] Halsted, *Romanticism*, 4. For older studies see Ernst Cassirer, *The Philosophy of the Enlightenment*, trans. F. C. A. Koelln and J. P. Pettegrove (Princeton, NJ: Princeton University Press, 1951), and Peter Gay, *The Enlightenment: An Interpretation*, 2 vols. (London: Weidenfeld & Nicolson, 1967–70). For studies which begin to employ more specific perspectives, see in particular Henry May, *The Enlightenment in America* (New York: OUP, 1976), and Roy Porter and Mikulas Teich (eds), *The Enlightenment in National Context* (Cambridge: CUP, 1981) and *Romanticism in National Context*

Priestley's role in all the complexity surrounding the Enlightenment-Romantic period of transition in ideas has never been assessed and his importance to the development of a new set of perspectives in historical understanding, both in secular and theological terms, has never been given the recognition it deserves. Priestley's historical work has always been sidelined in favour of his other talents, both by his own contemporaries and by modern writers. On 22 April 1804, two and a half months after Priestley's death, Joshua Toulmin, a founder of the Southern Unitarian Society, addressed a congregation at the New Meeting in Birmingham with a biographical tribute to the great polymath. Toulmin spoke in glowing terms of Priestley's fame in many fields, and of his 'great abilities and energy of mind'. He praised Priestley's numerous and impressive publications in 'belles-lettres, in natural and experimental philosophy, in metaphysics and in theology'. He told his attentive and respectful audience that, 'In the page of history...his name will live, with unsullied glory as an ornament to his country.'[4] This last comment was the only specific reference Toulmin made in his address that day to the subject of history—and it was with regard to Priestley *as* history rather than to Priestley as a *historian*.

Toulmin's failure to emphasize Priestley's powers in the analysis and understanding of the past is not particularly surprising. Both then and now the emphasis has tended to be upon Priestley's abilities in the many other areas of scholarship in which he was so well known. Secular history apart, it is also true that very little has been said about Priestley's historical Biblical criticism and, most importantly, its place in the development of historical understanding in the late eighteenth and early nineteenth centuries. In recent times, however, a most interesting analysis of Priestley's role of theologian as historian was made by Margaret Canovan, who rightly believed that he had been responsible for the evolution of a very sophisticated historical method which appears to have been absent from his secular historical thinking. In his treatment of these theological concerns Priestley exposed a more

(Cambridge: CUP, 1988). See also Martin Fitzpatrick, Peter Jones, Christa Knellwolf, Iain McCalman (eds), *The Enlightenment World* (London: Routledge, 2006).

[4] Joshua Toulmin, *A Biographical Tribute to the Memory of the Rev. Joseph Priestley* (Birmingham, 1804), 11, 25.

innovative side to his historical consciousness.[5] However, although her discussion revealed much of this side of Priestley's historical approach, Canovan never developed the idea in a wider sense.

A comprehensive, comparative analysis of Priestley's different perspectives as a historian is long overdue, and it is hoped to show that this persistent tendency to take insufficient note of the many and varied aspects of his keen historical insight is misguided. There are three parts to the following discussion. The first is concerned with Joseph Priestley the historian, the second with Priestley the theologian as historian and Biblical critic, and the third with the importance of his legacy in this latter respect. With regard to the second of these two subjects, a brief comparison is made between Priestley's approach to the relationship between religion and history and that of David Hume and Edward Gibbon, the two great historians of the eighteenth century. There are two works by Priestley which loom large in this analysis. The first is *Lectures on History and General Policy*, delivered at Warrington Academy in the late 1760s and revised and finally published in 1788, which deals with his secular approach to history. The second, *An History of the Corruptions of Christianity*, published six years earlier, in 1782, reveals a different approach to historical understanding, this time within a theological context.

JOSEPH PRIESTLEY, HISTORIAN

In very general terms, Priestley's approach to secular history is seen quite correctly as a full expression of his unbounded optimism about humankind's educational and moral progress. Like many other writers of the Enlightenment age he considered history to be educative in that it strengthened virtue and gave force and impetus towards the ethical perfection of mankind. In accordance with his belief in the consistency of Divine Providence, and his unshakeable conviction that all evil would be subsumed by good under its direction, he was certain that 'vices may be viewed as safely as virtues' for

[5] Margaret Canovan, 'The Irony of History: Priestley's Rational Theology', *P-PN*, 4 (1980), 16–25.

both equally 'teach virtue and good morals'. With his customary optimism, he added that history's account of the conduct of truly great men 'tends to inspire us with a taste for solid glory and real greatness'.[6]

However, not only did history assist moral improvement, it was also useful in that it was philosophy teaching by example. It instilled the capacity for good judgement and it eradicated prejudice. All improvements in the science of government were derived from history, and the histories of science itself, of commerce and of law would contribute inevitably towards the progress of mankind in these fields of human endeavour. History provided an 'anticipated knowledge of the world' which was a 'better guide to us, than any thing we would have learned from our own random experience'.[7] History for Priestley was an abundant crop of knowledge, example, and experience to be harvested eagerly in the quest for progress in the present and perfection in the future. In other words, the way in which we chose to make use of our appreciation and understanding of the past guided us towards the glories of the times that were destined to come.

It is in Priestley's *Lectures on History and General Policy* that we discover many of these bold and supremely confident sentiments founded upon a profound religious faith. It is here also that we discover him in his persona as the practical, rational historian whose approach and method reflected not only his own radical version of Enlightenment thought but also the general values of that age. Priestley's *Lectures* contain a wealth of practical historical wisdom and perceptive points on methodology, and indeed they represent a valuable guide to the study of history, one almost as relevant today as it was in the later decades of the eighteenth century. Contained within Priestley's work on secular history there were three important perspectives which grant the reader some insight into his historical vision and imagination and also show the care and attention he brought to his method. It may be useful to apply here a photographic analogy to illustrate the nature of Priestley's historical

[6] Joseph Priestley, *Lectures on History and General Policy*, ed. J. T. Rutt (London, 1840), 38. This volume contains the same text as in Rutt's edition of Priestley's works, published 1817–32, for which Rutt used the 1803 Philadelphia text of the *Lectures*.

[7] Priestley, *Lectures on History*, 29.

viewpoints. His clear identification and expert use of detailed historical sources give the reader a close-up view of some striking snapshots of the past, while his 'wide angle' perspective hovers high above the great sweeping landscape of history to its far horizons. Finally, the 'zoom lens' of the sharp Priestleyan historical eye moves in closer to investigate and record subjects which lend themselves to an approach which recognizes the place of the contextual within the whole. Priestley did not allow himself to remain at one fixed, specific vantage point from which he pursued his studies of the past, but instead moved closer or further away from his subject as the need arose.

On the question of the sources which he studied in close-up his historical sense was keen. He regarded oral traditions, for example, as an important storehouse of historical knowledge of ancient times before the development of the arts of writing, carving, and painting. His view was that in those unlettered ages every elderly person 'would be possessed of a little treasure of history', which would not only relate to his immediate family, but also to his own and neighbouring nations. Thus each person's individual perspective on the world, however limited, was of value, and such precious knowledge would pass inevitably to the next generation, for 'the natural talkativeness of old age, meeting with the natural inquisitiveness and curiosity of youth ... [was] favourable to the propagation of knowledge and instruction'.[8]

Most valuable also was the tradition, before the use of writing, of reciting important facts before an assembly of people and ensuring that what they heard was remembered. The North American Indian idea of representing each article of a complex treaty with a piece of wampum, and giving each to a separate listener to establish a coherent chain of memory, was cited as one example. The historical poems of the ancient European world constituted another accurate vehicle of knowledge. Their reliability as carriers of truth was derived from the very fact that they were poems and as such were less liable to alteration, for Priestley noted that 'a story reduced to any kind of metre would suffer little by repetition'.[9] Although he gave credit to Homer's *Iliad* for being to some extent founded upon facts, the whole concept of the classical myth itself suffered the sting of Priestley's

---

[8] Priestley, *Lectures on History*, 55, 56.   [9] Ibid. 61.

rational criticism. Later writers, such as the German classicist and philologist Christian Gottlob Heyne (1729–1812), who inspired Thomas Carlyle to write that Heyne 'carried the torch of philosophy towards, if not into, the mysteries of old time,[10] would tend to merge myth and history to a significant extent. Priestley, however, took a strictly reasoned approach to the problem of how to relate one to the other and rejected Greek myth as 'absurd'.[11] Although the content of myth was, in his view, irrational, the oral mechanisms which carried it down through the generations and diffused human memories, knowledge, and imagination he believed were entirely dependable.

In a similar category to knowledge gleaned from word of mouth he placed personal letters and diaries. Such sources were not, in his view, strictly historical, because they were not, like most other materials, contained in the writings of historians. They were nevertheless of great importance in that they reflected, often in an intimate and personal style, many interesting aspects and views of the time in question. Priestley cited as one fine example the letters of Cicero to his friends, and to Atticus in particular, although he acknowledged that the same could apply to letters written in any age. Cicero's letters were written with so much freedom that they contained a 'faithful history of the most active and critical period of his life,' and gave insight into how Cicero viewed the characters and events of his time.[12] This proved, Priestley suggested, that it was difficult for the historian to obtain a complete idea of things from historical books alone, and indeed much could be discovered from the writings of friend to friend.

Furthermore, in the absence of books, a great deal was to be learned from the inscriptions and pictorial representations found on monuments, coins, and medals. Like Joseph Addison's Philander,[13] Priestley was enthralled at the cultural mores and individual faces which gave life to ancient times. These images, carved in stone or etched

---

[10] Thomas Carlyle, 'Life of Heyne', in *Critical and Miscellaneous Essays, Works, The Ashburton Edition* (London, 1887), I, 314.

[11] Priestley, *Lectures on History*, 61.   [12] Ibid. 78.

[13] Joseph Addison, Dialogues upon the Usefulness of Ancient Medals (1721), in *The Miscellaneous Works of Joseph Addison*, ed. A. C. Guthkelch (London: G. Bell, 1914), II, 284.

in metal, had two functions. The first was to preserve tradition by representing national customs and commemorating historical events. The second, applying mainly to coins and medals, which Priestley described as a 'kind of portable monuments', was to 'give great light to history'. They carried the stark outlines of individual faces, they illustrated moments in civil and religious customs such as sacrifices and triumphs, they revealed the contours of ancient buildings, and they illustrated detailed and memorable images of aspects of the life of past ages. These tiny close-ups of ancient times were simple yet compelling, and historians were wrong to ignore them, for without these our vision of the life of the ancients would have been a great deal dimmer. Priestley recalled the point made by Addison, that 'without the help of coins...we should never have known which of the emperors was the first that ever wore a beard, or rode in stirrups'. Priestley was also quick to acknowledge, however, that there were serious limitations to the level of accuracy which was possible with regard to the images stamped upon ancient coinage. The historian could not, he argued, trust to coins for the characters of men for if he did 'Claudius would be as great a conqueror as Julius Caesar, and Domitian as good a man as Titus'.[14]

Roman coins did reveal, nevertheless, much about the taste of emperors. They brought to life the tyrant Nero with a fiddle, and revealed also, swathed in his lion's skin, the person of Commodus, that vicious and insane executioner who himself died violently in AD 192. It is through passages such as these which try to describe the images of ancient times that there shines a vivid historical imagination, and it is arguable that had he not excelled as a scientist, theologian, and philosopher Priestley would most certainly have made his mark as a historian alone. However, it is also arguable that Priestley's treatment of such sources—the treasured memories of an elderly person, the affectionate letters between friends, the elusive shred of fact within the myth, and lastly the haunting faces etched upon Priestley's coins and medals—produced little more than snapshots of the past. His approach to the historical circumstances and the images they reflected had no real sense of fluidity, movement, or historical change and they were little more than images frozen in time.

[14] Priestley, *Lectures on History*, 65, 68.

Priestley's mode of creation of historical pictures was similar in his evaluation of the economies of ancient nations in comparison to that of eighteenth-century England. His objective in assessing the costs of necessities in classical times was largely to estimate their wealth and compare it to that of his own. He was familiar with David Hume's essay on *The Populousness of Ancient Nations*,[15] and referred to this work in his general discussions about classical economies.[16] Priestley calculated the cost of labour and its purchasing power for necessities such as bread corn, establishing a set of economic criteria in relation to changes in the value of money for the purpose of comparison. For example, he worked out carefully that the price of corn in ancient Greece was about a third less than in his own time. In the Rome of Pliny the cost of the same commodity was much dearer than in eighteenth-century London, although the price of meat was much the same and wine was cheap.[17]

He went on to make other comparisons, for example, between the cost of items in Saxon times, the Middle Ages, and the London of his own age and also between the economies of England and France, whose money, Priestley estimated, had devalued more than our own.[18] Interesting though these must have been to the eighteenth-century reader, Priestley's comparisons were largely between the economic state of past ages and those of his own time. He never really looked in any meaningful way at the relative monetary fortunes of developing economies in a specific period. Ever mindful of his own concerns regarding the uniform progress of mankind in all his areas of endeavour, his economic comparisons tended to be on a trans-historical basis rather than related in any truly comprehensible way to one another.

Priestley's perspectives in his secular history, however, were by no means confined to close-up snapshots derived from the details and particulars of his historical sources, or trans-historical comparisons of the price of corn. He also took what may be termed a *wide angle view* of the historical landscape, one which was reflected in his

[15] See David Hume, *Political Discourses* (Edinburgh, 1752), Discourse X.
[16] Priestley, *Lectures on History*, 372, 379.
[17] Ibid. 113, 116–17.   [18] Ibid. 124.

comments about the value of history as what he called 'anticipated experience'. His idea was that

the experience of some ages should be collected and compared, that distant events should be brought together; and so the first rise, entire progress, and final conclusion, of schemes, transactions, and characters, should be seen, as it were, in one unbroken view, with all their connexions and relations.[19]

This description prefigured in historical terms the philosophical ideas of Priestley's necessitarian scheme, which was a mechanistic concept of uninterrupted cause and effect encompassing his holistic idea of God, man, and nature. For Priestley, whose arguments with his friend and fellow scholar Richard Price on this subject are well documented,[20] a particular cause would always produce the same effect and consequently the connection between cause and effect 'is concluded to be *invariable*, and therefore *necessary*'. It followed, Priestley wrote, that the chain of cause and effect could never be broken, for should such an event take place the very argument for the existence of God would be undermined. It was history that revealed God's workings in the world, which he famously believed could be perceived in 'the experiments made by the air pump; the condensing engine, or electrical machine, which exhibit the operations of nature, and the God of nature himself, whose works are the noblest subject of contemplation to the human mind'.[21] Priestley's world was atomistic and mechanistic, and into his historical thought in various ways he carried the imagery of the machine as the fundamental engine of human progress under God's guidance.

It was this desire to capture in a useful and coherent form a wide overview of history that inspired his enthusiasm for a chart of history imported from France, to which he added his own improvements. The chart gave a general outline of the fortunes of states throughout history relative to one another in terms of size, chronology, duration, and other factors. The representation of the power and progress of different nations was, however, constructed in a linear and

[19] Ibid. 53.
[20] See *A Free Discussion of the Doctrines of Materialism and Philosophical Necessity, in a Correspondence between Dr Price and Dr Priestley* (London, 1778). See also Chapter 3 above.
[21] Price and Priestley, *Free Discussion*, 10, 28.

mechanical fashion. In contrast, the great writer and critic Johann Gottfried von Herder (1744–1803) and his successors in the German Romantic movement preferred the outlines of organic symbols, such as trees perhaps, to represent those nations' birth, their growth, and their final decay. J. G. Herder wrote that 'Each nation must therefore be considered solely *in its place with everything that it is and has* ... [in] that great garden in which peoples grew up like plants.'[22] The French chart, however, Priestley described, without any feeling of life or growth, as

a picture of all history ... it renders visible to the eye ... the whole figure and dimensions of all history, general and particular; and so perfectly shows the origin, progress, extent, and duration of all kingdoms and states that ever existed, at one view, with every circumstance of time and place, uniting chronology and geography ... [23]

Despite its lack of biological imagery, this was a bold concept indeed. It would be hard to imagine a wider or more all-encompassing perspective on the past. Priestley hoped that the chart would inspire in historians an instant grasp of their subject of study as a vast, interconnected whole rather than as a series of disparate parts. Compared, however, with the supple, flowing, and flexible lines of the living tree, Priestley's linear representation of his wide historical vision appears rigid and unbending. Absent from his vision are the roots and branches, the growth and decay, the innumerable developmental variations, the strengths and weaknesses, and the light and shade envisaged by later historians.

From his vantage point above those great sweeping perspectives on history he moved in closer to see the various parts, the different cultures and contexts which made up the whole. His advice to the student who had chosen his particular area of study was, first, to consider his own period's relationship to that wider perspective, and secondly, to look more closely inside the period, to *zoom in*, as it were, and consider the relationships to one another of the different factors within the period itself. Priestley was anxious to show that linkages

---

[22] J. G. Herder, *Letters for the Advancement of Humanity* (1793–7), Tenth Collection, quoted in Michael N. Forster (ed.), *Johann Gottfried von Herder: Philosophical Writings* (Cambridge: CUP, 2002), 395.

[23] Priestley, *Lectures on History*, 133.

within specific historical contexts themselves were of a similar nature to those which connected that period to the whole, and also those which constituted the whole. His view of specific historical contexts was that 'so extensive is the connexion of things with one another, that everything written or done, in any period of time, is necessarily related, in a thousand ways, to many other things that were transacted at the same time'.[24] Here he emphasized the interdependence of factors in a historical context, within which it is impossible to separate the historical facts themselves from the particular circumstances of time and place. All historical factors within a period were related to one another, and therefore once again it is possible to detect the same frame of mind which produced the idea of the mechanistic interconnections of cause and effect in Priestley's doctrine of necessity.

With regard to context, various factors such as language, law, and ethics were highly relevant to Priestley in relation to the understanding of a people at a certain period, but not in the sense of a full appreciation of time, circumstances, and intrinsic historical value. *Language*, for example, ought to be recognized as a vital component in the make-up of any society. Priestley wrote that language was a great guide to a historian and that of all customs and habits that of speech was 'the most confirmed and least liable to change'.[25] It revealed much about the origins, condition, manners, customs, civil policy, and circumstances of that people.

Although it would appear that from the perspective of language Priestley had an appreciation of the diverse nature of historical contexts, in fact his ideas typified Enlightenment opinion on the subject of human tongues. Like the Enlightenment orientalist and philologist Sir William Jones (1746–94), who emphasized the common elements in languages rather than the differences,[26] Priestley believed that there had been a single origin of human speech which had been spoken

---

[24] Ibid. 77.   [25] Ibid. 78.

[26] See William Jones, *Discourses delivered at the Asiatick Society, 1785–1792* (1794; London: Routledge, Thoemmes Press, 1993), 188. This reprint from volume three of *The Works of William Jones* (London, 1807) contains an introduction by Roy Harris and a bibliography of eighteenth-century linguistics by Karen Thomson. For general studies on the history of language, see R. H. Robins, *A Short History of Linguistics*, 4th edn. (London: Longman, 1997) and Anna Morpurgo Davies, *Nineteenth-Century Linguistics* (1998), vol. 4 of *History of Linguistics*, ed. Giulio Lepschy (London: Longman, 1994–).

by the first family of the human race. Diversity in human tongues, Priestley thought, had been caused by the absence of the practice of writing, by the frequent admission of inflections into what was a simple and primitive form of speech, and also by differences in climate and ways of living.[27] Typically, Priestley's own preference would have been a *'philosophical and universal language*, which shall be the most natural and perfect expression of human ideas and sentiments'. In the meantime, however, he contented himself with the purpose of showing the variety of ways in which different languages expressed 'the same mental conceptions'.[28] Consequently, the tendency in Priestley's thought on language, as on other elements of human progress, was to appreciate and emphasize the most direct path towards uniformity rather than to stand aside and consider the nature and extent of real cultural diversity.

Similarly, the *laws* of a country were inextricably linked with everything else regarding the customs and nature of citizens. The Romans, for example, needed laws to prevent children being disinherited without just cause, suggesting that the state of paternal and filial affection amongst the Romans left a lot to be desired. Thus there was a close connection between the law and this particular trait in the character of Roman family life. Once again, however, an appreciation of a certain uniqueness here was not evident, for, as with all other aspects of law and its connection to different cultures, 'Customs and general maxims of conduct being of the nature of unwritten laws, give us the same insight into the state of things in a country.'[29] Consequently, despite the fact that laws specific to different cultures evolved in peoples and nations, law was for Priestley, like human nature, fundamentally universal.

Priestley's moral system had a truly Enlightenment pedigree. It was in the work of David Hartley that Priestley found the ideal *mechanism* to work alongside his own necessitarian ideas.[30] Priestley wrote of

---

[27] Joseph Priestley, *A Course of Lectures on the Theory of Language and Universal Grammar* (1762), reprint (Menston: Scolar Press, 1970), 288, 289–90. Priestley's lectures were given at Warrington Academy where he was tutor in languages and belles lettres.

[28] Priestley, *Lectures on the Theory of Language*, 8, 7.

[29] Priestley, *Lectures on History*, 82.

[30] *Hartley's Theory of the Human Mind, on the Principle of the Association of Ideas; with Essays relating to the Subject of it by Joseph Priestley* (London, 1775). See Chapter 3 above.

the nature of separate cultures with regard to ethics, but there was nothing in his ideas which suggested the existence of moral relativism. In his creation of a theory of moral progress he was attracted to the unbroken cohesion of the idea of association and the simplicity of the hypothesis.[31] Hartley, following the empiricist system of Locke, believed that moral knowledge could be explained by the association of ideas, and that this would actually *create* in man a moral sense which carried its own authority.[32]

The reasoning was that since men were all products of nature they were all designed in a similar way and were therefore equally responsive to the action of circumstance. The improvement of man's moral ideas was dependent on a process which was simultaneously natural and mechanical and directed by God. In time, the process, which operated in tandem with the idea of human nature as a constant factor and with the laws of natural philosophy, would facilitate the smoothing away of all particular differences of attitude and behaviour. Leslie Stephen's opinion of Hartley was that 'He seeks to do for human nature what Newton did for the solar system. Association is for man what gravitation is for the planets.'[33] The knowledge of virtue would come about by means of a process of abstraction in which the particulars of sense coalesced into a general, universal law 'as to appear but a simple idea'.[34] Such simple ideas became abstract and it was these moral abstractions which then guided man's behaviour.[35] Thus for Hartley and Priestley moral knowledge was distilled from man's sense experience into a general law which would be 'found to govern both the material and intellectual world'.[36] All men's better thoughts would be intensified by association, and all evils 'really and truly annihilated, in the idea of the greater good to which they are subservient'.[37]

[31] Priestley, *Hartley's Theory of the Human Mind*, p. xxiv.

[32] David Hartley, *Observations on Man, his Frame, his Duty, and his Expectations* (1749; London, 1791), 293–4.

[33] Leslie Stephen, *History of English Thought in the Eighteenth Century* (London, 1881), II, 66.

[34] Priestley, *Hartley's Theory of the Human Mind*, p. xxxiii.

[35] Barbara Bowen Oberg, 'David Hartley and the Association of Ideas', *Journal of the History of Ideas*, 37 (1976), 446.

[36] Priestley, *Hartley's Theory of the Human Mind*, pp. xxiv–xxv.

[37] Price and Priestley, *Free Discussion*, 110.

In his *Lectures on History*, Priestley wrote that 'even the sentiments of morality, which of all others one would expect to find the most invariable and uncorrupted, are found greatly perverted, and intermixed with notions that are foreign, and even contrary, to morality, in the minds of whole nations. So it was that the Tartars, who consider it a sin to beat a horse, would murder a man with impunity. The Arab who welcomes a stranger as his brother to his home, would have robbed and murdered him had he met him an hour earlier in the desert.' The weaknesses and inconsistencies in the human mind, wrote Priestley, were endless.[38] It would appear that although he did recognize the connection of moral behaviour to historical circumstance and the diversity of ethical standards which this implied, he saw this as an aberration from the general, universal law. He quoted the politician and historian Bolingbroke, agreeing with him that the student of history will collect general principles and rules of life and conduct which must always be true and will form 'a general system of ethics and politics on the surest foundations, on the trial of these principles and rules in all ages, and on the confirmation of them by universal experience'.[39] This universalism which was characteristic of Priestley's thought was intrinsic to his moral system. Because that system was founded upon the general laws of the natural world, of which man was a part, the moral law was common to all, and different ethical standards were regarded by him simply as deviations from the true path to human perfection.

His wider views of history as a whole and the contexts within it were bounded together by concepts which were built upon the mechanisms of his necessitarian scheme. In the historical–contextual setting, the system reflected the idea of unbroken links between all elements of a culture. This striking similarity between the foundations of Priestley's natural philosophy and other aspects of his thought was a trait correctly described by John G. McEvoy as 'synoptic'.[40] There is little doubt that that the fundamental

[38] Priestley, *Lectures on History*, 44.
[39] Henry St John, Viscount Bolingbroke, *Letters on the Study and Use of History* (London, 1752), letter iii, 54, quoted in Priestley, *Lectures on History*, 29.
[40] John G. McEvoy, 'Joseph Priestley, Aerial Philosopher: Metaphysics and Methodology in Priestley's Chemical Thought, from 1762 to 1781: Part One', *Ambix*, 25 (1978), 5.

characteristic of Priestley's intellectual position was that it projected the same frame of mind on to diverse areas of his thought.[41]

In the case of his moral system, his necessitarian views being applied to his understanding of historical contexts would suggest almost the idea of a relativism in cultural and moral terms which was more characteristic of thinkers of the Romantic period. In Priestley, however, this was not the case. In his biography of the polymath Robert Schofield argues that a great part of the *Lectures* shows how eighteenth-century history lacked the more truly historical sense of the nineteenth, which was concerned with a continuous process of development. Priestley's 'snapshots' of history were contained within a 'static world of abstractions in spatial deployment instead of temporal succession'.[42] Priestley never perceived history as moving or developing in an organic sense and his view was rather like that of Hume, whose efforts were dominated by a 'mechanical, atomistic conception of society'.[43] Priestley's understanding of history as educative may also be compared with similar ideas in Hume,[44] whose thoughts on the constancy of human nature were also similar to Priestley's own opinions. Like Hume, Priestley's objective was the illustration of timeless principles by reference to diverse contexts, periods and places and consequently his historical insights were limited in relation to movement, fluidity, or change. Such tendencies mark Priestley, once again like Hume,[45] as having the historical sensibilities of the eighteenth century.

[41] Alison Kennedy, 'John Kenrick and the Transformation of Unitarian Thought', PhD thesis (Stirling, 2006), 42–91.

[42] Sherman B. Barnes, 'Historians in the Age of Enlightenment', in Sherman B. Barnes and Alfred A. Skerpan (eds), *Historiography under the Impact of Rationalism and Revolution* (Kent, OH: Kent State University Press, 1952), 13, quoted in Schofield, II, 256.

[43] Thomas P. Peardon, *The Transition in English Historical Writing, 1760–1830* (New York: Columbia University Press, 1933), 62, 58–60, quoted in James T. Hoecker, 'Joseph Priestley as a Historian and the Idea of Progress', *P-PN*, 3 (1979), 31. See also Hume, *The History of Great Britain*, ed. Forbes, 50.

[44] J. B. Black, *The Art of History* (1926; New York: Russell & Russell, 1965), 85; David Womersley, *The Transformation of the Decline and Fall of the Roman Empire* (Cambridge: CUP, 1988), 20.

[45] Herbert Butterfield, *Man on his Past* (Cambridge: CUP 1955), 98. See also Benedetto Croce, *History, Its Theory and Practice*, trans. Douglas Ainslie (1920; New York: Russell & Russell, 1960), 269.

On the crucial question of the relationship between religion and history, however, comparisons between Priestley and historians such as Hume and Gibbon are more complex. There are fundamental differences between Hume and Gibbon on the one hand and Priestley on the other, and these are brought about by their attitudes to religious belief. Hume's view was that religion was a major factor in history, and in his *History of England* his primary focus in this respect was on the powerful influence of the Roman Catholic Church, its irrational doctrines, and the crimes of the popes.[46] Hume wrote that in the eleventh century, for example, it had been the church's decision to seize the right of investitures from the temporal power which had thrown Italy and Germany 'into the most violent convulsions'.[47] For Hume the Catholic religion was a 'strange superstition',[48] just as Protestant sectarianism was enthusiasm. His aversion to forms of religious belief had been evident from early in his life,[49] and later this was expressed by him in terms of religion as superstition, an inflamed imagination, or a faith which could never be defended on rational grounds.[50]

Likewise, Gibbon's idea of religion as a crucial factor in history was reflected in his argument in *The Decline and Fall of the Roman Empire* (1776–88) that Christianity had been a major cause of the decline of Rome. Gibbon believed that Christianity was the historical factor which weakened a Rome facing the barbarian threat and hastened the debilitating effects of luxury and despotism.[51] Gibbon wrote that while Rome was invaded and undermined by slow decay, a humble religion 'gently insinuated itself into the minds of men' and 'erected

---

[46] Rivers, II, 314–15.

[47] David Hume, *The History of England, from the Invasion of Julius Caesar to the Revolution in 1688* (1788), 6 vols (Indianapolis: Liberty Fund, 1983) I, 215.

[48] David Hume, *A Treatise of Human Nature* (Harmondsworth: Penguin, 1985), Book 1, sect. viii, 149.

[49] B. A. O. Williams, 'Hume on Religion', in D. F. Pears (ed.), *David Hume, A Symposium* (New York: Macmillan, 1966), 80. For more recent analyses of Hume and religion, see M. A. Stewart, 'Hume's Historical View of Miracles' and Christopher Bernard, 'Hume and the Madness of Religion', in M. A. Stewart and John P. Wright (eds.), *Hume and Hume's Connexions* (Edinburgh: Edinburgh University Press, 1994).

[50] Black, *Art of History*, 103.

[51] Womersley, *Transformation*, 102. For Gibbon's view of Christianity's role in the fall of Rome, see also J. G. A. Pocock, *Barbarism and Religion*, vol. II: *Narratives of Civil Government* (Cambridge: CUP, 1999).

the triumphant banner of the cross on the ruins of the Capitol'.[52] In chapters 15 and 16 of his history, Gibbon launched such a devastating critique of Christianity that he incurred the charge that he was a deist who was trying to destroy religion altogether.[53] Thus although both Hume and Gibbon recognized that religion was a factor in historical change, they also carried with them the idea that it was, in many respects, an unwelcome intrusion, *per se*, not only in historical terms but also in the life of man.

Priestley, however, was a deeply religious man and a believer in the power of faith as a force for good in the world. His understanding of the relationship between history, religion, and religious dogma found meaning within an entirely different configuration. Like Hume and Gibbon he believed in the importance of religion as a contingent element in history, but in Priestley's case the objective was not to reject religion but to rescue it. Priestley historicized religious dogma for the express purpose of showing how it had obscured and corrupted what had originally been a pure and simple faith. He employed history as a tool to remove the corruptions and irrationality with which Christianity had become entangled, thus revealing a pristine belief which he believed had been its original form. Unlike both Hume and Gibbon, Priestley was not a historian who wrote of religion as a historical factor which was adverse in its own right. Rather, he perceived human history itself as the prime cause of the corruption of the true religion.

JOSEPH PRIESTLEY, THEOLOGIAN AS HISTORIAN

In his religious concerns, which were paramount in his world view, Priestley became the historian as theologian, and showed in this rather different role a more sophisticated form of historical consciousness than he displayed in his secular historical ideas. Here was evidence of a keen historical understanding of the development of doctrine in relation to historical circumstances over time. Priestley's

---

[52] Edward Gibbon, *The History of the Decline and Fall of the Roman Empire*, ed. David Womersley, 3 vols. (Harmondsworth: Penguin Books, 1994), ch. xv, I, 446.

[53] Womersley, *Transformation*, 69.

need to fulfil his theological objectives had been initiated by his
religious pilgrimage from orthodoxy to Unitarianism, during which
he professed his disbelief in the doctrines of atonement, original
sin, Biblical inspiration, the Trinity, and the divinity of Christ. It
was this antipathy towards orthodox ideas that caused him to use
the 'historical method' to disprove such doctrines. All of them he
regarded as 'corruptions', which had accrued over the centuries and
had obscured the truth of what had been a pure and simple faith. He
wrote that everything he deemed to be a 'corruption' of Christianity
was a departure from the original scheme, and he added that

> It will also be seen, that I have generally been able to trace every such cor-
> ruption to its proper source, and to shew what circumstances in the state of
> things, and especially of other prevailing opinions and prejudices, made the
> alteration, in doctrine or practice, sufficiently natural, and the introduction
> and establishment of it easy.[54]

In order to achieve this, to show that Christianity had in fact been
corrupted by different cultural circumstances, Priestley first had to
identify these, and then trace the historical process whereby all this
had come about. His objective was then to discard such corruptions
and expound as true his own concept of Christian belief, which he
perceived as a simple faith which had the same resonance in all ages.
The key text in his analysis was *An History of the Corruptions of
Christianity*, first published in 1782. When the two volumes appeared
they caused great controversy and initiated Priestley's famous long-
running dispute with Samuel Horsley. The exchange of views lasted
for six years, from 1783 to 1789, and cast Priestley's radical ideas into
sharp focus.

   In order to disentangle the truth about early Christianity, which he
was convinced would prove the simple humanity of Christ and reveal
the falsehood of the Trinity and other doctrines, he had to identify
those cultural elements and circumstances within each age which had
been responsible for their creation. It was crucial that he established
by what means this primitive, original form of the Christian faith
had been obscured by the irrational dogma which had been formed
by time-bound ideas. The sources of these false doctrines had to

---

[54] Joseph Priestley, *An History of the Corruptions of Christianity*, 2 vols (Birmingham, 1782), I, p. xiv.

be identified, and the process whereby they had distorted the truth clearly explained, in order that there would be adequate justification for considering them flawed. This inevitably involved an appreciation on Priestley's part of the relationship between such perceived theological aberrations and the process over time which caused them to take shape. It was the adoption of this approach to doctrinal change which made him responsible for the evolution of a sophisticated historical method which was absent from his secular historical ideas.[55]

One example of how he tackled his historical Biblical criticism may be found in his treatment of the development of the doctrine of transubstantiation.[56] The simple direction of Christ to his disciples at the Lord's Supper, to eat bread and drink wine in remembrance of him, was corrupted over the centuries by custom, superstition, the use of language, priestly arrogance, and papal whim into a doctrine of supreme irrationality. Priestley cites the comments of Averroes, 'the great freethinker of his age [who] said that Judaism was the religion of children and Mahometanism that of hogs; but he knew no sect so foolish and absurd as that of the Christians, who adored what they ate'.[57] This simple direction first became a sacrament, then a mystery, for 'the Christians affected very early to call this rite one of the *mysteries of our holy religion'*, until Justin Martyr's idea that the bread and wine were the true flesh and blood of Christ became accepted.[58] Gradually enveloped in yet more mystery and symbolism, this view of the doctrine was endorsed by the Second Council of Nicaea in the fourth century and it became an article of faith at the Council of Trent in the sixth. In this century and the one which followed, it became the custom not only to make use of lights during the eucharist, but also of incense, and, wrote Priestley, 'both these appendages were borrowed from the heathen sacrifices'.[59] By the year 818 it was perceived that the doctrine went down well with the common people 'and that it promised to give a high idea of the dignity and power of the priesthood'.[60]

His method was essentially *historical.* He traced the various transmutations of this doctrine from the idea of sacrament to mystery to

[55] Canovan, 'Irony of History', 16–25.   [56] Priestley, *Corruptions*, II, 1–65.
[57] Ibid. II, 57–8.   [58] Ibid. II, 4, 8.
[59] Ibid. II, 32.   [60] Ibid. II, 41.

sanctifying power, and saw how different cultural circumstances and the use of language combined to bring about its development over the ages into the doctrine of transubstantiation. There are no linear concepts or mechanisms here. This is a truly historical account of the shifts and subtle alterations in thoughts, words, and meaning in relation to religious concepts as circumstances developed and changed. Priestley's consciousness of the cultural mores which brought about the fundamental alterations in the nature of the doctrine over time gave his theological concerns about the 'corruptions' of Christianity a truly historical perspective. Indeed, 90 years later, that most perceptive of commentators, the Unitarian biographer Alexander Gordon, credited Priestley with being a precursor of much later theories of theological development. Gordon believed that Priestley's greatest gift to theology was the application of historical method to problems of doctrine, and that he was an innovator in the historical treatment of Biblical questions.[61]

It was this method of understanding and recording the development of ideas in relation to cultural change that made Priestley in every sense a *historical* Biblical critic. Of his approach to the interpretation of the Scriptures and the exposure of flawed doctrines, Priestley himself argued that the historical method was a most satisfactory mode of argumentation to disprove those doctrines about the nature of Christ which had been gleaned from Scripture 'without any regard to the context, or the modes of speech and opinions of the times in which the books were written'.[62] Thus it would appear that the Priestley of *Corruptions* showed a much more developed historical consciousness than the Priestley of *Lectures on History*.

It was a measure of Priestley's expertise in this form of historical interpretation that his work was much admired by German scholars with similar concerns, and indeed some of Priestley's works were translated into German. Most notable of all was the publication of Priestley's *Corruptions* in Berlin and Hamburg in 1785, three years after it first appeared in England, under the German title of *Geschichte der Verfälschungen des Christenthums*. Consequently, this important

---

[61] Alexander Gordon, *Heads of English Unitarian History* (London: Philip Green, 1895), 120, 122.
[62] Priestley, *Corruptions*, I, 3.

work by Priestley, featuring a form of historical criticism which linked dogma to historical context, was read and absorbed by German scholars.

Conversely, Priestley depended on German scholarship to a surprising extent in his own work. In *Corruptions* there are more than 80 references to the work of the theologian Johann Lorenz von Mosheim (1694–1755). Mosheim, professor of divinity at Göttingen from 1747, was the Lutheran ecclesiastical historian who emphasized the importance of the objective, critical treatment of original sources, and who widened the contexts of church history to encompass secular historical themes. It was natural that Mosheim's rational, critical observations on Scripture would appeal to Priestley in his attempts to argue the Unitarian case on many important theological topics.

However, even before Priestley, there had already been established a tradition of intellectual cross-communication between the scholars of rational dissent and some German Biblical critics in relation to both Old and New Testaments. The earlier volumes of Nathaniel Lardner's vast work, *The Credibility of the Gospel History* (12 volumes, 1727–55) were translated into German, up to the fourth volume of 1751.[63] The translation of the first part of Lardner's work contained a lengthy preface written by Sigmund Jacob Baumgarten (1706–57), who taught both the orientalist J. D. Michaelis (1717–91) and the theologian J. S. Semler (1725–91).[64] Michaelis and Semler were both highly innovative historical critics whose radical ideas about Scriptural interpretation blossomed during the second half of the eighteenth century. Scholars such as these are usually credited with the invention of the techniques of modern Biblical criticism, and are now recognized as innovative thinkers whose ideas prefigured the historicism of the nineteenth century in Germany.[65] Consequently, Priestley was part of a Unitarian tradition which often looked to pre-historicist

[63] *Memoirs of the Life and Writings of the Late Reverend Nathaniel Lardner* (London, 1769), 124–6. See also Andrew Kippis, *The Life of Nathaniel Lardner* (London, 1778), pp. xciv–xcv. See, in addition, Booklets with Notes, Notes on Nathaniel Lardner, DWL, MS. 12.54.

[64] Johann David Michaelis was professor of philosophy from 1746 and oriental languages from 1750 at Göttingen. Johann Salomo Semler became professor of theology at Halle in 1753.

[65] See Peter Hanns Reill, *The German Enlightenment and the Rise of Historicism* (Berkeley and Los Angeles: University of California Press, 1975).

German thinkers for inspiration with regard to the methodology of historical Biblical criticism.

However, attempting to argue what he believed to be false proved rather different in terms of perspective than validating what he thought to be true. Priestley's objectives were not only to expose irrational doctrines, but also to convince his detractors of what were the original truths about Christianity. For example, he was certain that the idea of the simple humanity of Christ was probably a common belief amongst the common people of the apostolic age, and those who discussed Christ's divinity were aware of just how unpopular their opinions were.[66] Alexander Gordon noted correctly that with regard to the identification of an original period in which the real truth about Christ and his teachings were known, Priestley's historical method threw into sharp relief the idea that there was some 'primitive nucleus whence developments proceed'.[67] This pinpoint of clarity, this unassailable and untainted purity of faith which Priestley was intent upon revealing to the world, was, however, a truth which was eternal. Priestley's 'primitive nucleus' of truth about the origins or 'springhead' of the Christian religion was universal and relevant to all ages. Thus his angle of vision had shifted to one which used the contextual to validate the truth of something which was essentially universal and therefore trans-historical. Consequently, in his historical Biblical criticism also, there were complexities of perspective which created tensions between the historical–contextual and the universally valid. Although Priestley, unlike, for example, the German Enlightenment thinker Gotthold Ephraim Lessing (1729–81), was not conscious of this paradox, it remains one which reflects the contradictions which appeared during a period of transition in historical thought.

It is important to understand all the complexities of Priestley's historical and theological historical approaches, for his method of Biblical criticism went on to become very important to the scholarship of rational dissent. Priestley was a figure of great influence in Unitarian historical Biblical scholarship during and after his own

---

[66] Joseph Priestley, *An History of Early Opinions Concerning Jesus Christ, Compiled from Original Writers, Proving that the Christian Church was at First Unitarian*, 4 vols. (Birmingham, 1786), IV, 311.

[67] Gordon, *English Unitarian History*, 120.

lifetime and his efforts to prove his radical theological beliefs were closely bound up with this rather sophisticated historical method. He rejected the idea of divine inspiration with regard to the actual content of the gospels and the general theme of his approach to the Scriptures was that their credibility should be ascertained by historical evidence alone. His own fundamental maxim was that the critic should consider the gospel historians in the same light as other historians in order to form a true picture. The credibility of any fact in the Scriptures must be supported by evidence recorded by contemporary historians and also by those who were regarded as reliable sources at the time. Thus Priestley's engagement with the Scriptures, intended to prove the falsehood of doctrines such as the Trinity, the virgin birth, and the divinity of Christ, was founded entirely on a rational, historical basis which recognized the relationship between doctrine and historical change. There are many perspectives evident here, but arguably this final point is one of the most important for the analysis of the development of historical thought itself in this period. This conclusion takes us a step further, to propose the idea that Priestley's contribution as a historical biblical critic may be seen as an important element in a pattern of development of the rational interpretation of the Holy Scriptures which stretched all the way from John Locke and Nathaniel Lardner to later eighteenth- and early nineteenth-century scholars.

PRIESTLEY'S HISTORICAL LEGACY

Priestley's successors were characteristically writers in the Socinian mould of the late eighteenth and early nineteenth centuries who, like Priestley himself, sought to disprove orthodox doctrines. They employed the same kind of scholarship, one which began to take on a form of historical understanding which prefigured in some ways the more historical methods of the later nineteenth century. The Unitarian divine Thomas Belsham (1750–1829), an ardent follower of Priestley, wrote, for example, that he had discovered 'the falsehood of those monstrous, absurd and idolatrous doctrines by which the beauty of Christianity has been defaced', and vowed to contribute to the 'purification of the gospel'.[68] Over the following decades Belsham contributed a great deal to scriptural interpretation, often in the columns of the Unitarian journal, *The Monthly Repository*.[69] In 1819 he encouraged scholars to interpret the sacred writings in the same way as other ancient works, by the use of a correct text and the philological approach, and to pay attention to the 'context, to the object and design of the writer, to the habits of thinking, and the peculiar phraseology of his age and country'.[70] At Daventry, Thomas Belsham taught both Timothy Kenrick (1759–1804), father of the classical scholar John Kenrick (1788–1877), and also the scholar and Biblical critic John Kentish (1768–1853), who was the young Kenrick's private tutor for two years from 1805 to 1807. They were all responsive to Priestley's ideas about historical scholarship of the Bible and also to ideas which came from Germany. Timothy Kenrick wrote that in order to understand the full truth about Christ's discourses, it was necessary to take some account of the historical context in which the Scriptures were written and 'to consider the circumstances and present temper of his hearers'.[71] The contents of his three volumes on New Testament interpretation took the form of a careful analysis of Scripture, verse by verse, and an account of the contexts of the gospel passages.

John Kentish's approach was rather similar. He selected short passages of Scripture and discussed their meaning from historical and philological viewpoints. Ever present here also was the theme of the rejection of false doctrine in favour of a rational, historical analysis of Biblical topics from a contextual perspective. In his *Notes and Comments on Passages of Scripture*, published in 1844, Kentish's comments on the Sermon on the Mount, for example, concentrated upon the style of expression adopted by Jesus. Kentish wrote that 'It

---

[68] John Williams, *Memoirs of the Late Reverend Thomas Belsham* (London, 1833), 376, 379.

[69] See *The Monthly Repository*, First Series, 1806–26.

[70] Thomas Belsham, *Monthly Repository*, 14 (1819), 403, quoted in Francis Mineka, *The Dissidence of Dissent: The Monthly Repository, 1806–1838* (Chapel Hill, NC: University of North Carolina Press, 1944), 132. Although this quotation comes from an anonymous refutation of objections to a Unitarian 'Improved Version' of the New Testament, Mineka is quite certain that the author was Thomas Belsham.

[71] Timothy Kenrick, *An Exposition of the Historical Writings of the New Testament*, 3 vols (Birmingham, 1807), I, 35.

abounds with imagery ... [and] this characterises some of the beatitudes'.[72] This did not mean, however, that Christ's style was necessarily unusual or obscure, for the people of the East at this time were quite used to such a method of expressing themselves and accordingly this was Christ's accustomed manner of instruction. There was a clear link established here between Christ's way of conveying his simple doctrine to the multitude and the form of linguistic imagery related to that particular time and place. Kentish was also closely engaged with the ideas of German critics in the period. In his *Notes and Comments* there were almost 270 sources listed, of which around 35 were German. Kentish, like Belsham, was receptive to the discoveries of German writers such as Johann Gottfried Eichhorn (1752–1827), whose interpretation of Old Testament passages, particularly those of Genesis, incorporated the idea that the story of Creation may have been simply a myth.

It was, however, Kentish's pupil John Kenrick, who became professor of history and literature at Manchester College in York in 1840, who took the historical ideas of the Unitarians a stage further. Kenrick did this by means of adapting elements of this particular historical–Biblical frame of mind to secular classical history. Kenrick, who was also a Socinian in the Priestleyan mould, inherited from his predecessors the desire to define the nature of early Christianity by seeking out its origins and sources. He was also, like some of his teachers, a diligent student of German who absorbed the ideas of German scholars, not only in the field of historical Biblical criticism, but also in the study of the interpretation of classical myth.

Kenrick was a historian first and foremost, and it was with the historian's eye that he considered the context of the Scriptures themselves. The most impressive passages of the prophets, he wrote, would be unintelligible did we not know the relations in which Israel and Judah stood towards Egypt, Assyria, and Tyre, when those prophecies were delivered. Similarly, in the New Testament, many of the words and actions of the Saviour himself derived their significance from the context in which they took place. Kenrick thought that the

---

[72] John Kentish, *Notes and Comments on Passages of Scripture* (London, 1844), 161. Kentish's many articles on the subject of Biblical criticism were collected together and published in this volume. Two other editions followed, in 1846 and 1848.

difference between religious and secular history was that the former was more liable to corruption and the only way to redress the balance was to attain historical truth by ascending 'as near as possible to its springhead'.[73]

Always in the background were Kenrick's strong Unitarian beliefs, which had encouraged him to seek Priestley's vision of a primitive Christian faith. This frame of mind was a crucial factor, and Kenrick used methods he had learned from his historical criticism in his approach to classical myth. In a very early unpublished essay of 1816, entitled 'A Specimen of the application of Historical Principles to the Explanation of the Greek Mythology', written while he was a tutor at Manchester College in York and three years before he left for a study year in Göttingen and Berlin, Kenrick discussed history, myth and the local origins of myth.[74]

There are several aspects of the essay which are striking. First, Kenrick made the point that the principles contained in it were new. This was certainly true, for the whole essay was constructed around two crucial, original ideas of the German scholar Heyne: that history and myth were interactive and could not be separated, and that the origins of myths were localized and unique to each separate people who created them.[75] Accordingly, the critic's method, Kenrick wrote, should be to ascertain the oldest fables of the Greeks respecting their gods, and 'to trace them upwards, as far as historical evidence will enable him to do it to their local origin'.[76] This revealed Kenrick's agreement with Heyne on the two important elements of mythic interpretation: the German's conviction that myth and history were complementary to one another (apart from the case of the most ancient Greek deities), and that the origins of myth were localized. Also, however, the quotation cast light on Kenrick's intended method,

[73] John Kenrick, *Biblical Essays* (London, 1864), 64. This work, which Kenrick published later in his life, was a collection of works previously aired to the public in various articles and other minor publications.

[74] John Kenrick, 'A Specimen of the application of Historical Principles to the Explanation of the Greek Mythology', DWL, Kenrick Papers, 24.107.50 (n).

[75] Christian Gottlob Heyne, 1. 'Interpretation of Myths', and 2. 'An Interpretation of the Language of Myths or Symbols Traced to their Reasons and Causes and Thence to Forms and Rules', in Burton Feldman and Robert D. Richardson, *The Rise of Modern Mythology, 1680–1860* (Bloomington, IN: Indiana University Press, 1972), 221, 223.

[76] Kenrick, 'Historical Principles', 5.

which he himself regarded as original, for he wrote that he proposed a course of proceeding 'which as far as he [the writer] has observed has not been adopted by any of those who have written on this subject'.[77] He saw his essay as original not only because it contained these important new ideas of Heyne's regarding history, myth, and its origins, but also on the grounds that his own methodology, the way in which he himself intended to *develop* Heyne's ideas, was indeed also new.

Crucially, Kenrick's method of interpreting myth was formed along the same conceptual lines and was analogous to the approach he had used in biblical criticism. He incorporated into the interpretation of classical myth concepts from the Unitarian tradition of historical analysis. Early in the essay, Kenrick wrote that he was convinced that more might be done towards establishing the outlines of a method of interpretation of Greek mythology which would establish its 'source and primary meaning... if we would be guided by history and not by the love of a pre-established system'. By the latter he meant that form of analysis in which not only is there no distinction between the myths of different ages, but in which the marriages and births, the genealogies, and adventures of deities are taught 'in the same affirmative historical time, as if they were the truths of our own religion'. Little care, he added, had been taken in the discrimination of the evidence for the existence of those opinions related to the 'age, the country, the character, or the prejudices of the writer who furnishes it'.[78] The descriptions of terms related to the importance of true historical origins, as opposed to the falsity of later, composite, a-historical versions, were in many respects analogous to the Unitarian historical Biblical method of interpretation.

Even Homer himself, wrote Kenrick, was guilty of the distortion of myth. Twenty years earlier, the whole question of the authorship of the Homeric poems had been raised in the *Prolegomena ad Homerum* of F. A. Wolf (1759–1824), a small volume which had shaken the world of classical studies to the core. Sensationally, Wolf had contended that there had been no single author of the great classical epics, *The Iliad* and *The Odyssey*, but that later editors had compiled them from a series of ballads of much earlier origin. Wolf's work was

---

[77] Ibid. 4.   [78] Ibid. 1, 4.

eagerly read by contemporary critics who had already grasped the
notion of original, natural, primitive poetry, and Homer was the poet
most under discussion from that time onwards.[79]

Kenrick's own view of Homer's compilation was that it was unhis-
torical. Homer was like other writers such as, for example, a Neopla-
tonist 'seeking to spiritualise the grossness of the ancient mythology',
or even a Christian apologist 'not averse from exaggerating its defects'.
The combination of all these testimonies produced a 'system' which
'certainly was never received at any one period as the general belief'.
The interpreters of myth had 'applied their systems' to a mass of
heterogeneously composed primitive fables, poetical embellishments,
and philosophical refinements, with the result that the historical truth
about the origins of myth had been distorted.[80]

His frame of mind in the essay on these points was strikingly similar to that which already had been revealed in his Biblical criticism. In
Unitarian Biblical criticism the general theme had been a rejection of
the systematic, the presupposed, and the artificially constructed way
of understanding the past in favour of a direct, concrete historical
approach to seeking out original sources and truths. It seems that
he applied an analogous set of ideas to the interpretation of ancient
myth. In the essay, Kenrick expressed himself in the language of
the Unitarian Biblical critic, and in his analysis reflected some of
those concepts with which he was familiar in this respect. Although
the context was clearly different, his proposed method repeated the
importance of finding the origins and the truth about the source and
the beginnings of things.

In Kenrick, there had been a projection of the frame of mind which
had dealt with Unitarian Biblical criticism into the problem of the
interpretation of classical myth. Kenrick's method, derived from what
he had learned about the objectives of Unitarian Biblical scholarship
to seek for the primary origins, was applied to the pre-Romantic precepts of Heyne. While clearly these were aspects of two sets of diver-
gent thoughts, in this particular instance they locked together with
the ease of two parts of a well worn jigsaw. Kenrick's development of

[79] For a concise account of the content and influence of Wolf's *Prolegomena*, see
Rudolph Pfeiffer, *History of Classical Scholarship from 1300 to 1850*, 2 vols. (Oxford:
Clarendon Press, 1976), II, 173–7.
[80] Kenrick, 'Historical Principles', 4.

Heyne's ideas was guided by that fundamental element of Unitarian Biblical criticism which sought the 'springhead' or 'primitive nucleus' of truth about a simple Christian faith. Consequently, Kenrick's way forward was directed to the discovery of the original sources of myths, to the beginnings of races and their languages, and in general to truly historical ideas about origins, development, diversity, and relativism in a cultural sense.

In Kenrick's thought it is clear that there had developed a parallel set of ideas between his methods in Biblical criticism and those in classical history. It became a strong characteristic of his thought that just as the purity of Christianity had been corrupted by the dogma of later ages, so it was that the truth about the origins of classical myths had been obscured by the mythological 'systems' constructed at a later period by writers such as Homer. This frame of mind inspired an appreciation of the importance of the search for the truth about origins in the secular historical world, all of which contributed greatly to ideas about the uniqueness of cultural and national characteristics and the development of peoples along very different and diverse routes. These intellectual traits and others, including an appreciation of organic development in historical terms, identify Kenrick as a transitional figure who tended in many respects towards the more truly historical consciousness of the Romantic period. He was not the only Unitarian and rational dissenter to absorb some of the more historical ideas of the nineteenth century, but he is most interesting in being one who in some respects reached this point via the historical Biblical criticism which had been so carefully crafted by Joseph Priestley.

There were, then, many complex historical perspectives in Priestley's mind. If we step back and try to form our own view of him, we should understand him within the history of ideas of the eighteenth and nineteenth centuries with regard to the changes and development of historical consciousness. Priestley is an important figure who ought to be recognized as part of this development, for his historical Biblical criticism held the seeds of some new ideas about the understanding of history which emerged in the nineteenth century. Although these ideas were expressed more readily in terms of Herder's organisms than Priestley's machines, the thought of Priestley the historian as theologian in particular may nevertheless be considered an important step towards a new historical consciousness which manifested itself in some ways in later Unitarians such as John Kenrick.

If we concentrate on a wide-angle view of Joseph Priestley, we may see that in a period during which were entangled together the threads of both Enlightenment and Romantic thought he was a historian of fundamental importance. It is true that he was limited in his ideas about movement and change in secular history. Nonetheless, Priestley the theologian as historian did have a deep understanding of the development of the relationship between dogma and the ages which produced it, and carefully scanned the Scriptures for proof of his own theology. His legacy was one of historical perspectives which were slanted differently, first, in relation to aspects of his secular history and, secondly, to what was of course most important to him, his theological concerns. Like clear rays of light reflected through a slowly rotating prism, Priestley's historical perspectives frequently altered their angles and distances. Fragmented and incomplete as they were, his perspectives on the past left an important legacy, the outlines of which assisted some of those scholars who came after him to develop the Unitarian consciousness a stage further towards the historical thought of the nineteenth century.

7

Joseph Priestley in America*

Jenny Graham

THE EXODUS FROM ENGLAND

In the closing years of the eighteenth century, an almost unprece-
dented number of Englishmen emigrated to the United States of
America. 'Let us see,' wrote Talleyrand, the emigrant French politician
and diplomat, in the summer of 1794,

what sort of emigration England sends today to America: mechanics, craftsmen who flee from the burden of taxes and . . . a few men excited about theological questions whom the Anglican church has tried to persecute because
alarmed by the discussion of its dogmas. The first can perfect here their craft,
the second found colleges.[1]

In this description of the emigration of the 1790s—'the numbers . . . are astonishing,' wrote one observer, of this 'rage for going
to America'[2]—Talleyrand was surely misleading. Without doubt,

---

* I wish to gratefully acknowledge permission granted from the Librarians and
Curators of manuscripts at the American Philosophical Society, Bowdoin College,
Birmingham City Archives, Dr Williams's Library, the Historical Society of Pennsylvania, the Library of Congress, Massachusetts Historical Society, and Warrington
Borough Council—Library, Museum & Archives Service, for permission to reproduce
material in their Archives. I would also like to thank Dr Colin Bonwick for kindly
reading and commenting on an earlier draft of this chapter.

[1] *Talleyrand in America as a Financial Promoter, 1794–6. Unpublished Letters and
Memoirs*, ed. and trans. Hans Huth and Wilma Jennings Pugh, American Historical
Association, Annual Report, 1941, vol. II (Washington, 1942), 37–8.

[2] T. Cooper to J. Watt, Jr., 24 Aug. 1793, MS 3219/6/2/C/117, BCA, JWP. Catharine
Cappe, *Memoirs of the Life of the Late Mrs Catharine Cappe Written by Herself*

this emigration consisted of large numbers of skilled artisans and craftsmen, as well as more than one prominent dissenting minister.[3] A significant portion of this extraordinary exodus of talent— 'there are gone to America,' declared one radical newspaper, '... the best farmers, mechanics and men of the truest science'[4]—consisted, however, of political radicals, large numbers of whom were, indeed, Protestant dissenters, suffering much harassment. It was the political opinions of many of these refugees, however, in the years 1793–4 in particular, which had put them in imminent danger not only of mob violence, which was widespread, but of government prosecution.

Joseph Priestley, who was—for all his elaborate disclaimers to the contrary prior to his departure[5]—implicated in more than one way in the activities of the English radicals, fell very largely into this category. Priestley departed in some haste for America in April 1794, at the urgent pleading of his friends, alarmed, as was he, by the animosity which his more extreme pronouncements on the need for reform in England, and his outspoken partisanship for the cause of France, had brought upon him.[6]

Priestley's decision to leave England was not taken lightly, and was above all influenced by the spate of government prosecutions of reformers in 1793 and 1794, many of them his personal friends. 'I cannot in a letter,' he wrote to one of his correspondents in America, the Vice-President John Adams, 'give you an idea of the prosecutions by which many of my friends are continually harassed, the infamous informers that are encouraged, and the disposition of the country to

---

(London, 1822), 263; see Graham, *Reform Politics*, 502–3, 512–20, and Graham, 'Revolutionary in Exile', 28ff., 174.

[3] W. C. Frank, Jr., ' "I Shall Never be Intimidated". Harry Toulmin and William Christie in Virginia', *TUHS*, 19.1 (1987), 24–37; Graham, 'Revolutionary in Exile', 33n., 65n., 78 & n., 116 & n., 165.

[4] *Cambridge Intelligencer*, 22 Mar. 1794.

[5] Joseph Priestley, *The Present State of Europe compared with Ancient Prophecies. A Sermon, Preached at the Gravel Pit Meeting in Hackney, February 28, 1794... with a Preface, Containing the Reasons for the Author's Leaving England* (London, 1794), pp. ixff. See the *Preface* to Joseph Priestley, *A Sermon Preached at the Gravel-Pit Meeting, in Hackney, Apr. 19, 1793* (London, 1793), pp. iii–xvi. See also Jenny Graham, 'Revolutionary Philosopher', part one, 47–8; part two, 42.

[6] Ibid., part two, 14–46.

listen to them.'[7] He was much shaken by the successful prosecution of the dissenting minister William Winterbotham (1763–1829): 'It shews that no man who is obnoxious, however innocent, is safe.'[8] And he was further alarmed by the fate of another dissenting minister, Thomas Fyshe Palmer (1747–1802), and his fellow reformer, the lawyer, Thomas Muir (1765–99), condemned to transportation to Botany Bay. 'The case of men of education and reflection,' he wrote,

(and who act from the best intentions with respect to the community) committing what only *state policy* requires to be considered as *crimes*, but which are allowed on all hands to imply no moral turpitude, so as to render them unfit for heaven and happiness thereafter, is not to be confounded with that of common felons. There was nothing in the conduct of Louis XIV. and his ministers, that appeared so shocking, so contrary to all ideas of justice, humanity and decency, and that has contributed more to render their memory execrated, than sending such men as Mr. Marolles, and other eminent Protestants, who are now revered as saints and martyrs, to the gallies, along with the vilest miscreants. Compared with this, the punishment of death would be mercy.[9]

Throughout 1793, Priestley was coming to his reluctant conclusion that emigration to America was necessary. 'I perceive your resolution, and approve of it,' he wrote to William Russell, the Birmingham reformer, and Priestley's close political friend and ally, on the latter's almost certain decision to emigrate to America, 'and I take it for granted that I shall very soon be compelled to adopt the same measure'.[10] He was in correspondence with his former pupil, John Vaughan, in Philadelphia, who had settled in America in 1782, taking with him letters of recommendation from Priestley. Vaughan was by 1791 Treasurer of the American Philosophical Society, investing in the American funds for his mentor, and foremost amongst those urging

---

[7] Priestley to Adams, 20 Aug. 1793, Adams family papers, Mass. Hist. Soc., Reel 376.

[8] Priestley to Wilkinson, 2 Dec. 1793, WPL; Priestley, *The Present State of Europe*, pp. xviii–xix. For Winterbotham, see Graham, *Reform Politics*, 468 and n., 503–4 and n., 505n.

[9] Priestley, *The Present State of Europe*, Preface, pp. xviiin.–xixn.

[10] Priestley to Russell, 3 Apr. 1793, Rutt, I ii, 199. See Samuel Henry Jeyes, *The Russells of Birmingham in the French Revolution and America, 1791–1814* (London: George Allen, 1911).

him to emigrate to America.[11] Priestley's own preference was for France, in which he was joined by his eldest son, Joseph, and almost certainly by his two other sons, William and Harry.[12] This had, however, been made increasingly impossible by the descent of that country into chaos and anarchy: 'the conduct of the French has been such as their best friends cannot approve,' wrote Priestley. 'France, I fear, will long be in a lamentable state.'[13] He wrote to Vaughan of Joseph's intention to sail for America, to spend 'a year in looking about him'. He himself would, in all probability, follow.[14] 'No son of mine can settle to advantage in this country,' Priestley wrote to his brother-in-law, the wealthy iron-master, John Wilkinson.[15] And his decision to emigrate was undoubtedly influenced by the departure of his sons.

In August 1793, two of Priestley's sons, Joseph and Harry, departed for America, provided with many letters of introduction from their father.[16] 'I am now,' wrote Priestley to Theophilus Lindsey, '... a great deal occupied about the departure of my sons for America. Mr. Cooper goes with them, and Mr. Walker ... will follow.'[17] Thomas Cooper (1759–1839) and Thomas Walker (1749–1817), two of the most prominent of the English radicals, were under both actual and imminent threat of prosecution for their activities in 1793. A bill of indictment was found against Thomas Walker,[18] and in the event it was only Cooper, for whom Priestley had a great admiration both as a fellow scientist and as a man of strong radical opinions,[19] who

[11] Graham, 'Revolutionary in Exile', 22–4, 29, 174–5.

[12] Ibid. 21, 29, 69n., 174; Graham, *Reform Politics*, 128, 343 and n., 509.

[13] Priestley to Withering, 15 Apr. 1793, *Scientific Correspondence*, 135; Priestley to Wilkinson, 16 May 1793, WPL.

[14] Priestley to Vaughan, 6 Feb. 1793, APS, BP 931, Graham, 'Revolutionary in Exile', 29, 174–5.

[15] Priestley to Wilkinson, 6 Apr. 1793, WPL.

[16] Graham, 'Revolutionary in Exile', 32–3.

[17] Priestley to Lindsey, 5 Aug. 1793, Rutt, I ii, 205.

[18] Frida Knight, *The Strange Case of Thomas Walker: Ten Years in the Life of a Manchester Radical* (London: Lawrence & Wishart, 1957); Graham, *Reform Politics*, 505–6, 534–5, 602. For Priestley's concern, see Priestley to Lindsey, 5 Aug. 1793, Rutt, I ii, 205; Priestley to Wilkinson, 19 Aug. 1793, WPL; Priestley to Adams, 20 Aug. 1793, Adams family papers, Mass. Hist Soc., Reel 376.

[19] Dumas Malone, *The Public Life of Thomas Cooper* (New Haven, CT: Yale University Press, 1926); Graham, 'Revolutionary in Exile', 30–1 & nn.; Schofield, II,

accompanied his sons to America.[20] Cooper left England in a state of great apprehension of writs being taken out against him, and when he returned, on his own, early in 1794, it was 'incog.,' as he described it.[21] He brought with him the news of his, John Vaughan's, and Joseph Priestley Jr.'s plan for a consortium to buy a tract of land in upstate Pennsylvania, for a settlement for English emigrants. 'I cannot help thinking it very hazardous for him,' wrote Priestley, one of the few to be apprised of Cooper's return.[22]

Yet another of Priestley's friends, Benjamin Vaughan—the pupil whose interests were most attuned to his[23]—was to make a precipitate departure from England. Benjamin Vaughan (1751–1835), brother of John,[24] close friend of Franklin, strenuous supporter of the cause of revolutionary France, and almost certainly instrumental in persuading Priestley to invest in the French funds,[25] was compromised by one of the most extreme and incautious of this radical fraternity, Priestley's Unitarian disciple, John Hurford Stone (1763–1818). Hurford Stone was now resident in Paris, and in regular correspondence not only with his brother, the London merchant, William Stone, but with Priestley.[26] Benjamin Vaughan fled England early in May 1794, to France, thence to Switzerland, returning to France in 1796, before his eventual arrival in America in 1797.[27] 'I think,' Priestley was to write after his own safe arrival, 'that if I had continued in England I could not have escaped being involved with some of my friends, and

275–6. For Joseph Priestley, Jr. and Cooper, see Graham, 'Revolutionary in Exile', 21n., 29, 31n., 69 n.

[20] Graham, 'Revolutionary in Exile', 31–2.

[21] Cooper to Rogers, 14 Dec. 1793, Peter William Clayden, *Early Life of Samuel Rogers* (London: Smith Elder, 1887), 285–6; Graham, *Reform Politics*, 513–14, 602; Graham, 'Revolutionary in Exile', 31–5.

[22] Priestley to Wilkinson, n.d. (Feb. 1794), WPL; see Clayden, *Early Life of Rogers*, 286.

[23] Joseph Priestley, *Lectures on History and General Policy* (Birmingham, 1788), Dedication; Priestley to Russell, 10 Nov. 1795, Rutt, I ii, 322.

[24] See above, n. 11.

[25] Craig C. Murray, *Benjamin Vaughan (1751–1835), The Life of an Anglo-American Intellectual* (New York: Arno Press, 1982); Graham, 'Revolutionary in Exile', 22 and n.

[26] Graham, *Reform Politics*, 345–6, 350, 355–7, 361 & n., 362 & n., 387 & n., 508, 575–8; Graham, 'Revolutionary in Exile', 25, 28, 34, 36–7.

[27] Murray, *Benjamin Vaughan*, 338–81; Graham, *Reform Politics*, 611; Graham, *Revolutionary in Exile*, 37–8.

therefore I think myself happy in being where I am, and wish more of my friends were with me.'[28]

There were many other political activists in this flight from England.[29] Others, however, in particular in the aftermath of the State Trials, when the imminent threat of government prosecution was lifted, decided to remain. Amongst these were Thomas Walker and many of the radicals of Norwich, from where came a plea, in their publication, *The Cabinet*, for a halt to the torrent of emigration.[30] 'If *good men* would *not* leave us,' wrote Felix Vaughan to Thomas Cooper, 'what might we not attempt for the good people of England'.[31] Early in 1795, moreover, the administration led by George Washington, first President of the United States, passed its controversial Naturalization Act.[32] This, while motivated to a great extent by a fear of the influence of fleeing French aristocrats, was another factor in reducing the number of emigrant English. 'The present governing powers have shewn a ridiculous jealousy of democratical emigrants,' Priestley lamented, in what was for him an anticlimactic year, when many of his initial plans and the expectations arising from his welcome less than a year earlier had been dashed. 'From a dread of them, as Mr. Adams acknowledges to me, they have, in the last congress, made naturalization more difficult than before.'[33]

[28] Priestley to Lindsey, 5 Jul. 1794, DWL MSS., 12.12, passage omitted by Rutt; Priestley to Thomas Belsham, 27 Aug. 1794, Rutt, I ii, 273; and Graham, 'Revolutionary in Exile', 60 & n., 69.

[29] Michael Durey, *Transatlantic Radicals and the Early American Republic* (Lawrence, KS: University Press of Kansas, 1997); see also Graham, *Reform Politics*, 512ff; Graham, 'Revolutionary in Exile', 60 & n.

[30] Graham, *Reform Politics*, 602–3, 641–4.

[31] Felix Vaughan to Cooper (Jul. 1794), Thomas Walker, *The Original*, ed. William Blanchard Jerrold, 2 vols. (London, 1874), I, 87. See also Cooper to (T. and R. Walker), 4 July 1795, MS 3219/ 6/2/C/126, BCA, JWP; Graham, 'Revolutionary in Exile', 82.

[32] John Bach McMaster, *A History of the People of the United States, from the Revolution to the Civil War* (New York: D. Appleton & Company, 1900), II, 208–12.

[33] Priestley to Lindsey, 12 Jul. 1795, Rutt, I ii, 312; and Priestley to Lindsey, n.d. (1795), Rutt, I ii, 303–4. For some continuing emigration, see, however, Graham, *Reform Politics*, 645; and Sarah Vaughan to F. W. Vaughan, 7 Sept. 1795, Charles Vaughan Papers, George G. Mitchell Department of Special Collections & Archives, Bowdoin College Library, Brunswick, Maine (hereafter Charles Vaughan Papers, Bowdoin College).

PRIESTLEY'S ARRIVAL IN AMERICA

Priestley's arrival in America, where he landed, in New York, on 4 June 1794, was, as more than one observer recorded, little short of triumphant. As one eminent American historian emphasized, he was seen as a symbolic figure in this flight across the Atlantic from governmental repression and persecution. 'They hailed him as a martyr, and overwhelmed him with attention.'[34] His arrival 'was soon known through the city, and next morning the principal inhabitants of New York came to pay their respects and congratulations,' wrote a visiting Englishman.'... No man in any public capacity could be received with more respect than he was.'[35] It was a reception which Priestley could not but enjoy: 'it shews the difference of the two countries'.

I feel as if I were in another world. I never before could conceive how satisfactory it is to have the feeling that I now have, from a sense of perfect security and liberty, all men having equal rights and privileges, and speaking and acting as if they were sensible of it... With respect to myself, the difference is great indeed. In England, I was an object of the greatest aversion to every person connected with Government; whereas here, they are those who shew me the most respect.[36]

'As to the government,' he wrote, 'it is nearly every thing we can wish, and the few imperfections will be easily removed when it is the general interest and wish that they should be so; and here the majority bear rule.'[37] 'The preachers,' however, as he wrote, in his only note of dissatisfaction, 'though all civil to me, look upon me with dread, and none of them have asked me to preach in their pulpits.'[38]

It was in New York that Priestley first met many members of Congress, on their return from Philadelphia. 'Without exception,' he wrote, 'they seem to be men of first-rate ability, though some of them plain in their manners.' He described, however, the growing party discord:

---

[34] McMaster, *History of the People of the United States*, II, 207; see also Schofield, II, 324–5.
[35] D. J. Jeremy (ed.), 'Henry Wansey and his American Journal, 1794', *Memoirs of the American Philosophical Society*, 82 (1970), 85.
[36] Priestley to Lindsey, 6, 15 June 1794, Rutt, I ii, 246, 255–6.
[37] Priestley to Belsham, 16 June 1794, Rutt, I ii, 259.
[38] Priestley to Lindsey, 15 June 1794, Rutt, I ii, 256–7.

The parties are the Federalists and Anti-Federalists, the former meaning the friends of the present system, with a leaning to that of England, and friendship with England; the latter wishing for some improvements, leaning to the French system, and rather wishing for war. With a little more irritation, the latter will certainly prevail.[39]

In a controversial move, he replied to the Addresses of the Societies who welcomed him to America. One of these was the Francophile Democratic Society, one of many which had spread across the country, their aim to keep a watchful eye on government. Their activities were deplored by the Federalists, and by Washington in particular, and encouraged by the opponents of a close American connection with England, and the rupturing of ties with France.[40] Priestley spoke of his relief at having reached a country where he could enjoy 'that protection from violence which laws and government promise in all countries'. In England, he declared to the Republican Natives of Great Britain and Ireland, 'all liberty of speech and of the press, as far as politics are concerned, is at an end'. And to the Democratic Society he added a remark which one who was to become his chief scourge in America—William Cobbett, another English emigrant—was to seize upon.[41] He could not, he declared, 'promise to be a better subject of this government than my whole conduct will evince that I have been to that of Great Britain'.[42]

The New York Addresses and Priestley's replies were published 'in the Gazettes'.[43] Although Priestley wrote to Lindsey of the general 'satisfaction' he believed he had given by 'the caution I have observed in my answers,'[44] it was to a clearly apprehensive John Vaughan that, on 8 June, he composed a letter, intended for publication in New

[39] Priestley to Lindsey, 15 June 1794, Rutt, I ii, 256–8; see also Priestley to Benjamin Vaughan, 30 July 1794, WPL, Graham, 'Revolutionary in Exile', 176–7.

[40] Philip Sheldon Foner, *The Democratic–Republican Societies, 1790–1800* (Westport, CT and London: Greenwood Press, 1976), 3; and Stanley Elkins and Eric McKitrick, *The Age of Federalism: The Early American Republic, 1788–1800* (New York and Oxford: OUP, 1993), 456ff., 484–5.

[41] William Cobbett, *Observations on the Emigration of Dr. Joseph Priestley, and on the Several Addresses Delivered to him, on his Arrival at New-York* (Philadelphia, 1794), 29.

[42] Rutt, I ii, 248, 253. For the Addresses, see Rutt, I ii, 241–3, 247–55.

[43] Cobbett, *Observations*, 37n.

[44] Priestley to Lindsey, 15 Jun. 1794, Rutt, I ii, 257.

York and Pennsylvania, setting out his political principles, and the course of action he intended to pursue while in America. He intended to be, as he had been in England, 'as little as can well be supposed of a political character, having only been an advocate for general liberty, & a free representation of the people as the foundation of it'. He rather disingenuously declared that he took no interest in the political parties of America. He defended the existence of clubs and political associations, and the need for some form of opposition to government, however 'fundamentally good' was that of America. 'As to myself, I have seen & felt so much of the greater abuses of government, that I shall perhaps be even too little attentive to smaller ones. For these ought to be narrowly watched, lest they should lead to greater.'[45]

On 18 June, the Priestleys departed for Philadelphia, where the Addresses and Priestley's replies were published by the Francophile Benjamin Franklin Bache, grandson of Franklin, in his paper, the *General Advertiser*.[46] In Philadelphia, Priestley met with a reception similar to that in New York, 'received with the most flattering attention by all persons of note,'[47] although, as in New York, regarded with 'jealousy and dread' by the preachers.[48] He was introduced to Washington by Thomas McKean, Chief Justice of Pennsylvania,[49] and he received a deputation from the Philosophical Society—to which in 1785 he had been elected a member.[50] Amongst those who paid their respects was the eminent Philadelphia physician, Dr Benjamin Rush, whom Priestley was to find one of the most congenial spirits in America.[51] The Society delivered an

[45] Priestley to John Vaughan, 8 Jun. 1794, APS, Miscellaneous Manuscripts Collection, Graham, 'Revolutionary in Exile', 175–6. See also Schofield, II, 331.

[46] Graham, 'Revolutionary in Exile', 54. For Bache, see James Tagg, *Benjamin Franklin Bache and the Philadelphia Aurora* (Philadelphia, PA: University of Pennsylvania Press, 1991).

[47] Priestley to Wilkinson, 27 Jun. 1794, WPL.

[48] Priestley to Lindsey, 24 Jun. 1794, Rutt, I ii, 263.

[49] Washington to McKean, 9 Jul. 1794, McKean Papers, III. 2, HSP; Graham, 'Revolutionary in Exile', 54.

[50] *Minutes of the American Philosophical Society* (Philadelphia, 1884), 223; see also D. W. Bronk, 'Joseph Priestley and the Early History of the American Philosophical Society', *Proceedings of the American Philosophical Society*, 86 (1943), 103, 106.

[51] Priestley to Rush, 14 Sept. 1794, *Scientific Correspondence*, 140.

Address,[52] signed by the great mathematician and astronomer, David Rittenhouse, who was also to become a personal friend.[53] 'I am confident,' wrote Priestley in his reply,

> ... from what I have already seen of the spirit of the people of this country, that it will soon appear that republican governments, in which every obstruction is removed to the exertions of all kinds of talents, will be far more favourable to science and the arts than any monarchical government has ever been.[54]

PRIESTLEY AND AMERICA

It was, indeed, as a long-standing friend of the Americans and their experiment in republican government, as much as for his persecution in England for his outspoken support for France, that Priestley was given such a rapturous welcome in the summer of 1794. Friend of Franklin—'his letters to me would have made a very large volume',[55] propagandist for the colonists, in 1774, at Franklin's behest,[56] and member not only of the Philosophical, but also of the American Academy of Arts and Sciences,[57] Priestley, with so many other radicals of his generation, followed the fortunes of the new republic across the Atlantic with an anxious interest.[58] He 'rejoiced,' he wrote to Joseph Willard, the President of Harvard, on receiving his membership of the American Academy of Arts and Sciences, 'that, after so noble and successful a struggle for your *liberties*, you are now, in time of peace, attending to matters of *science*'.[59] On one of his annual visits

---

[52] Rutt, I ii, 261–2.   [53] Graham, 'Revolutionary in Exile', 55, 89.

[54] Rutt, I ii, 262–3.

[55] Joseph Priestley, *Letters to the Inhabitants of Northumberland and its Neighbourhood, on Subjects Interesting to the Author, and to Them*, 2nd edn. (Philadelphia, 1801), 15. See also Graham, 'Revolutionary Philosopher, Part One,' 58, 60–2; Graham, 'Revolutionary in Exile', 6.

[56] Graham, 'Revolutionary Philosopher', part one, 58–9; Joseph Priestley, *An Address to Protestant Dissenters of all Denominations, on the Approaching Election of Members of Parliament* (London, 1774); see also Joseph Priestley, *The Present State of Liberty in Great Britain and her Colonies* (London, 1769), 'Revolutionary Philosopher,' part one, 56–7.

[57] Priestley to Joseph Willard, 23 Jun. 1785, *Proc. Mass. Hist. Soc.*, 43 (1910), 619.

[58] Graham, *Reform Politics*, 48ff.   [59] Priestley to Willard, 23 Jun. 1785.

to London, where he mingled with the supporters of America,[60] he became 'well acquainted' with John Adams, the then Minister to Great Britain.[61] From late in 1792 onwards, the two men were in correspondence on the subject of Priestley's emigration. 'It would give me great personal pleasure to see you in America,' wrote Adams, 'yet I cannot but think your removal would be a great loss to the philosophical and literary world.'[62] On Priestley's arrival in New York, he wrote to Adams, and received a reply, urging him to settle in Boston, which, Adams believed, was 'better calculated for him than any other part of America'.[63]

In the spring of 1793, Priestley had, indeed, inclined to settle in Boston, if emigration were to be his lot. To Willard, President of Harvard, he wrote of his preference for 'a situation near your university'. His youngest son, Harry, of whom he had fond hopes of 'succeeding him in his *Theological* and *Philosophical* Pursuits,' could, 'if he do not prefer Agriculture or Commerce,' there be placed under Willard's care. 'Should this take place,' he wrote, 'I promise myself much satisfaction from your society.'[64] To the dismay of some, however, his initial inclination was overridden by the powerful persuasion of others—Thomas Cooper, John Vaughan, and his eldest son, Joseph, who had developed what was to prove to be their disastrously over-ambitious scheme for the purchase of land in upstate Pennsylvania. 'The scheme of purchasing a tract of land is Mr. Vaughan's,' wrote

[60] Graham, *Reform Politics*, 56; Graham, 'Revolutionary in Exile', 6–8; see also S. P. Stetson, 'The Philadelphia Sojourn of Samuel Vaughan,' *PMHB*, 73 (1949), 459–74; Graham, *Reform Politics*, 50–1; Bronk, 'Joseph Priestley and the Early History of the American Philosophical Society,' 105.

[61] Rutt, I ii, 234 n.; Graham, *Reform Politics*, 56 & n.

[62] Adams to Priestley, 12 May 1793, Adams family papers, Mass. Hist. Soc., Reel 116; see also Priestley to Adams, 20 Dec. 1792, Mass. Hist. Soc., Reel 375; Priestley to Adams, 23 Feb. 1793, Mass. Hist. Soc., Reel 376; Adams to Priestley, 27 Feb. 1793, cit. Schofield, II, 333n.; Priestley to Adams, 20 Aug. 1793, Adams family papers, Mass. Hist. Soc., Reel 376.

[63] Jeremy (ed.), 'Henry Wansey and his American Journal, 1794,' 89; Graham, 'Revolutionary in Exile', 48 & n.

[64] Priestley to Willard, 10 Apr. 1793, *Proc. Mass. Hist. Soc.*, 43 (1910), 640. See also Rutt, XV, 523 n.; Priestley to Lindsey, 2 Jun. 1791, DWL, cit. Schofield, II, 406; Priestley to Adams, 23 Feb., 20 Aug. 1793, Adams family papers, Mass. Hist. Soc., Reel 376, Adams to Priestley, 12 May 1793, Mass. Hist. Soc., Reel 116, and also Graham, 'Revolutionary in Exile', 33, 48n., for Priestley, Jr.'s intention of visiting Boston (and also Priestley to Willard, 10 Apr. 1793).

Priestley, 'who, as he lives in America, is the best judge of it, and as he himself embarks as a principal, I am disposed to think well of it.'[65]

It was this plan which Thomas Cooper, on his return to England in 1794, had been at pains to promote. In his *Some Information Respecting America*, written in response to the 'many enquiries' with which he had been beset concerning America and the means of living there, Cooper decisively rejected the states of New England, on account of climate, which, he opined, made farming too difficult. The states of the south he rejected likewise: the heat was oppressive, the system of slave labour intolerable.[66] Cooper had left England with letters of introduction to Thomas Jefferson, at that time still Secretary of State. He met, by his own account, many members of Congress, and he was undoubtedly pressed by both Jefferson and James Madison, one of the authors of *The Federalist*, to bring the Priestleys to Virginia.[67] What was to prove to be a crucial decision had, however, been made. Early in July 1794, Priestley and his wife set out from Philadelphia, on an uncomfortable and hazardous journey of 130 miles 'through an almost impassable road', to inspect the lands for the proposed settlement on the banks of the Susquehannah, where they were undoubtedly hoping to be joined by many of their English friends.[68]

PRIESTLEY'S EARLY YEARS IN PENNSYLVANIA

Northumberland, situated 'within the forks of the Susquehannah River', was a township consisting of less than 100 houses. From the outset, Priestley was acutely aware of the chief drawback for him in this situation—a lack of proper communication with the outside

[65] Priestley to Wilkinson, 25 Jan. 1794, WPL. For the most comprehensive account, see Jeremy (ed.), 'Henry Wansey and his American Journal', 78–80.

[66] Thomas Cooper, *Some Information Respecting America, Collected by Thomas Cooper, Late of Manchester* (London, 1794), p. iii, 2ff.

[67] Graham, 'Revolutionary in Exile', 33, 173–4; Cooper, *Some Information*, p. iii; Jefferson to Priestley, 18 Jan. 1800, *Papers of Jefferson*, XXXI, 320.

[68] Anne Durning Holt, *A Life of Joseph Priestley* (London: OUP, 1931),186; and Hannah Lindsey to Catharine Cappe, *Memoirs of the Life of Catharine Cappe*, 264; Priestley to John Vaughan, 21 Jul. 1794, Dreer Collection, HSP; see also Priestley to Lindsey, 5 Jul. 1794, Rutt, I ii, 268–70; and Jeremy (ed.), 'Henry Wansey and his American Journal,' 79n., 80n.

world.[69] In September, there came the additional blow of the failure
of the settlement.[70] At this very time, he was offered the Chair of
Chemistry in the University of Pennsylvania, an offer which he did
not reject out of hand, but which, by 11 November, he had resolved
to decline. His heart failed him, he wrote, at the prospect of leaving
his wife for four months of the year.[71] 'Had this proposal been made
to me before the removal of my library and apparatus hither, the
case would have been different; but this being now done, at a great
risk and expense, I am, at all events, fixed for the remainder of my
life.'[72] The news of these developments was received with conster-
nation by his friends in England.[73] His situation was, as he wrote
to Lindsey, 'distant' from his 'original views'.[74] He was still hoping
for the establishment of a college, the plans for which were, however,
never realized.[75]

Throughout 1795, Priestley was concerned for his sons, all now
to become farmers, and he described his own labouring in the fields
alongside Harry: 'Two or three hours I always work in the fields, along
with my son. The weather beginning to be hot, I do this early and
late.'[76] Harry, he wrote,

works with his men, like one of them, and here there is little difference
between master and servant. Indeed, those terms are unknown. If there
was more subordination, it would be better for them all. There are no

---

[69] Graham, 'Revolutionary in Exile', 61, 65, 71ff.; Schofield, II, 345–6; and Jenny
Graham, 'A Hitherto Unpublished Letter of Joseph Priestley,' *E & D*, 14 (1995), 96–7.

[70] Jeremy (ed.), 'Henry Wansey and his American Journal,' 79; Graham, 'Revolutionary in Exile', 63–4, 178.

[71] Priestley to Rush, 14 Sept., 28 Oct., 3, 11 Nov. 1794, *Scientific Correspondence*,
139–45.

[72] Priestley to Rush, *Scientific Correspondence*, 145; see also Priestley to Lindsey, 12
Nov. 1794, Rutt, I ii, 280.

[73] William Vaughan to John Wilkinson, 25 Oct. 1794, WPL, Graham, 'Revolutionary in Exile', 178; Hannah Lindsey to Catharine Cappe, *Memoirs of Catharine Cappe*,
265; Sarah Vaughan to Charles Vaughan, 15 Aug. 1794, Charles Vaughan Papers,
Bowdoin College, 'Revolutionary in Exile', 71n.

[74] Priestley to Lindsey, 22 Feb. 1795, Rutt, I ii, 295; and to Adams, 13 Nov. 1794,
Adams family papers, Mass. Hist. Soc., Reel 378; Graham, 'Revolutionary in Exile', 68.

[75] Schofield, II, 330–1, 339–40; Priestley to Wedgwood, 17 Mar. 1795; Priestley to
Withering, 27 Oct. 1795, *Scientific Autobiography*, 285–9. See also Priestley to Lindsey,
10 Feb. 1795, n.d. (1795), 12 July, 12 Aug. 1795, Rutt, I ii, 293, 303–4, 312, 314; and
Graham, 'Revolutionary in Exile', 77–8.

[76] Ibid. 80–1; Priestley to Lindsey, 12 Jul. 1795, Rutt, I ii, 311.

beggars here, or in the country; but though they are miserably housed, hardly clothed, and feed no better than their cattle, they will not go to service.[77]

The difficulty of keeping even the servants whose passage had been paid across the Atlantic afflicted the Priestleys from their arrival in New York onwards.[78] In October, Mary Priestley was described as 'much pester'd & provok'd from the impossibility of getting or keeping Servants,'[79] and Priestley wrote of her great 'trials' in this respect.[80] In the spring of 1796, he expressed himself forcibly on the subject to the wife of the English Minister in Philadelphia.[81] By that time, indeed, the Priestleys were employing 'a black slave,' hired 'by the week'; and Thomas Cooper was considering purchasing 'a set of negroes ... They are purchaseable here till they are 28 Years old'.[82]

With Thomas Cooper, an ardent opponent of the slave trade and slavery,[83] and outspoken on his arrival on the need for the abolition of the latter in America,[84] Priestley, in contrast to the intellectual circles in which he moved when in Philadelphia,[85] had been forced by harsh circumstance to adapt himself to his surroundings. By the mid-1790s, the institution of slavery in Pennsylvania was in steep decline. In 1796, however, it was still the case that, as stipulated in a compromise clause in the Abolition Act passed by the Pennsylvania Assembly on 1 March 1780, 'all children of slave mothers were to be required to serve their mother's master until age twenty eight'.[86]

---

[77] Priestley to Lindsey, 12 Jul. 1795, Graham, 'Revolutionary in Exile', I ii, 310.

[78] Priestley to Lindsey, 24 Jun. 1794, DWL MSS, 12.12, passage omitted by Rutt.

[79] N. B. Wilkinson, 'Mr Davy's Diary', *Pennsylvania History*, 20 (1953), 258, 3 Oct. 1794: passage omitted in Rutt's extracts from Davy (Rutt, I ii, 278–9nn).

[80] Priestley to Wilkinson, 12 Nov. 1794, 17 Dec. 1795, WPL.

[81] Henrietta Liston to her uncle, 14 Aug. 1796, *WMQ*, 3 Ser. 11 (1954), 602.

[82] Graham, 'Revolutionary in Exile', 87 & nn.

[83] Joseph Priestley, *A Sermon on the Subject of the Slave Trade; Delivered to a Society of Protestant Dissenters at the New Meeting, in Birmingham* (Birmingham, 1788); Thomas Cooper, *Letters on the Slave Trade* (Manchester, 1787); Thomas Cooper, *Supplement to Mr. Cooper's Letters on the Slave Trade* (Warrington, 1788); see also Malone, *Cooper*, 19–22.

[84] Rutt, I ii, 254.

[85] Gary B. Nash and Jean R. Soderlund, *Freedom by Degrees: Emancipation in Pennsylvania and its Aftermath* (New York and Oxford: OUP, 1991), 158–9.

[86] Nash and Soderlund, *Freedom by Degrees*, 103; see also Arthur Zilversmit, *The First Emancipation: The Abolition of Slavery in the North* (Chicago and London: The

It was at this stage of his fortunes in Pennsylvania, when, as he declared in an unguarded moment to the wife of the English Minister in Philadelphia, 'the *Servants* alone are sufficient to render a native of Britain miserable in this Country',[87] that a visiting Frenchman, de Liancourt, called upon the Priestleys in Northumberland. De Liancourt professed to find Priestley's 'modes of life and dress...nearly the same as in England, the wig excepted, which he has laid aside'.[88] The Russells, on their arrival in Northumberland in September 1795, were, however, much dismayed by the situation in which they found their friends. Had they 'been banished by law' to such a place, declared Thomas Russell, 'they would have been right to make the best of the situation. But to retire [there] into voluntary exile, appeared to him extraordinary and unaccountable'.[89] From another English emigrant, Ralph Eddowes, there had come criticism of Thomas Cooper's over-optimistic account of the lands in Pennsylvania. It was a criticism of which Cooper was clearly aware. He had heard, he wrote in a letter to England in the summer of 1795, 'that People say Dr. Priestley & I are dissatisfied with the country: I desire, *&* the Dr. *desires*, this may be contradicted, for I do not believe either he or I have felt that sentiment—for a moment. I have nothing to unsay about the Country, but,' he nevertheless added, 'I shall recommend it to no one any more'.[90]

The Russells departed, to Priestley's deep regret, for New England, and he had by now heard of Benjamin Vaughan's intention to settle on his family estate in Maine. 'I can only say that I wish,' he wrote, 'he was nearer to me.' 'His being *here* would be a great addition to my satisfaction in the place. What I chiefly want is such society as his.'[91] In the wake of these disappointments, a further series of blows befell him. In December 1795, young Harry died of an ague, contracted in his labours on his farm. 'Considering how delicate his constitution was,' wrote Priestley, 'and that his education was for a

University of Chicago Press, 1967); E. R. Turner, 'The Abolition of Slavery in Pennsylvania,' *PMHB*, 36.2 (1912), 129–42.

[87] Henrietta Liston to her uncle, 14 Aug. 1796, *WMQ*, 3 Ser. 11 (1954), 602.

[88] François Alexandre Frédéric, Duc de La Rochefoucauld Liancourt, *Travels through the United States of America* (London, 1799), 75.

[89] Graham, 'Revolutionary in Exile', 84; Jeyes, *The Russells*, 169, 197–9.

[90] Graham, 'Revolutionary in Exile', 86–7.

[91] Ibid. 84, Murray, *Benjamin Vaughan*, 381.

learned profession, it was something extraordinary that he should so cheerfully submit to all the drudgery of a common farmer.' 'Had he been bred a farmer, he could not have been more assiduous than he was ... and it was always said that he was better served than any other farmer in this country.'[92] From this disaster, Mary Priestley did not recover. Her death, in September 1796, put further to the test the fortitude Priestley had summoned on the death of his son. 'I never stood in more need of friendship than I do now,' he wrote to Lindsey. '... This day I bury my wife.' 'It has been a happy union to me for more than thirty four years,' he wrote to his brother-in-law, John Wilkinson, 'in which I have had no care about anything in the world; so that, without any anxiety, I have been able to give all my time to my own pursuits. I always said I was only a lodger in her house.'[93] In the following January, he wrote of feeling 'quite unhinged, and incapable of the exertions I used to make'.[94] And it is possible that, with Mary Priestley's restraining influence no longer present,[95] what some were to regard as Priestley's errors of judgement in the ensuing years might have been avoided.

It was in the aftermath of the death of his wife that Priestley's increasingly unsettled thoughts dwelt upon the possibility of removing to France, for, among other reasons, his at times urgent need to realize his investments in the French funds.[96] He was in correspondence with Hurford Stone, who, in 1796, published a *Letter* to him in Paris.[97] This, while distancing itself from the horrors perpetrated by the Jacobins, was a lengthy tribute to the virtues of French republicanism in general, and the current French constitution in

---

[92] Priestley to Wilkinson, 17 Dec. 1795, WPL; Priestley to Lindsey, 17 Dec. 1795, Rutt, I ii, 327–9: See also William Bakewell, 'Some Particulars of Dr Priestley's Residence at Northumberland, America,' *Monthly Repository*, 1 (1806), 396; Schofield, II, 348, 349n.

[93] Priestley to Lindsey, 19 Sept. 1796, Rutt, I ii, 354; Priestley to Wilkinson, 19 Sept. 1796, WPL; Priestley to William Vaughan, 1 Nov. 1796, *Scientific Correspondence*, 151–2. See also Schofield, II, 348–9; H. J. McLachlan, 'Mary Priestley. A Woman of Character,' in Schwartz and McEvoy, 251–62.

[94] Priestley to Wilkinson, 25 Jan. 1797, WPL; and Schofield, II, 348–9 & n.

[95] Rutt, I ii, 367n.

[96] Graham, 'Revolutionary in Exile', 97–8, 179; Schofield, II, 350.

[97] John Hurford Stone (pseud. Plotinus), *A Letter from John Hurford Stone to Dr. Priestley* (Paris: the English Press, IV year of the Republic).

particular. It ended with the hope that Priestley might return from his state of exile to Europe: 'either to France, where liberty is established; or to England, about to be restored to more than her ancient freedom.'[98]

PRIESTLEY IN PHILADELPHIA

Despite his inclination to remove to France, and the difficulties attending his way of life in Northumberland, Priestley, in particular after his visit to Philadelphia in 1796, was increasingly identifying himself with America. 'Every thing here is the reverse of what it is with you,' he wrote to Lindsey: 'Indeed, I do not suppose there ever was any country in the world in a more flourishing and promising way.... But great numbers,' he continued, 'find themselves, on one account or other, disappointed, and return, I understand, with very unfavourable ideas of the country; and for this I see no remedy. I have been careful not to encourage any person to emigrate, though I admire this country very much.'[99] Priestley delivered a set of thirteen discourses in the Universalist church in Philadelphia in the spring of 1796 to crowded audiences, including John Adams, to whom they were dedicated, and many members of Congress.[100] This was in striking contrast to his stay in Philadelphia in 1794. He would not, he had written to John Vaughan from Northumberland, 'be reduced to a disgraceful silence by the bigotry and jealousy of the preachers'.[101]

It was this visit by Priestley to Philadelphia which prepared the ground for the founding of the first Unitarian congregation in the city. Among the congregation who organized themselves in the summer of 1796 were several prominent English emigrants, including

---

[98] *A Letter from John Hurford Stone*, 152.

[99] Priestley to Lindsey, 15 Feb. 1796, Rutt, I ii, 332–3.

[100] Graham, 'Revolutionary in Exile', 88–9; Joseph Priestley, *Discourses relating to the Evidences of Revealed Religion, Delivered in the Church of the Universalists at Philadelphia* (Philadelphia, 1796). Schofield, II, 327, wrongly gives the date of the discourses as 1794. See also Elizabeth M. Geffen, *Philadelphia Unitarianism, 1796–1861* (Philadelphia: University of Pennsylvania Press, 1961), 28, 32.

[101] Priestley to John Vaughan, 6 May 1795, APS, BP 931.

William Russell. 'They were all English families. Not a single native American joined them,' Priestley was later to write.[102]

Lodging in the house of William Russell in the spring of 1796, Priestley was received cordially by Washington; he dined with the eminent Professor of Natural Philosophy, Provost Ewing, of the University; he was on close terms with the Professor of Chemistry, James Woodhouse; he paid several visits to Rittenhouse, before the latter's untimely death; he was a frequent attender at the Philosophical Society, and was not long afterwards invited to be their President, an invitation he was to refuse.[103] It was at one of these meetings that he certainly renewed his acquaintance with Talleyrand, who was shortly to depart for France.[104] Talleyrand was also an acquaintance of the Russells. He and Priestley had met at Hurford Stone's house in London in 1792. And that Priestley was still considering removing to France can be seen in the remark Talleyrand made on his own departure: 'The last thing he said to me,' wrote Priestley, 'was, that he expected to see me in France'.[105]

In Philadelphia in the spring of 1796 Priestley also attended debates in Congress, including that of 28 April, after which he spoke with awe of the oratory of the Federalist, Fisher Ames,[106] in his dramatic speech in support of the notorious Treaty with England, negotiated by the Chief Justice, John Jay. The Treaty had provoked widespread outrage and popular demonstrations in the previous year, both for the secrecy of the Senate's deliberations, and for its contents, when they were eventually published, by Bache, in the Philadelphia *Aurora*, shortly

[102] Priestley to Lindsey, 11 Sep. 1796, Rutt, I ii, 352–3; Priestley to Lindsey, n.d. received 'March 16, 1801,' Rutt, I ii, 453. See also Geffen, *Philadelphia Unitarianism*, 32–45.

[103] Graham, 'Revolutionary in Exile', 88–9; Lucy E. L. Ewing, *Dr. John Ewing and Some of his Noted Connections* (Philadelphia: printed for the author, The John C. Winston Company, 1930). Ewing was also a Vice-President of the Philosophical Society. See also Bronk, 'Joseph Priestley and the Early History of the American Philosophical Society,' 107; Priestley to B. S. Barton, 8 Oct. 1796, *Scientific Autobiography*, 291–2.

[104] J. L. Earl, 'Talleyrand in Philadelphia, 1794–1796,' *PMHB*, 91 (1967), 294 & n.

[105] Jeyes, *The Russells*, 203; Michael Rapport, 'Stone, John Hurford (1763–1818)', *Oxford DNB*; Priestley to Hurford Stone, 20 Jan. 1798, Rutt, I ii, 394.

[106] Charles Caldwell, *Autobiography of Charles Caldwell* (Philadelphia, 1855), 114; Graham, 'Revolutionary in Exile', 90 and n. See also McMaster, *History of the People of the United States*, II, 280–1; Elkins and McKitrick, *Age of Federalism*, 448.

before Independence Day.[107] There can be no doubt that Priestley shared the Republicans' outrage,[108] if it was not until later that he expressed himself in print: 'In this proceeding I see nothing of the fairness and openness that I should have expected from a republican government'.[109]

Priestley was to make a second visit to Philadelphia in the winter and spring of 1797, by which time the actions of the retiring French Minister, Pierre Auguste Adet, distinguished chemist and certainly not unknown to Priestley,[110] had further inflamed Federalist opinion. For Adet, acting on orders from the Directory—whose members now formed the government of France and who, 'angered and dismayed by the Jay Treaty,' were adopting an increasingly belligerent stance towards America—published, in Bache's *Aurora*, four diplomatic notes, announcing 'the new policy of the Directory,' instructing all Frenchmen in America to wear the tricolor cockade, and effectively appealing to the American people to support the Republican party, and Jefferson in particular, in the forthcoming presidential election.[111] This blatant attempt to influence American politics largely failed. Jefferson was elected Vice-President, and it was now that Priestley, through the good offices of Benjamin Rush, expressed his wish to meet this effective leader of the opposition to Washington's Anglophile policies—due to arrive in Philadelphia from his long retreat at Monticello.[112] It was a desire which, as a letter from Jefferson to Rittenhouse attests, was reciprocal.[113] And in the spring of 1797, the two men, so closely linked in spirit, in philosophy and

---

[107] McMaster, II, 212ff., Elkins and McKitrick, 415ff.; Tagg, *Bache and the Philadelphia Aurora*, 239–63.

[108] Priestley to Lindsey, 12 Aug. 1795, Rutt, I ii, 315.

[109] Priestley, *Letters to Inhabitants of Northumberland*, 72–3.

[110] Graham, 'Revolutionary in Exile', 97–8 & n., 105; and see Schofield, II, 355, for their chemical controversy.

[111] McMaster, *History of the People of the United States*, II, 287–9, 300–1; Merrill Daniel Peterson, *Thomas Jefferson and the New Nation: A Biography* (New York: OUP, 1970), 555–6; Tagg, *Bache and the Philadelphia Aurora*, 293–4.

[112] Rush to Jefferson, 4 Feb. 1797, *Letters of Benjamin Rush* ed. Lyman Henry Butterfield (Memoirs Amer. Phil. Soc., vol. 30, part 2, Princeton University Press, 1951), II, 786; and *Papers of Jefferson*, XXIX, 284. See also Priestley to B. S. Barton, 8 Oct. 1796, *Scientific Autobiography*, 291–2.

[113] Thomas Jefferson to David Rittenhouse, 24 Feb. 1795, *Papers of Jefferson*, XXVIII, 279.

politics, finally met, and laid the foundation for the friendship which was to be Priestley's greatest satisfaction in America. 'I have seen a good deal of him,' he wrote to Thomas Belsham, his and Lindsey's closest friend in London.[114]

On this visit to Philadelphia, during and after which the attitude of his old friend Adams, now elected to the presidency, underwent a marked change towards him,[115] Priestley delivered, in the University Hall, his discourse entitled *The Case of Poor Emigrants*. This was, as Schofield has rightly emphasized, a response to the increasingly xenophobic policies of the Federalists.[116] What harm, Priestley asked, in a characteristic utterance, could political refugees of any complexion do to the great good sense and inherent stability of America:

where the great body of the people are so fully enlightened with respect to the principles of good government, that they easily discern the just medium between them; and what is more, daily see them exemplified to their own unspeakable advantage in practice. In this state of things, those emigrants themselves will soon learn to correct their own errors.... If the emigrants be men of information and discernment, you may even receive benefit from the lights they may give you. Where there is perfect liberty of speaking and writing, no principles can be dangerous. In these circumstances *truth* has a decided advantage, and will certainly prevail in the end.[117]

In this discourse, Priestley was also soliciting support for a society, already in existence, for the assistance of emigrants of all classes and political creeds. He gave an account of its achievements to date, in finding employment and other material assistance for emigrants, 'from the reports of the acting committee'; and an account, 'from the reports of the physician,' of the 'pecuniary and medical assistance' it had also provided for 'sick and needy emigrants'.[118] It seems very probable that this society was that founded in 1794 by, among others, two members of the Unitarian congregation—the Philadelphia

[114] Priestley to Belsham, 14 Mar. 1797, Rutt, I ii, 373. See also Graham, 'Revolutionary in Exile', 88n., 96n.; Peterson, *Thomas Jefferson and the New Nation*, 576.

[115] Graham, 'Revolutionary in Exile', 95, 97, 99–100.   [116] Schofield, II, 332.

[117] Joseph Priestley, *The Case of Poor Emigrants, Recommended in a Discourse, Delivered at the University Hall in Philadelphia, on Sunday, February 19, 1797* (Philadelphia, 1797), 25–6.

[118] Ibid. 28–9.

Society for the Information and Assistance of Persons Emigrating from Foreign Countries.[119]

A year later, as relations between America and France deteriorated further, and discord between Federalists and Republicans became increasingly vituperative, Priestley published anonymously, in Bache's *Aurora*, his *Maxims of Political Arithmetic*. These demonstrate, as does his *Case of Poor Emigrants*, his increasing identification with the social and political trials facing America. In the *Maxims*, he expounded the Jeffersonian philosophy of developing the natural resources of America—improving her agriculture and internal communications, and expanding her literary and scientific institutions— in response to the Federalist policy of building an expensive navy to protect the commercial interest, in the face of French aggression. It was, however, he wrote, perhaps 'the wise plan of Providence' to involve America 'in the vortex of European politics, and the misery of European wars; and to prevent the importation of the means of knowledge till a better use would be made of them'. And he commented on the prospect for the Union—possible civil war, with many lives lost—were the present level of party animosity to continue.[120]

PRIESTLEY UNDER FEDERALIST ASSAULT

By the time of these two public statements concerning the American political scene, the substantial house in Northumberland which Mary Priestley had planned in 1794 was finally near to completion. 'Excepting Philadelphia, and its neighbourhood, there are perhaps few that are equal to it in the whole State,' Priestley was to write. His 'library and philosophical apparatus' were, he believed, 'superior to any thing of the kind in this country'.[121] And yet, throughout 1798,

[119] Geffen, *Philadelphia Unitarianism*, 44; J. Thomas Scharf and Thompson Westcott, *History of Philadelphia, 1609–1884*, 3 vols (Philadelphia, 1884), I, 480.

[120] [Joseph Priestley] *Maxims of Political Arithmetic, Applied to the Case of the United States of America, First Published in the Aurora for February 26 & 27, 1798, by a Quaker in Politics*. For their subsequent publication by Priestley, see below, n.141.

[121] Schofield, II, 347; and Priestley, *Letters to Inhabitants of Northumberland*, 4.

Priestley was still considering removing to France.[122] In January of that year he wrote to Hurford Stone, rejoicing 'in the success of the French'. He was, he wrote, 'subject to more coarse abuse, as a friend of France, than I was in England'.[123] He was, indeed, as a friend of France, now so unpopular in Philadelphia that even John Vaughan declined to receive him.[124] He was, nevertheless, commenting in an unguarded fashion to a Unitarian congressman in Philadelphia on the rapidly worsening relations between France and America. These had plumbed new depths with the behaviour of the Directory, and Talleyrand in particular, towards the American envoys sent to Paris by Adams to negotiate.[125] The publication of the news of this insult 'produced,' as Jefferson himself wrote, 'such a shock on the republican mind as has never been seen since our independence'.[126] If Jefferson's reaction was modified by disapproval of Adams's policies, the general reaction in America amounted to a state of political hysteria. The country was put on a war footing, and in June and July the Alien and Sedition Acts were passed,[127] as a result of which some hundreds of immigrant French, including Volney, 'the peripatetic French rationalist' and acquaintance of Jefferson and Priestley,[128] made a rapid departure from America.[129] In July, Priestley had the mortification to discover that his correspondence with the Unitarian congressman, George Thatcher, had been bruited abroad in Philadelphia. In this, he had deplored the Directory's military aggression, and their behaviour towards America: their 'successes, like those of the Romans, appear to have made them ... equally void of fear or shame'. He nevertheless deplored Adams's policies: 'If ever there be a restoration of harmony,

---

[122] Graham, 'Revolutionary in Exile', 102, 105.

[123] Priestley to J. Hurford Stone, 20 Jan. 1798, Rutt, I ii, 393.

[124] Graham, 'Revolutionary in Exile', 105 & n.

[125] McMaster, *History of the People of the United States*, II, 368ff.; Elkins and McKitrick, *Age of Federalism*, 571ff.

[126] Peterson, *Jefferson and the New Nation*, 596; and see Jefferson to James Madison, 6 Apr. 1798, *Papers of Jefferson*, XXX, 250–1.

[127] McMaster, *History of the People of the United States*, II, 393–7; Elkins and McKitrick, *Age of Federalism*, 590–3; James Morton Smith, *Freedom's Fetters: The Alien and Sedition Laws and American Civil Liberties* (Ithaca, NY: Cornell University Press, 1956).

[128] Peterson, *Jefferson and the New Nation*, 520, 576.

[129] Ibid. 604, 618; McMaster, *History of the People of the United States*, II, 396.

his abusive language must be retracted, or suppressed'. And he spoke with certainty, 'whether there be peace or war,' of revolution in England.[130]

Priestley was now, as he was well aware, in danger of deportation from America by his old friend Adams.[131] In August came the most damaging blow, delivered by Hurford Stone. Stone's intercepted letters to Priestley, and to another, anonymous correspondent in America, praising the achievements, civil and military, of the French republic, making clear the latter's friendship with Talleyrand, deriding the Americans, eagerly awaiting the conquest of England, and anticipating Priestley's return to France or England, '*as England will then be*,'[132] were published in England in May, and seized upon with triumph by Cobbett. 'PRIESTLEY COMPLETELY DETECTED,' he proclaimed on 20 August, and he called on Adams to deport him without delay.[133] This, Adams, in spite of having in his possession a potentially compromising note from Priestley, resolutely refused to do.[134]

In the wake of this disaster, Priestley certainly did not distance himself from Hurford Stone. He was, he declared, a friend of many years' standing, and 'a zealous friend of the American and French Revolutions, which sufficiently accounts for his corresponding with me'. He could not, however, be 'answerable for what he or any other person may think proper to write to me'.[135] He revealed, moreover, the identity of the other intended recipient, Benjamin Vaughan, and, although this had been more than hinted at in Hurford Stone's letter, the furore this aroused in Boston, and amongst Vaughan's family, was intense.[136] Vaughan chose to maintain silence. In the following year, however, Priestley published his *Letters to the Inhabitants of*

---

[130]   Graham, 'Revolutionary in Exile', 108–10.

[131]   Ibid. 109–10, 133, 147, 180–1.

[132]   John Hurford Stone, *Copies of Original Letters Recently Written by Persons in Paris to Dr Priestley in America. Taken on Board of a Neutral Vessel* (2nd. edn., London, 1798); Graham, 'Revolutionary in Exile', 110–13.

[133]   *Porcupine's Gazette*, 20 Aug. 1798; Graham, 'Revolutionary in Exile', 110, 113.

[134]   Graham, 'Revolutionary in Exile', 125 and n., 126n., 179.

[135]   Priestley to Cobbett, 4 Sep. 1798, Rutt, I ii, 406–7, Graham, 'Revolutionary in Exile', 114.

[136]   Priestley to Cobbett, 4 Sep. 1798; Stone, *Letters*, 28; Graham, 'Revolutionary in Exile', 114–15; Murray, *Benjamin Vaughan*, 416–22.

Northumberland, to defend himself from the obloquy with which he was beset. In these he set out, in extraordinary detail, the extent of his political interest—so much of which he had previously denied; he declared his pride in his citizenship of and association with republican France in 1792; he wrote of the pleasure he received from Hurford Stone's correspondence. He denied, somewhat sophistically, any wish to leave America. But he wrote again of his certainty that revolution was inevitable in England—'tho' I wish it may be effected peaceably, and without the interference of any foreign power'. 'Shocked,' as he was, by 'the enormities which have been committed in France,' he refused to join the prevailing fashion of exclaiming against '*all revolutions* indiscriminately, and all the *principles* that lead to them.'[137]

In the second part of his *Letters*, Priestley spoke freely of his views on the American Constitution, and of Adams's abuse of the power of the executive. The laws lately passed in Congress were, he wrote, 'in some respects...more severe than those in England'. The Sedition Act he compared to the fetters placed upon the press in France under the Ancien Regime. Of the Alien Laws, he said that 'had those laws been made six years ago, there would not have been an Englishman in this place'.[138]

The *Letters to the Inhabitants of Northumberland* mortified Priestley's friends in England, alienated John and Benjamin Vaughan, and aroused much Federalist ire.[139] The Vaughans believed their old mentor to have been under the influence of Thomas Cooper, whose own *Political Essays*, an eloquent attack on Adams, were also published in 1799.[140] In his *Letters*, in his chapter once more enunciating Jeffersonian principles of the development of the natural resources of America and the avoidance of war, Priestley recommended Cooper's *Essays*. Cooper, he claimed, 'independently of me, adopted the same principles, and has enforced them in his excellent manner. 'A nation,' he wrote,

---

[137] Priestley, *Letters to Inhabitants of Northumberland*, 3ff, 23–5.

[138] Ibid. 62–9.

[139] Graham, 'Revolutionary in Exile', 127–31, 137, 141, 144–5.

[140] Thomas Cooper, *Political Essays Originally Inserted in the Northumberland Gazette, with Additions* (Northumberland, 1799); and see Malone, *Public Life of Thomas Cooper*, 91ff.

conducting its affairs on these maxims, defending its territory by a well disciplined militia, remonstrating against injuries from other nations, but never revenging them, and withal acting justly and generously on all occasions, could not fail to be respected, and would not be subject to many insults. It would insure the invaluable blessing of *peace*. It would employ its hands, and its capital, in the improvement of the country, in making bridges, roads, and navigable canals, in encouraging science, agriculture, and manufactures. It would contract no debts, and have occasion for few taxes; and therefore could not fail to flourish more than any country has ever yet done.[141]

Priestley's *Letters* and Cooper's *Essays* earned both men the gratitude of more than one leading American Republican, Jefferson in particular. 'The papers of Political arithmetic both in your's & Mr. Cooper's pamphlets are the most precious gifts that can be made to us,' he wrote, on receiving them from Priestley: 'for we are running navigation-mad, & commerce-mad, and navy-mad, which is worst of all.' He commiserated with Priestley on 'the persecutions' to which even in America he had been subjected, he asked his advice on the proposed University of Virginia, and invited him to Monticello. In a second letter, he wrote of his conviction that 'the temporary delirium which has been excited here' was 'fast passing away'.[142] Jefferson distributed Priestley's *Letters* amongst his friends in Virginia; in New York, an edition was printed by the leading Republican, Chancellor Livingston; and in Philadelphia the *Letters* swiftly sold out, and went into a second edition.[143] They were regarded by more than one observer, including Adams himself, as having played an

---

[141] Priestley, *Letters to Inhabitants of Northumberland*, 79. Priestley's *Maxims of Political Arithmetic*, published in the *Aurora* in 1798, were appended to this chapter in both the 1799 and 1801 editions of the *Letters*.

[142] Jefferson to Priestley, 18, 27 Jan. 1800, *Papers of Jefferson*, XXXI, 319–22, 339–41. See also Priestley to Jefferson, 30 Jan., 8 May 1800, *Papers of Jefferson*, XXXI, 346–7, 567–70, Schofield, II, 340–2, for Priestley's replies, and his 'Hints concerning Public Education'; and Graham, 'Revolutionary in Exile', 143.

[143] Jefferson to Priestley, 18 Jan. 1800; Priestley to Russell, 7 Feb. 1800, Priestley to Lindsey, 29 May 1800, Rutt, I ii, 427, 435–6; Priestley to Jefferson, 30 Jan. 1800, *Papers of Jefferson*, XXXI, 346; Priestley to Livingston, 17 Apr. 1800, *Scientific Autobiography*, 303; and see Madison to Jefferson, 4 Jan. 1800, *The Republic of Letters: The Correspondence between Thomas Jefferson and James Madison 1776–1826*: vol. II *1790–1804*, ed. James Morton Smith (New York and London: W. W. Norton & Company, 1995), 1124.

influential role in securing his defeat in the bitterly contested Election of 1800.[144]

PRIESTLEY'S FINAL YEARS UNDER JEFFERSON

On Jefferson's election, Priestley wrote of his relief: 'The measures of the late administration are now almost universally reprobated', he wrote to Lindsey.[145] And he had the satisfaction of a letter from Jefferson, welcoming him to America, tendering him 'the homage of its respect & esteem,' assuring him 'of the protection of those laws which were made for the wise and good like you', and disclaiming 'the legitimacy of that libel on legislation, which, under the form of a law, was for some time placed among them'. 'The storm,' he wrote, was 'now subsiding, and the horizon becoming serene.'[146] In his First Inaugural, Jefferson had expressed his confidence in republican principles of government, and in the free expression of opinion, the foundation on which it rested.[147] Priestley wrote, also, of his satisfaction 'in the glorious reverse that has taken place ... This I flatter myself will be the permanent establishment of truly republican principles in this country, and also contribute to the same desirable event in more distant ones'.[148]

After Jefferson's first annual message to Congress, in December 1801, Priestley's admiration for his Presidency increased. 'He is every thing that the friends of liberty can wish,' he wrote to Hurford Stone.[149] For Jefferson proposed to abolish all internal taxation, the elimination of the national debt within 16 or 17 years, and the

---

[144] Graham, 'Revolutionary in Exile', 144, 165–6; Schofield, II, 339.

[145] Priestley to Lindsey, 25 Dec. 1800, Rutt, I ii, 451.

[146] Jefferson to Priestley, 21 Mar. 1801, Lib. Cong. Mss.; *The Works of Thomas Jefferson*, ed. Paul Leicester Ford, 12 vols. (New York and London: G. F Putnam's Sons, 1904–5), IX, 216–19. See Graham, 'Revolutionary in Exile', 147–8n.

[147] *Thomas Jefferson, Writings*, ed. Merrill Daniel Peterson (New York: Library of America, 1984), 492–6.

[148] Priestley to Jefferson, 10 Apr. 1801, Lib. Cong. Mss., and Graham, 'Revolutionary in Exile', 180–1.

[149] Priestley to Hurford Stone, 19 Feb. 1802, Rutt, I ii, 476.

reduction of the standing army and navy.[150] 'You will see by the message of our President to the Congress the uncommonly pleasing prospect that is before us in this country', wrote Priestley to Lindsey. 'It is such as was never made by the chief magistrate of any nation before ... It must, I should think, make his administration universally popular, great as the prejudices were that had been raised against him by the opposite party.'[151]

It was under Jefferson's administration that Priestley was consulted by the Quaker congressman, George Logan, on the new President's measures;[152] and that he found himself 'for the first time in my life ... in any degree of favour with the governor of the country in which I live'.[153] In 1802, he dedicated the second volume of his *Church History* to Jefferson:

Many have appeared the friends of the rights of man while they were subject to the power of others, and especially when they were sufferers by it; but I do not recollect one besides yourself who retained the same principles, and acted upon them, in a station of real power.[154]

In 1803, Priestley published a new edition of his *Lectures on History and General Policy*, adding a chapter expressing his renewed confidence in the Constitution of America, although, with Jefferson, he had finally abandoned hope for France.[155] 'Tell Mr. Jefferson,' he wrote, in one of his last surviving letters, 'that I think myself happy to have lived so long under his excellent administration; and that I have

---

[150] Peterson, ed., *Writings of Jefferson*, 501–9; Peterson, *Jefferson and the New Nation*, 684–9.

[151] Priestley to Lindsey, 19 Dec. 1801, APS, BP 931, Graham, 'Revolutionary in Exile', 181–3.

[152] Ibid. 154.

[153] Priestley to Logan, 26 Dec. 1801, Logan Papers, V. 43, HSP; Graham, 'Revolutionary in Exile', 153–4.

[154] Graham,'Revolutionary in Exile', 154–5, 183–4; Joseph Priestley, *A General History of the Christian Church, from the Fall of the Western Empire to the Present Time* (Northumberland, 1802), p. iv.

[155] Graham, 'Revolutionary in Exile', 159–61; Joseph Priestley, *Lectures on History and General Policy; to which is Prefixed, an Essay on a Course of Liberal Education for Civil and Active Life; and an Additional Lecture on the Constitution of the United States* (Philadelphia, 1803).

a prospect of dying in it. It is, I am confident, the best on the face of the earth, and yet I hope to rise to some thing more excellent still.'[156]

Marred as they had been by much personal tragedy, as well as political obloquy, Priestley's years in America were eventually to secure him a position of lasting esteem. In England, his political intervention in the wake of the French Revolution had brought upon him only harassment and violence. It was in America that he had the satisfaction of seeing his political ideals, first enunciated at an early stage in his career, put into practice. As their author, it was in America also that his contribution to democratic thought was gratefully acknowledged.

[156] Priestley to Logan, 25 Jan. 1804, Barton Papers, p. 65, HSP; Graham, 'Revolutionary in Exile', 164.

Selected Bibliography

The aim of this bibliography is to provide the reader with a brief guide to (a) Priestley's most important writings in his main areas of interest and (b) useful secondary works on or relevant to Priestley, arranged alphabetically under the following headings: Collections of Essays on Priestley; Life and Correspondence; Religion, Theology and Dissent; Education and Historiography; Science; Philosophy; Politics. No attempt is made to describe the complex publishing history of Priestley's works, most of which went through multiple editions. R. E. Crook, *A Bibliography of Joseph Priestley, 1733–1804* (London: The Library Association, 1966) is a valuable checklist of Priestley's publications. For further works by Priestley and other eighteenth-century authors and for more specialist secondary works the reader should consult the notes to individual chapters. For names without titles and for short titles see the List of Abbreviations.

COLLECTIONS OF ESSAYS ON PRIESTLEY

Anderson & Lawrence.
Bowden & Rosner.
E&D, 2 (1983), Joseph Priestley 1733–1804 celebratory issue.
Kieft, Lester and Bennett R. Willeford, Jr. (eds), *Joseph Priestley: Scientist, Theologian, and Metaphysician* (Lewisburg, PA: Bucknell University Press, 1980).
Oxygen and the Conversion of Future Feedstocks: The Proceedings of the Third BOC Priestley Conference (London: Royal Society of Chemistry, 1984).
Schwartz & McEvoy.

LIFE AND CORRESPONDENCE

Priestley's Writings

'Memoirs and Correspondence, 1733–1804', in Rutt I i and I ii.

Memoirs of Dr Joseph Priestley, to the Year 1795, Written by Himself: With a Continuation, to the Time of his Decease, by his Son, Joseph Priestley (Northumberland [PA], 1806; London, 1806).

Scientific Autobiography.

Scientific Correspondence.

Secondary Works

Clark, John Ruskin, *Joseph Priestley, a Comet in the System: Biography* (San Diego, CA: Torch Publications, 1990).

Fitzpatrick, Martin, 'Priestley Caricatured', in Schwartz & McEvoy, 161–218.

Graham, 'Revolutionary in Exile'.

Holt, Anne, *A Life of Joseph Priestley*, with an introduction by Francis W. Hirst (London: OUP, 1931).

Schofield, I and II.

Schofield, Robert E., 'Priestley, Joseph (1733–1804)', *Oxford DNB.*

RELIGION, THEOLOGY, AND DISSENT

Priestley's Writings

An Appeal to the Serious and Candid Professors of Christianity ([London?], 1771). [No copy of the 1770 Leeds edn. appears to have survived.]

Considerations on Church-Authority; Occasioned by Dr. Balguy's Sermon on that Subject (London, 1769).

Disquisitions Relating to Matter and Spirit. To which is Added, the History of the Philosophical Doctrine concerning the Origin of the Soul (London, 1777).

An History of the Corruptions of Christianity, 2 vols. (Birmingham, 1782).

The Importance and Extent of Free Inquiry in Matters of Religion: A Sermon, Preached Before the Congregations of the Old and New Meeting of Protestant Dissenters at Birmingham. November 5, 1785. To Which are Added, Reflections on the Present State of Free Inquiry in this Country (Birmingham, 1785).

Institutes of Natural and Revealed Religion, 3 vols (London, 1772–4).

A Letter to the Right Honourable William Pitt... on the Subjects of Toleration and Church Establishments, 2nd edn., corr. & enlarged (London, 1787).

Letters to Dr. Horsley, in Answer to his Animadversions on the History of the Corruptions of Christianity (Birmingham, 1783).

The Proper Constitution of a Christian Church, Considered in a Sermon Preached at the New Meeting in Birmingham, November 3, 1782 (Birmingham, 1782).

The Conduct to be Observed by Dissenters in Order to Procure the Repeal of the Corporation and Test Acts (Birmingham, 1789).

Secondary Works

Bolam, C. Gordon, Jeremy Goring, H. L. Short, and Roger Thomas, *The English Presbyterians: From Elizabethan Puritanism to Modern Unitarianism* (London: George Allen & Unwin, 1968).

Bradley.

Canovan, Margaret, 'The Irony of History: Priestley's Rational Theology', *P-PN*, 4 (1980), 16–25.

Ditchfield, G. M., 'Anti-Trinitarianism and Toleration in late 18th-Century British Politics: the Unitarian Petition of 1792', *JEH*, 42 (1991).

_____ ' "How Narrow will the limits of this Toleration Appear?" Dissenting Petitions to Parliament, 1772–1773', in Stephen Taylor and David L. Wykes (eds), *Parliament and Dissent* (Edinburgh: Edinburgh University Press, 2005), 91–106.

_____ 'The Preceptor of Nations: Joseph Priestley and Theophilus Lindsey', *TUHS*, 23 (2004), 495–512.

Fitzpatrick, Martin, 'Joseph Priestley and the Cause of Universal Toleration', *P-PN*, 1 (1977), 3–21.

_____ 'Latitudinarianism at the Parting of the Ways: A Suggestion', in John Walsh, Colin Haydon and Stephen Taylor (eds), *The Church of England c.1689–c.1833: From Toleration to Tractarianism* (Cambridge: CUP, 1993).

Gordon, Alexander, *Heads of English Unitarian History with Appended Lectures on Baxter and Priestley* (London: Philip Green, 1895).

Griffiths, Olive M., *Religion and Learning: A Study in English Presbyterian Thought from the Bartholomew Ejections (1662) to the Foundation of the Unitarian Movement* (Cambridge: CUP, 1935).

Oliver, W. H., *Prophets and Millennialists: The Uses of Biblical Prophecy in England from the 1790s to the 1840s* (Auckland: Auckland University Press; Oxford: OUP, 1978).

Richey, Russell E., 'Joseph Priestley: Worship and Theology', *TUHS*, 15 (1972), 41–53, 98–103.

_____ 'The Origins of British Radicalism: the Changing Rationale for Dissent', *Eighteenth-Century Studies*, 7 (1973–4), 179–92.

Rivers.

Seed, John, ' "A set of men powerful enough in many things": Rational Dissent and Political Opposition in England, 1770–1790', in Haakonssen, 140–68.

Watts, Michael, *The Dissenters: From the Reformation to the French Revolution* (Oxford: OUP, 1978).

Webb, R. K., 'The Emergence of Rational Dissent', in Haakonssen, 12–41.

Young, B. W., *Religion and Enlightenment in Eighteenth-Century England: Theological Debate from Locke to Burke* (Oxford: OUP, 1998).

EDUCATION AND HISTORIOGRAPHY

Priestley's Writings

A Course of Lectures on Oratory and Criticism (London, 1777).

A Course of Lectures on the Theory of Language, and Universal Grammar (Warrington, 1762).

A Description of a Chart of Biography with a Catalogue of all the Names Inserted in it, and the Dates Annexed to Them (Warrington, 1765).

A Description of a New Chart of History (London, 1769).

An Essay on a Course of Liberal Education for Civil and Active Life ([London], 1765).

An History of the Corruptions of Christianity, 2 vols. (Birmingham, 1782).

'Joseph Priestley's Journal While at Daventry Academy, 1754', ed. Tony Rail and Beryl Thomas, *E & D*, 13 (1994), 49–113.

Lectures on History and General Policy; to which is Prefixed, an Essay on a Course of Liberal Education for Civil and Active Life (Birmingham, 1788).

The Rudiments of English Grammar: Adapted to the Use of Schools. With Observations on Style (London, 1761).

Secondary Works

Fitzpatrick, Martin, ' "Through the glass of history"; Some Reflections on Historical Knowledge in the Thought of Joseph Priestley', *E&D*, 17 (1998), 172–209.

Schofield, I and II.

Watts, Ruth, 'Joseph Priestley and Education', *E&D*, 2 (1983), 87–93.

Wykes, D. L., 'The Contribution of the Dissenting Academy to the Emergence of Rational Dissent', in Haakonssen, 99–139.

_____ 'Sons and Subscribers: Lay Support and the College, 1786–1840' in Barbara Smith (ed.), *Truth, Liberty, Religion: Essays Celebrating Two Hundred Years of Manchester College* (Oxford: Manchester College, 1986), 31–77.

SCIENCE

Priestley's Writings

Experiments and Observations on Different Kinds of Air, 3 vols. (London, 1774–7).

Experiments and Observations Relating to Various Branches of Natural Philosophy, 3 vols. (London, 1779, 1781; Birmingham, 1786).

The History and Present State of Discoveries Relating to Vision, Light, and Colours, 2 vols (London, 1772).

The History and Present State of Electricity, with Original Experiments (London, 1767).

The Doctrine of Phlogiston Established and that of the Composition of Water Refuted (Northumberland, PA, 1800).

Scientific Autobiography.

Secondary Works

Anderson & Lawrence.

Brooke, John Hedley, *Science and Religion: Some Historical Perspectives* (Cambridge: CUP, 1991), ch. 5, 'Science and Religion in the Enlightenment.

Crosland, M. P., 'Priestley Memorial Lecture: A Practical Perspective on Joseph Priestley as a Natural Philosopher', *British Journal for the History of Science*, 16 (1983), 223–38.

_____ ' "The Image of Science as a Threat": Burke versus Priestley and "Philosophic Revolution" ', *British Journal for the History of Science*, 20 (1987), 277–307.

Golinski.

McEvoy, John G., 'Joseph Priestley, "Aerial Philosopher": Metaphysics and Methodology in Priestley's Thought, 1772–1781', *Ambix*, 25 (1978), 1–55, 93–116, 153–75; 26 (1979), 16–38.

McEvoy, John G. and J. E. McGuire, 'God and Nature: Priestley's Way of Rational Dissent', *Historical Studies in the Physical Sciences*, 6 (1975), 325–404.

Partington, James R., 'Priestley', *A History of Chemistry*, vol. 2 (London: Macmillan, 1962), 237–97.

Schaffer, Simon, 'Priestley's Questions: An Historiographical Survey', *History of Science*, 22 (1984), 39–55.

Schofield, Robert E., *The Lunar Society of Birmingham: A Social History of Provincial Science and Industry in Eighteenth-Century England* (Oxford: Clarendon Press, 1963).

Schofield, I and II.

PHILOSOPHY

Priestley's Writings

Disquisitions Relating to Matter and Spirit. To Which is Added, the History of the Philosophical Doctrine Concerning the Origin of the Soul (London, 1777).

The Doctrine of Philosophical Necessity Illustrated (London, 1777).

An Examination of Dr. Reid's Inquiry into the Human Mind on the Principles of Common Sense, Dr. Beattie's Essay on the Nature and Immutability of Truth, and Dr. Oswald's Appeal to Common Sense in behalf of Religion (London, 1774).

A Free Discussion of the Doctrines of Materialism and Philosophical Necessity, in a Correspondence between Dr. Price and Dr. Priestley (London, 1778).

Institutes of Natural and Revealed Religion, 3 vols. (London, 1772–4), especially part 1 and the preface to part 3.

A Letter to the Rev. Mr. John Palmer, in Defense of the Illustrations of Philosophical Necessity (Bath, 1779).

Letters to a Philosophical Unbeliever, part 1 (Bath, 1780).

Works edited by Priestley

Hartley's Theory of the Human Mind, on the Principle of the Association of Ideas; with Essays relating to the Subject of it (London, 1775).

A Philosophical Inquiry Concerning Human Liberty. By Anthony Collins, Esq. Republished with a Preface by Joseph Priestley (Birmingham, 1790).

Secondary Works

Allen, Richard C., *David Hartley on Human Nature* (Albany, NY: State University of New York Press, 1999), for Priestley's relation to Hartley.

Harris, James A., *Of Liberty and Necessity: The Free Will Debate in Eighteenth-Century British Philosophy* (Oxford: OUP, 2005), for Priestley and Reid.

—— 'Joseph Priestley and 'the proper doctrine of philosophical necessity', *E&D*, 20 (2001), 23–44, for Priestley and Hume.

Martin, Raymond, and John Barresi, *Naturalization of the Soul: Self and Personal Identity in the Eighteenth Century* (London and New York: Routledge, 2000).

Popkin, Richard, *The High Road to Pyrrhonism* (San Diego, CA: Austin Hill Press, 1980), 213–26, for Priestley and Hume.

Schofield I, ch. 7, and Schofield II, ch. 2, for Priestley and natural religion.

Sell, Alan P. F., 'Priestley's Polemic against Reid', *P-PN*, 3 (1979), 41–52.

—— 'Priestley's Polemic against Reid: An Additional Note', *E&D* 2 (1983), 121.

Stephens, John, 'Samuel Horsley and Joseph Priestley's *Disquisitions Relating to Matter and Spirit*', *E&D*, 3 (1984), 103–14.

Yolton, John W., *Thinking Matter: Materialism in Eighteenth-Century Britain* (Minneapolis: University of Minnesota Press, 1983).

POLITICS

Priestley's Writings

An Address to Protestant Dissenters of all Denominations, on the Approaching Election of Members of Parliament (London, 1774).

The Case of Poor Emigrants, Recommended in a Discourse, Delivered at the University Hall in Philadelphia, on Sunday, February 19, 1797 (Philadelphia, 1797).

An Essay on a Course of Liberal Education for Civil and Active Life (London, 1765).

An Essay on the First Principles of Government, and on the Nature of Political, Civil and Religious Liberty (London, 1768).

Lectures on History and General Policy; to which is Prefixed, an Essay on a Course of Liberal Education for Civil and Active Life (Birmingham, 1788).

Lectures on History and General Policy; to which is Prefixed, an Essay on a Course of Liberal Education for Civil and Active Life; and an Additional Lecture on the Constitution of the United States (Philadelphia, 1803).

Letters to The Right Honourable Edmund Burke Occasioned by his Reflections on the Revolution in France, 2nd edn. corrected (Birmingham, 1791).

Letters to the Inhabitants of Northumberland and its Neighbourhood, on Subjects Interesting to the Author, and to Them, 2nd edn. (Philadelphia, 1801).

Maxims of Political Arithmetic, Applied to the Case of the United States of America (Philadelphia, 1798).

The Present State of Liberty in Great Britain and Her Colonies (London, 1769).

Priestley: Political Writings, ed. Peter N. Miller (Cambridge: CUP, 1993).

Secondary Works

Canovan, Margaret, 'Two Concepts of Liberty: Eighteenth Century Style', *P-PN*, 2 (1978).

—— 'Paternalistic Liberalism: Joseph Priestley on Rank and Inequality', *E&D*, 2 (1983), 23–37.

—— 'The Un-Benthamist Utilitarianism of Joseph Priestley', *Journal of the History of Ideas*, 45 (1985), 435–50.

Dickinson, H. T., *Liberty and Property: Political Ideology in Eighteenth-Century Britain* (London: Weidenfeld & Nicolson, 1977).

—— review of Isaac Kramnick, *Republicanism and Bourgeois Radicalism: Political Ideology in Late Eighteenth-Century England and America*, in *E&D*, 11 (1992), 124–5.

Dybikowski, James, review of *Priestley: Political Writings*, ed. Peter N. Miller, in *E&D*, 15 (1996), 118–27.

Fruchtman, Jack Jr., *The Apocalyptic Politics of Richard Price and Joseph Priestley: A Study in Late Eighteenth-Century English Republican Millennialism* (Philadelphia: The American Philosophical Society, 1983).

Garrett, Clarke, *Respectable Folly: Millenarians and the French Revolution in France and England* (Baltimore and London: Johns Hopkins University Press, 1975).

Graham, 'Revolutionary Philosopher', parts one and two.

Gunn, J. A. W., *Beyond Liberty and Property: The Process of Self-Recognition in Eighteenth-Century Political Thought* (Kingston and Montreal: McGill-Queens University Press, 1983).

Kramnick, Isaac, 'Religion and Radicalism: English Political Theory in the Age of Revolution', *Political Theory*, 5 (1977), 505–34.

―――― 'Eighteenth-Century Science and Radical Social Theory: The Case of Joseph Priestley's Scientific Liberalism', *JBS*, 25 (1986), 1–30, both reprinted in Kramnick, *Republicanism and Bourgeois Radicalism: Political Ideology in Late Eighteenth-Century England and America* (Ithaca and London: Cornell University Press, 1990).

Miller, Peter N., *Defining the Common Good: Empire, Religion and Philosophy in Eighteenth-Century Britain* (Cambridge: CUP, 1994).

Mudroch, Vilem, 'Joseph Priestley on Morals and Economics: Reconciling the Quest for Virtue with Pursuit of Wealth', *E&D*, 20 (2001), 45–87.

Philp, Mark, 'Rational Religion and Political Radicalism', *E&D*, 4 (1985), 35–46.

―――― 'The Fragmented Ideology of Reform', in Mark Philp (ed.), *The French Revolution and British Popular Politics* (Cambridge: CUP, 1991), 50–77.

―――― 'English Republicanism in the 1790s', *The Journal of Political Philosophy*, 6 (1998), 235–62.

Tapper, Alan, 'Priestley on Politics, Progress and Moral Theology', in Haakonssen, 272–86.

Thomas, D. O., 'Progress, Liberty and Utility: The Political Philosophy of Joseph Priestley', in Anderson & Lawrence, 73–80.

Index